CUISINE TO KILL FOR

RECIPES & TRUE CRIME STORIES

FROM THE WORLD'S MOST HAUNTED PLACES

AMY BRUNI

HARPER Celebrate

Cuisine to Kill For

Published by Harper Celebrate, an imprint of HarperCollins Focus LLC.

Note: This book is meant for information and entertainment purposes only. Much of the content of this book is a result of the author's lifetime of work, including books read beginning in childhood, guided tours, conversations, investigations, handwritten notes and journals, and personal experiences. The author has done their best to include sources where possible. If you find one of the stories particularly interesting or curious, the author and publisher invite you to explore the subject more closely for yourself, as the world of the paranormal is always being researched and studied, with new theories presented regularly.

A Note About Egg Safety: Some of the recipes in this book call for uncooked or partially cooked eggs. Consuming raw or undercooked eggs may increase your risk of foodborne illness, especially if you have certain medical conditions.

Cover and food photography: Emily Dorio
Food styling: Tami Hardeman
Prop styling: Colson Horton
Photography assistant: Joel Micah Dennis
Food styling assistant: Matthew Mosshart
Prop styling assistant: Khaki Stanford
Cover design and art direction: Tiffany Forrester
Interior typesetting: Kait Lamphere

ISBN 978-1-4002-5502-3 (HC)
ISBN 978-1-4002-5507-8 (audiobook)
ISBN 978-1-4002-5506-1 (ePub)

Printed in Malaysia

26 27 28 29 30 PJM 5 4 3 2 1

To Jimmy, my rock of a partner in life.
You may not believe in ghosts,
but you certainly believe in me.

CONTENTS

CHAPTER 5

BEHIND LOCKED DOORS

CHAPTER 6

UNSAVORY CHARACTERS

FOREWORD

When Amy told me she was working on a book that combined food, history, serial killers, and ghosts, I didn't even blink. Of course she was. This is exactly who Amy is—a brilliant collector of the eerie and the delicious.

Cuisine to Kill For is more than just a cookbook or a haunted history lesson. It's a portal into the mind of someone who sees connections where others don't, who finds meaning in the strange, and who isn't afraid to stir a little darkness into the stew.

When you've spent as many years navigating the paranormal world as Amy and I have, you start to notice a few recurring themes: The dead don't always stay quiet, history is never as buried as it seems, and the best investigators—the ones who truly get it—possess an unwavering commitment to a passion that will never die. This isn't just a book; it's an experience. It's Amy, with her characteristic warmth, inviting you to pull up a chair—perhaps at a haunted table, one graced by a spectral guest, a notorious killer, or a grieving loved one—and encouraging you to listen, to taste, and to wonder.

Amy possesses an uncanny ability to seamlessly connect the dots between the eerie and the familiar, to unearth the humanity within the horror, and to make even the darkest tales feel strangely inviting. *Cuisine to Kill For* is precisely that brand of magic. It's clever, it's chilling, and it's packed with the kind of tasty details only Amy could unearth. In the years we've spent investigating, dining, and laughing together, she has always approached every moment with infectious curiosity, profound depth, and a refreshing dose of humility. I'm incredibly grateful for our longtime friendship and proud to introduce this uniquely thrilling book.

Just don't read it on an empty stomach—or alone at night.

Steve Gonsalves

Star of *Ghost Hunters*

Bestselling author of *A Life with Ghosts*

INTRODUCTION

Over the last few years, food and death have become my life. When I originally floated the idea of a cookbook highlighting the history and recipes of haunted locations, no one could have predicted the career trajectory shift I was about to initiate.

For as long as I can remember, I've lived by the adage "do what you love," and having been a paranormal investigator and researcher, I've always looked for ways to make spookiness my career. But those projects, the kind where I'd go exploring some creepy old building looking for ghosts, were far more predictable than a haunted cookbook. We're talking ghost hunting television shows, college lectures, writing magazines and books. But all that changed when one day, on a whim, I thought, *I really enjoy cooking. And I really enjoy ghosts—how can I make that into a project?* Famously, I was inspired by Lizzie "Lizbeth" Borden's meat loaf recipe, written on a recipe card at the Fall River Historical Society. But time and time again I heard a nagging voice in my head: *Do people really want to cook historic recipes while thinking about some of the most terrifying things on earth?*

My first cookbook, *Food to Die For*, taught me that emphatically, yes, a lot of you do. Like, *so many of you.* Not only did that make me feel less alone in the weirdness, but I also became increasingly inspired to take this a step further. I owe that largely to readers and fellow cooking enthusiasts. My inbox was filled with your messages, requesting locations further away and stories that were even darker. Most importantly, you adored the twist of terrifying cooking just as much as I did. You wanted more recipes, more history, and more ghosts. It's a want I'm happy to oblige because, well . . . it turns out I really like cooking while also thinking about really awful things.

This time around, I wanted to incorporate more than just ghosts. I wanted to highlight true crime–related hauntings specifically. Additionally, I wanted to take this show on the road, so in *Cuisine to Kill For*, we've ventured across the globe and jumped around in time: from the dark, blood-stained history of "Blood Countess" Elizabeth Báthory to Dracula's Bran Castle in Romania, to more "modern" killers, like H. H. Holmes in Chicago, believed to be America's first serial killer. Researching these tragic tales spawned not only remarkable stories of the supernatural but also remarkable connections to food, sometimes delicious, sometimes not—you'll see.

Countess Elizabeth Báthory, 1585

For those of you who are new to this macabre marriage of cooking and history, it's important to note a few things as you proceed. First of all, and please repeat this to yourself as much as possible: "Most of these recipes are delicious, but some are very *historic*." Meaning, if you're going to delve into the world of Shrimp Wiggle, a seafood dish once served to the unfortunate residents at Pennhurst State School and Hospital in Spring City, Pennsylvania (which was closed due to extreme neglect and disgusting living conditions), you may want to have your expectations in check. At the same time, that recipe was found with measurements based on fifty servings. What you see here is the result of paring it down and testing it to make it a little more suitable for an average kitchen. Of course, if you have fifty friends who you think might like Shrimp Wiggle, feel free to reach out; I'll give you the original recipe.

Another interesting conundrum when choosing recipes for this book is my natural desire to highlight history and historical locations and to also give credit to the eateries that now inhabit some of these spaces. Brushy Mountain State Penitentiary, for example: Yes, I probably could have found an actual recipe served to inmates when Brushy was a working penitentiary. But I love that an actual barbecue restaurant is operating out of a place that was once notorious for its harsh treatment of prisoners. And, according to reviews and locals, it's the best barbecue in town. I suppose, yes, I could have tortured you with some horrendous slop once served to prisoners there, but instead, I opted to grace you with a killer turnip greens recipe.

As you prepare these recipes, I urge you to recognize the unorthodox form of time travel we're engaging in here. I find preparing these dishes to be an almost spiritual experience as I ponder the history behind them while mixing ingredients and stirring pots. The act of cooking can be very ritualistic in nature, filling your food with intention as you take in some of the most terrifying ghost stories in the world, including historical accounts of extremely bloody and awful deaths. It's an experience you can savor just for yourself, but it's also perfect for sharing. Who doesn't want to dig into a helping of Meat Stew with Polenta and Egg from Bran Castle while discussing Vlad the Impaler and his penchant for, well, impaling? And what kind of host would you be if you served a Marilyn cocktail from Bobby Mackey's Music World and *didn't* debate whether a young lady's head was actually thrown down the well in the basement? Come to think of it, does anyone have thoughts on where her ghost will go now that the legendary honky-tonk has been torn down?

I'm glad you're here on this global journey with me as we explore all kinds of cuisine to kill for.

A NOTE ON THE CONTENT: We all know that what's considered acceptable today is very different from what was acceptable two hundred years ago (or in some cases, even twenty years ago). There are terms in this book that are historically accurate to a particular time period that we wouldn't use today. When you're reading, please remember that you're diving into the past, rough terminology and all.

Also, there are murders. And ghosts. A lot of them. Read at your own risk (or morbid curiosity). You did buy a book called *Cuisine to Kill For*, after all.

CHAPTER 1

CENTURIES-OLD CHILLS

As I've walked through haunts and halls where some of history's most heinous crimes have occurred, I've noticed something: Due process was not often afforded the accused. Perhaps that's why so many of the places featured in this chapter seem to have ghosts lurking at every corner.

It appears some of these spirits are seeking revenge or vindication. Some are lost souls looking only to be found and recognized. And of course, there's a sprinkling of those who seem intent on enjoying their debaucherous ways well into the afterlife.

Thrillingly (or terrifyingly?), the locations aren't secret; these are places where you can walk in and ask point-blank for a good story, and the caretakers will often oblige you. But if you'd rather not risk having one of the very brazen spirits stow away in your suitcase, perhaps preparing one of these signature dishes will satisfy your paranormal cravings.

PARIS CATACOMBS

PARIS, FRANCE

Deep beneath the streets of Paris lies a city of the dead. Stretching five stories into the ground, the Paris Catacombs include more than 150 miles of corridors lined floor to ceiling with human bones. An estimated 550,000 (living) people explore the macabre attraction every year. And as they enter, each visitor reads the same warning: "Stop! This is the Empire of Death."

Experts estimate that the remains of six million people are interred in the catacombs, moved from the crowded city's overflowing cemeteries to tunnels underground. In the late 1700s, Paris cemeteries had become so overcrowded after centuries of burials that the stuff of horror movies began to become a regular occurrence.

"People would be drinking, eating, or dancing in a cellar tavern or cabaret when a wall would collapse and decomposing bodies fall in on them. Just imagine the scene," forensic pathologist Philippe Charlier told *The Guardian* in 2024.

The first remains were disinterred in 1785 from one of Paris's oldest churches, the Saints Innocents Cemetery, and in 1860, the catacombs' final remains were laid to rest. But by the time the last bones were interred, the catacombs had already become a tourist attraction. The ossuary—a room that holds the bones of the dead—is one of the largest in the world.

When the tunnels were first designated as catacombs, bodies were simply thrown down old quarry shafts and into the tunnels, which had been used for quite a while as sources of stone to build the city. But in the early 1800s, nobleman Louis-Étienne Héricart de Thury transformed the bone-filled tunnels into a place that showed more respect for the dead. Bones were sorted and arranged into artful, decorative walls.

Suddenly the catacombs could be visited not just by mourners, but also by tourists bent on thinking more about their own mortality as a philosophical exercise. One of those musings carved underground: "Think in the morning that you may not make it to the evening, and in the evening that you may not make it to the morning."

Engraving of Paris Catacombs, 1889

Visit today, and you'll notice that those deep subterranean tunnels are eerily silent, a stark contrast to the noise of the busy city above. The quiet makes it all the easier to hear unexplainable things. Visitors to the catacombs will sometimes emerge with stories of seeing apparitions, hearing whispers from disembodied voices, and feeling touched by invisible hands. Though most of the remains of people in the catacombs were moved from other locations, a handful of deaths happened inside. Philibert Aspairt became lost underground in 1793, and his body wasn't discovered for eleven years. In 2016, a man attending an illegal party in the tunnels died of a heart attack.

While the majority of the bones interred in the catacombs were moved from other locations, some found the tunnels to be their first and final resting place. The only known murders in the catacombs took place in 1824. (I will note, though, that the only record of this incident was published in *The London Journal* in 1845, more than twenty years after the alleged crime.) Alexandre Francornard, who worked as a torchbearer for visitors who wanted to walk through the catacombs, had developed an interest in wealthy Parisian widow Eugenie Marsac. One night, Marsac and her three-year-old daughter visited Francornard in the catacombs, but later, he emerged alone. The woman and child were later discovered in the tunnels, brutally murdered. Francornard disappeared but was found six months later and was beheaded for the crimes in 1825.

The story is horrific, but thankfully it's the only account of a violent crime in the catacombs that I could find. To prevent the crime of stealing bones, catacombs employees check visitors' bags at the exit.

But one very large crime was committed in the catacombs recently—and it was, even by my standards, a pretty weird one.

In 2017, thieves took to the underground burial tunnels on a mission. But they weren't looking for anything in the catacombs themselves. They were looking for access to a private apartment, tunneling through the catacombs' walls, in search of one specific thing: wine. Those thieves bored through a wall to pilfer from the wine cellar of a home in the sixth arrondissement, stealing more than three hundred bottles of rare and vintage fine wine. The total value of the heist? About €250,000 at the time, worth nearly $330,000 today. (If anyone knows who did it, let me know—especially if they're willing to share.)

COQ AU VIN

What better way to celebrate France's spookiest wine heist than with one of the country's signature dishes—one that puts wine at the center of the show. The secret to a great coq au vin is to choose good-quality wine for the sauce. I've skimped on the wine before and picked the cheapest bottle, thinking it wouldn't matter. But trust me—it does. A light- to medium-bodied red like Beaujolais or Burgundy works best. It's also delicious as a wine pairing on the table.

Prep Time: 20 minutes | Cook Time: 2 hours 25 minutes | Yield: 6 servings

INGREDIENTS

12 pieces dark meat chicken (drumsticks and/or thighs), bone-in, skin-on

Salt and black pepper, to taste

2 tablespoons neutral cooking oil, divided

10 slices thick-cut bacon, cut crosswise into 1/2-inch pieces

3 large carrots, peeled and chopped

3 celery stalks, chopped

1 medium white onion, diced

1 (750 mL) bottle of light- to medium-bodied red wine (like a Beaujolais or Burgundy), divided

1/2 cup tomato paste

12 sprigs fresh thyme

6 sprigs fresh rosemary

4 cups chicken broth

1 pound baby bella or cremini mushrooms, sliced

INSTRUCTIONS

1. Pat the chicken pieces dry, and season all over with salt and pepper.
2. In a large Dutch oven over medium-high heat, heat 1 tablespoon of the cooking oil. Working in batches, brown the chicken well, about 5 minutes per side. Remove the chicken from the pot and set aside.
3. Add the bacon to the same pot and cook over medium-high heat until the bacon has started to crisp and the fat is rendered, about 5 minutes. Remove to a paper towel–lined plate to drain. Add the carrots, celery, and onion to the same pan. Cook until the onion is translucent, about 8 minutes.
4. Add about a quarter of the bottle of wine and the tomato paste. Simmer, stirring often, for about 5 minutes. Add the bacon back in, pour in the rest of the wine, and simmer about 20 minutes, until the liquid in the pot is reduced by half.
5. Preheat the oven to 350°F.
6. Tie the herbs together with kitchen twine (they'll be easy to fish out later) and add the bouquet to the pot. Pour in the chicken broth, and add the chicken pieces back in. Bring the mixture to a boil.
7. Put the lid on the pot and place in the oven. Cook the mixture until the chicken is falling off the bone, about an hour.

(recipe continues)

(recipe continued from page 5)

8. While the chicken is braising, in a large skillet over medium-high heat, cook the mushrooms in the remaining 1 tablespoon of cooking oil until browned, about 5 minutes. Pour off any excess liquid. Set the mushrooms aside.

9. When the chicken reaches an internal temperature of 165°F, remove the pot from the oven. Remove the chicken from the pot and set aside. Discard the herbs.

10. Place the pot back on the burner, and simmer the sauce for about 20 minutes, until it's reduced by about one-third. Season to taste with salt and pepper. Once the sauce is reduced, add the chicken and mushrooms to the pot. Heat until everything is warm and ready to eat.

11. You can serve this dish immediately—but it tastes even better the next day.

SHANGHAI TUNNELS

PORTLAND, OREGON, USA

Underneath the oldest neighborhood in Portland, Oregon, there's a hidden network of tunnels. Today they're mostly sealed off, but in centuries past the tunnels were a vital network for transporting goods to downtown businesses in the area known today as Old Town Chinatown. If the legends are to be believed, the tunnels were also used for a darker purpose: to kidnap and sell able-bodied men to sea captains in need of manual labor on their ships, and to kidnap women and force them into prostitution. Today, the only reason to descend into the "Shanghai Tunnels," as they're commonly known, is to walk in the footsteps of those who came before—and, of course, to find the ghosts that people report encountering in the underground halls.

Officially called the "Portland Underground," the tunnels connected Portland's waterfront to the basements of nearby hotels, restaurants, and bars, a way of easily transporting supplies without interference from inclement weather or crowded streets. Using the tunnels was also, more likely than not, a convenient way for mafiosos to conduct their "business" away from prying eyes and for visitors of opium dens and gambling parlors to escape police raids. But as the city's ports grew and the area gained an increasingly rough reputation, stories started to circulate. Men would be drugged, their drinks laced with opium, or they were beaten unconscious. When they woke up, they'd be on ships sailing to Asia, with no option but to work on board or to perish at sea.

Women also started to vanish. They would be disappeared, made victims of sex trafficking, held captive sometimes in Portland, sometimes in far-off locales.

To be *shanghaied*, as the action came to be known, wasn't a respectful term. The phrase is linked to James "Shanghai" Kelly, the owner of several boardinghouses and bars in San Francisco. In the latter half of the nineteenth century, Kelly was a known *crimp*, a person who would kidnap and sell men to the boats (to *shanghai* someone is also known as "crimping"). During the Gold Rush, sea captains often found themselves in a particular predicament: They would sail ships full of supplies from Asia to California, where sailors would jump ship, literally, to go seek their fortunes. Without a crew, ships couldn't make the arduous return trip back across the Pacific. So when captains couldn't hire enough sailors in America for the return journey, they sometimes resorted to enslaving people to get their work done. Kelly was the most infamous of the San Francisco crimps, known for drugging, beating, or swindling men to get them on the boats. According to Bay area publication The Bold Italic, Kelly once sold off one hundred men on a single night after renting a steamer ship for his birthday and drugging everyone aboard, then getting them to waiting captains.

Research suggests that crimping was much more prevalent in San Francisco than Portland, and some say the rumors that inspired the nickname of one of Portland's most notorious landmarks are overblown. Regardless, what's very real is the public's ongoing fascination with the tunnels. Every year, thousands of visitors explore the city's underground so they can see the trapdoors built into bar floors that dropped people into barred cells before ferrying them into servitude.

According to tour company Portland Ghosts, a spirit named Sam is a frequent guest on paranormal tours of the tunnels. He's believed to turn off lights in bar basements and to make his presence known to tunnel visitors by moving things around or even shouting his own name. People on the tours also report feeling tugs at their clothing and hair or hearing whistling while they walk underground.

When captains from Asia couldn't hire enough sailors in America for the return journey, they sometimes resorted to enslaving people to get their work done.

Old Town Pizza & Brewing, housed in what was once the Merchant Hotel, is built directly above some of the tunnels. The restaurant has a house ghost named Nina (pronounced *Nigh-na*). She's believed to be a woman who, while working at the hotel more than a hundred years ago, was crimped and became a victim of human trafficking. According to Old Town's website, she attempted to purchase her freedom by sharing information with missionaries working to end the practice. But soon after, she was found dead, having been thrown down an elevator shaft. Today, Nina watches over the restaurant and the tunnels below, sometimes appearing to guests in a black dress or sometimes just with a slight wafting of perfume.

TIPSY CHARLOTTE

As I was researching the cuisine a weary sailor might have eaten in Portland a century ago, one dish stood out immediately—and it happens to share a name with my daughter. It'll be quite a few years before my Charlotte eats this decadent, boozy dessert, adapted from the 1885 *Web-Foot Cook Book* by the San Grael Society of Portland's First Presbyterian Church. But that's fine! More for us grown-ups.

Prep Time: 25 minutes	Cook Time: 10 minutes	Yield: 10 to 12 servings

INGREDIENTS

½ cup granulated sugar

¼ cup cornstarch

¼ teaspoon salt

2½ cups whole milk

4 large egg yolks

½ teaspoon almond extract

1 tablespoon unsalted butter

2 cups cream sherry

1 cup water

About 48 ladyfingers

4 cups sliced almonds, divided

1 cup heavy cream

2 tablespoons powdered sugar

INSTRUCTIONS

1. In a medium saucepan, off the heat, whisk together the granulated sugar, cornstarch, and salt. Gradually pour in the milk, whisking constantly, until the cornstarch is fully dissolved. Whisk in the egg yolks.
2. Gently warm the saucepan over medium heat, whisking constantly, until the mixture is just starting to bubble, about 5–7 minutes. Reduce the heat to low and cook 1 more minute, whisking constantly.
3. Remove the saucepan from the heat. Into a medium mixing bowl, strain the custard through a fine-mesh sieve. Stir in the almond extract and the butter. Let the custard cool for about 30 minutes.
4. In a small mixing bowl, combine the sherry and the water. Hold a ladyfinger between your fingers and dip the top side of the cookie into the mixture. Shake off the excess, then place the cookie in a 9 x 13-inch casserole dish. Repeat until you've completed a single layer at the bottom of the dish.
5. Sprinkle about a third of the almonds over the cookies. Repeat with two more layers of dipped cookies and almonds, reserving a small scoop of almonds for garnish.
6. Spread the custard evenly over the top layer of ladyfingers a. Cover the casserole dish with plastic wrap, making sure the plastic wrap touches the custard to avoid a skin forming on the custard. Refrigerate at least 8 hours or overnight.
7. Just before serving, make the whipped cream. In the bowl of a stand mixer fitted with a whisk attachment, whip the cream on medium-high, gradually sprinkling in the powdered sugar, until stiff peaks form.
8. Gently spread the whipped cream over the unwrapped custard mixture, then sprinkle with the remaining almonds. Serve immediately. Store any remaining dessert in the refrigerator.

THE NATIONAL EXCHANGE HOTEL

NEVADA CITY, CALIFORNIA, USA

During the Gold Rush, tiny towns in the American West became bustling cities overnight. Fortune seekers flooded previously unknown destinations—sometimes founding towns based on mining claims where no settlements had previously stood. Many of these Gold Rush towns were abandoned once the lodes dried up, or when the ore prices dropped and made mining no longer financially viable. But some of the cities built up by golden riches are still thriving today. Nevada City (near my hometown of Placerville, California, and where we filmed *Historically Haunted*) is one of those towns. Built up by the wealth brought out of the ground, Nevada City is now sustained by the people who settled there and those who continue to travel there, drawn to the town's creative energy and historic preservation.

When tourists go to Nevada City looking for ghosts—which, make no mistake, are easy to find—they almost all head to the National Exchange Hotel. Built in 1856, the hotel was an upscale destination from the start, a place for wealthy forty-niners and mine owners to stay while visiting from San Francisco and regions beyond. Just a few years ago, the building was in a state of disrepair, but a change of ownership and a two-year renovation brought it back to its former glory.

Every day the staff receives questions from visitors asking if the building is *really* haunted, the National Exchange Hotel's events manager, Anthony Jones, told me. And his answer is always the same: "You tell us."

The hotel was a high-end destination, with luxury accommodations fitting for guests of a certain distinction. Jones told me that while suffragettes would have tea, "you also had the ladies of the evening [at the hotel], because it was a brothel, too." The building also housed the post office, a bank, and meeting space, so it was almost a de facto town square.

When the hotel gives its Haunted by History tours, Jones said, "We don't romanticize the Gold Rush. We explain that the people coming over here did lead to displacing people who were originally here. The folks coming here—mainly men, 20,000 people in a town that now has about 3,500—were in really harsh conditions. It was a hard life. It was seedy and dangerous because all of it was revolving around gold and greed."

Many of the establishment's resident ghosts are believed to be tied to that time. People frequently report seeing Victorian-era spirits, including a woman floating across the dining room, a little girl chasing after a ball, and a man who politely greets guests on the stairs, according to Mark Lyon's *Haunted Nevada City and Grass Valley*. Many staff members also report water glasses breaking on their own and hearing phantom piano music or unseen entities say their names out loud.

There are darker stories, too. In 1897, a woman registered as Mrs. Frances Zeitler was found murdered at the hotel. When she was discovered, her body had been dragged into a shed and staged to look like she died by suicide, but her head wounds indicated otherwise. More recently, a man ended his own life in room 402, a room that had once been a jail cell and even a stable. Near the same area, a prostitute is said to have been murdered, but details are hazy.

But like my favorite hotel in the world, the Omni Mount Washington in New Hampshire (more on that in chapter 3), the National Exchange manages to be both haunted and welcoming at the same time. "That room [402] has a lot of history to it, but honestly where most people experience stuff is just the hotel in general," Jones said. "They say that the feeling of it is very feminine and very comforting. If there is anything there, it's in communion with everyone who's there."

The National Exchange Hotel, 1894

FRENCH ONION SOUP

Today, the National Exchange Hotel is a beautifully preserved relic of the Gold Rush era, thanks to a multi-year renovation. The hotel reopened in 2021 with a fine dining restaurant, Lola. The eatery was named after performer Lola Montez, whose "spider dance" made her a nineteenth-century sensation. This recipe is courtesy of Alan Gosker, the executive chef of Lola at the National Exchange Hotel.

Prep Time: 10 minutes	Cook Time: 1 hour 20 minutes	Yield: 4 servings

INGREDIENTS

1 tablespoon unsalted butter

1 tablespoon olive oil

2 pounds yellow onions, thinly sliced

4 large cloves garlic, thinly sliced

Salt, to taste

1/3 cup red wine

1 sprig fresh thyme

4 bay leaves

3 cups beef bone broth

1/4 cup brandy

8 baguette slices

1 cup grated Gruyère cheese

INSTRUCTIONS

1. In a heavy-bottomed pot over medium heat, melt the butter with the olive oil. Add the onions, garlic, and a pinch of salt. Cook slowly, stirring occasionally, until the onions are deeply caramelized, about 45–60 minutes.
2. Once the onions are caramelized, preheat the oven to 425°F.
3. To the soup pot add the red wine, thyme, and bay leaves. Simmer until the wine is almost completely reduced, about 10–15 minutes. Stir in the bone broth and bring to a gentle simmer for 10 minutes. Add the brandy, then remove the thyme and bay leaves. Taste the soup and adjust the seasoning with salt as needed.
4. Toast the baguette slices, and reserve.
5. Ladle the hot soup into individual oven-safe crocks or bowls, about 12 ounces each, making sure to leave about a half inch of space at the top. Place two toasted baguette slices on top of each soup crock. Generously pile the grated Gruyère over the bread, covering the bread completely.
6. Place the crocks on a baking sheet. Bake for 10 minutes, or until the cheese is melted and bubbling. Remove from the oven and serve immediately.

THE OLD TALBOTT TAVERN

BARDSTOWN, KENTUCKY, USA

Built in 1779, the Old Talbott Tavern offers services today that look pretty similar to what it offered back then—providing refreshment to guests and lodging to weary travelers. The building is believed to be the oldest in Kentucky *and* the oldest Western stagecoach stop still in operation, according to Alan Brown's *Stories from the Haunted South*. Its downstairs bourbon bar, which the restaurant claims is the oldest in the world, regularly wins international awards for its two-hundred-bottle selection.

George Talbott bought the tavern in 1886. And while the business was a success, he faced enormous personal loss. In the first two years of owning the place, six of his and wife Ann's ten children died within its walls, including one by falling down the stairs and another who died by suicide.

Throughout its nearly 250-year history, the tavern has seen many guests of historical significance. General George Rogers Clark, leader of the Virginia Militia, used the tavern as a base of operations during the Revolutionary War. Future presidents Andrew Jackson, William Henry Harrison, and Abraham Lincoln stayed at the inn long before their White House stints were a twinkle in their eyes. Other notable visitors include renowned naturalist John James Audubon, pioneer Daniel Boone, General George Patton, Queen Marie of Romania, and Louis-Philippe, the final king of France, who stayed at the inn after he abdicated the throne during the French Revolution of 1848.

One of the tavern's most infamous frequenters was Jesse James, the notorious outlaw who robbed banks and trains and led the James–Younger Gang. James's crimes have made him a legend; after fighting alongside Confederate guerrillas during the Civil War, he turned his energy toward stealing money from those in power, positioning himself as giving it to those in need (though there's no record of him sharing his spoils). Through his robberies of banks, trains, and stagecoaches, James left a wake of murder and ruin behind him, killing innocent people and sometimes leaving press releases to drum up attention for his flagrant lawbreaking. During his time at Talbott, he left his mark on the place, literally—he drunkenly shot at the birds painted on a wall mural and left bullet holes that remain to this day. His revolver remains on display in the tavern today.

There are journals in each room so guests can record their thoughts on their stays. One woman wrote that she woke up to find the spirit of James next to her in bed. Another spotted the outlaw at their window. Even staff members have seen him walking the restaurant late at night.

Other reports include shower curtains opening on their own and toys moving in the middle of the night. The staff members say sometimes objects like silverware and glasses move without anyone touching them, or that disembodied voices will speak to them when they're alone. Occasionally, spirits show themselves through phantom music from a piano or footsteps from an unseen person.

"Guests have reported doorknobs jiggling with no one on the other side, flashes of light, orbs moving in their room, furniture moving, personal items being tossed off of chairs, and the apparitions of those who have stayed here in the past," manager Chuck Wood told the *The Louisville Courier-Journal* in 2022. "They play a lot of tricks but nothing malicious. It's just something we are living and working with every day."

Wood also shared a spectral story of his own. In the General's Quarters room, there's an antique doll that once belonged to a girl who died in the tavern after falling down the stairs. Though staff ask guests not to touch the doll, Wood broke his own rule one night as he was getting ready to sleep in the room. "I decided I didn't want the doll looking at me, so I picked it up and turned it around so it was facing the wall across from the bed," he said. The next morning, the doll wasn't just looking at Wood—it was at the end of the bed.

The tavern's "lady in white" is believed to be the spirit of Ann Talbott, George's wife. When the chandeliers shake, staff interpret that to mean members of the Talbott family are present. Ann is believed to make one chandelier shake, but if two are moving, Ann and George's twins are the culprits.

The Old Talbott Tavern seems to be a place where the living and the dead peacefully coexist. I love to think about the Talbotts' spirits together in their home, spending their afterlife together as a family.

"I never believed in ghosts before I worked here, but sometimes you have to throw that out the window and believe what you see or hear or feel," Wood added. "I can't explain what is going on here. I just know I've had great experiences."

THE OLD TALBOTT TAVERN PIE

This citrus custard pie is so simple and delicious. It's been on the menu at the Old Talbott Tavern for more than three decades. And now, thanks to the restaurant, you can have it at home, whether your backyard is bluegrass or badlands. If you're feeling fancy—or you just love a lemon meringue pie—whip up a meringue rather than topping the custard with whipped cream.

Prep Time: 5 minutes	Cook Time: 10 minutes, plus chilling time	Yield: 8 servings

INGREDIENTS

3/4 cup granulated sugar

1/2 cup all-purpose flour

1/4 teaspoon salt

1 1/4 cups water

2 egg yolks, beaten

1 tablespoon orange zest

1/2 cup orange juice

2 tablespoons lemon juice

1 tablespoon powdered gelatin

One 9-inch pie shell, baked

Whipped cream, for serving

INSTRUCTIONS

1. In the top of a double boiler, off the heat, combine the sugar, flour, and salt. Add the water and stir until smooth. Cook over medium heat, stirring constantly, for 5 minutes.
2. Remove the double boiler from the heat. Add the yolks to the mixture and return the double boiler to the heat. Cook 5 minutes longer, stirring constantly.
3. Remove the double boiler from the heat. Stir in the orange zest, orange juice, lemon juice, and gelatin.
4. Transfer the mixture to a medium bowl, and cover with plastic wrap, making sure the plastic wrap touches the custard directly to avoid a skin forming on the custard. Chill the custard mixture for at least an hour, then spread the custard mixture into the baked pie shell. Chill the pie for several hours or overnight.
5. Just before serving, top the pie with whipped cream.

VALLEY INN RESTAURANT

PORTSMOUTH, RHODE ISLAND, USA

The Valley Inn Restaurant is the kind of place that fills up the minute the doors open, especially the coveted bar seats the locals know are the best spots in the house. But nearly four centuries ago, it was the site of a death that prompted one of the most infamous murder cases in American history.

Thomas and Rebecca Cornell left England in 1638 and were among Boston's earliest settlers before moving to Portsmouth in 1644. After Thomas's death, Rebecca put their son Thomas Cornell Jr. in charge of the estate, and soon after, Thomas Jr. moved his own family into the estate to live with his mother. Rebecca had an altercation with her son's second wife, Sarah. The younger woman had threatened her stepson with violence, a child Thomas had with his first (and late) wife, even chasing him with an axe until Rebecca intervened. Thomas, for his own part, didn't care well for his seventy-three-year-old mother. He'd barely heat the house in winter, if at all, and forced her to labor around the farm. Things got so bad for Rebecca that she began to make plans to leave the home and move in with her son Samuel instead.

But the move never happened.

In early 1673, Rebecca was found dead on the floor of her bedroom, half inside the fireplace, with burns all over her head and torso. The coroner concluded that it was an accident, that possibly she had fallen asleep and ash from her pipe had dropped onto her body.

But a few days later, another story emerged. John Briggs, Rebecca's brother, claimed to have been visited by an apparition. According to the New England Historical Society, John later testified that he awoke when "he felt something heave up the bedclothes twice." At first, he thought someone had climbed into his bed, and when he sat up, a bright light began to shine in the room, revealing the appearance of a woman standing by his bed.

"In the name of God, what art thou?" he cried out.

"I am your sister Cornell," the ghost said to him. "See how I was burned with fire."

And indeed, the woman appeared to be badly burned.

When John shared his story, officials reopened the investigation into Rebecca's death and discovered a wound in her stomach. Thomas Jr. was charged with murder. Among the things that put suspicion on him, Thomas had said, "that his Mother in her life time had a desire to have a good fire, and [he] further said that he thought God had answered her ends, for now she had it."

Thomas was sentenced to death by hanging and was executed in May 1673. Rebecca Cornell's murder is the only court case in American history to use spectral evidence—testimony by a ghost—to convict a killer.

That home burned down in the mid-1800s, and a new building that incorporated the surviving sections of the house replaced it. The home remained in the Cornell family until 1957, when Mario Occhi purchased it and turned it into the Valley Inn. Today, his son Joe Occhi owns the restaurant.

Joe himself has witnessed some strange happenings and heard interesting stories from guests. Once, a woman dining in the restaurant was drawn to the residential part of the building, crouching down and talking to an unseen person in front of a fireplace. Later, the guest said she'd been trying to communicate with a woman she'd seen in that spot, who was holding a bleeding child. At the same time this happened, a bottle flew off a shelf in the bar area.

Another incredible facet of this place's history: Lizzie "Lizbeth" Borden was directly descended from Thomas Jr. and Sarah's daughter, Innocent Cornell. Innocent was born after Thomas's hanging and was likely named as a tribute to her father.

Readers who have listened to my podcast, *Haunted Road*, or watched *Kindred Spirits* already know what a remarkable experience my investigating partner and costar Adam Berry and I had at the restaurant, where we were able to make contact with John Briggs and the younger Thomas Cornell. When we heard Thomas proclaiming his own innocence, we began to question our assumptions about John's testimony. John said Rebecca had told him, "See how I was burned with fire," *not*, "I was killed by my son."

Because Thomas Jr. died in disgrace, he was buried away from the rest of the family. The Cornell family cemetery is still standing on what's now a nearby property. But the younger Thomas was buried at the farthest possible spot away from the rest of the family, next to what's now the parking lot of the restaurant. We asked him if he wanted to be moved near the rest of his family, and he said no. I really can't blame him.

PENNE ALLA VODKA

Because this place is so close to my heart, I desperately wanted to include the Valley Inn in *Food to Die For*. I've eaten there many times, and I love the food, but I've learned one thing: Don't ask too many questions about their closely guarded family recipes, which have been passed down through generations. For *this* book, I finally wore down owner Joe Occhi. This pasta comes from him and his son, Chef Mario Occhi. They've given me their recipe for Penne alla Vodka, but it's not exact: Theirs relies on a house-made marinara sauce. The most they'd tell me about that sauce is that it's made with onions, celery, peppers, and both crushed and peeled tomatoes. This version of their pasta is delicious, but make no mistake—if you visit the Valley Inn, theirs will be just a little bit better.

Prep Time: 10 minutes	Cook Time: 30 minutes	Yield: 4 servings

INGREDIENTS

2 teaspoons salt, divided

1 pound penne pasta, fresh or dried

3 tablespoons unsalted butter

2 cloves garlic, minced

1/2 teaspoon black pepper

1/2 teaspoon red pepper flakes

3/4 cup vodka

2 cups marinara sauce

3/4 cup heavy cream

2 cups chopped fresh spinach

1/4 cup chopped fresh Italian parsley

1/4 cup chopped fresh basil, plus whole leaves for garnish

1/4 cup grated Parmesan cheese, plus more for garnish

INSTRUCTIONS

1. Fill a large pot with water and add 1 teaspoon of the salt. Bring the salted water to a boil. Cook the pasta according to package instructions, removing the pasta 1 minute before the indicated cooking time (the pasta will finish cooking in the sauce). Reserve 1 cup of the pasta water and set aside. Then drain the pasta and set aside.
2. While the pasta is cooking, prepare the sauce. In a large skillet over medium heat, melt the butter. Add the garlic, the remaining 1 teaspoon salt, the black pepper, and red pepper flakes. Cook for about 1 minute, stirring constantly. Don't let the garlic burn.
3. Add the vodka to the pan. Cook the mixture for 2–3 minutes, or long enough to reduce the liquid by half (this will also cook off the alcohol). Reduce the heat to medium-low.
4. Add the marinara sauce, followed by the heavy cream. Bring the mixture to a simmer, then add the spinach, parsley, and basil. Reduce the sauce until thickened, about 10–15 minutes.
5. Add the pasta to the sauce and toss to coat. Add in a splash of pasta water to help bind the pasta to the sauce, then add the Parmesan cheese. Cook, stirring frequently, for 2–3 minutes. If the sauce is too thick, add a bit more pasta water to thin the sauce to your desired consistency.
6. Serve the pasta garnished with more Parmesan and fresh basil.

LA CABOTINA

TRIORA, ITALY

High up in the Ligurian Alps, a tiny village holds a thousand years of history. One of the one hundred most beautiful Italian towns (as officially designated by I Borghi più belli d'Italia), Triora is famous for its medieval architecture—including the ruins of a castle—and for its unusually delicious bread. But it's also famous for another reason. In the 1500s, as witch hunts were sweeping Europe, Triora became known as "The Village of Witches," where Italy's most notorious witch trials were held. Today, it's often referred to as the "Salem of Europe" for its associations with America's most notoriously witchy city.

Every August, the city celebrates a festival of witches, called the Strigòra, with a medieval market, roving performers, and a procession through the streets. According to Borghi di Riviera, "The aim of the Strigòra event is to reevaluate and demystify the figure of the poor witches, unjustly condemned, among stalls, old-time games, lots of music and shows."

But that history is there every day, in the art and architecture depicting witches, and in La Cabotina, Triora's "house of witches," the place where the village's alleged practitioners of dark arts enacted their occult rituals. "The Cabotina was where the bàgiue, or witches, mixed their magical herbs and prepared potions," according to the blog Agriturismo Le Girandole. "It is said that, under the effects of their mixtures, they would indulge in obscene dances and orgies with the devil, who often took animal forms.

Stone archway in Triora

They would then kidnap the children of the village, left to play unattended in the open air, and turn themselves into pumpkins, waiting to be plucked by the lover and then cause him torment."

In 1587, conditions were bad in Triora. Bad harvests were causing famine, and people were dying. Desperate to find a solution, villagers started blaming witchcraft. Local authorities arrested about thirty women, torturing them so badly that one of them died during interrogation. Eventually those women gave up other names, which set off two years of witch trials in the village. It became the epicenter of Italy's witch hunts, which quickly spread throughout neighboring areas. In Triora, at least four women were burned at the stake.

Local authorities in Triora arrested about thirty women, torturing them so badly that one of them died during interrogation.

Today, people claim that the spirits of those wrongly accused women still walk the streets. I haven't seen a lot of evidence of this happening, but I believe it. The village faces its past and honors those women, throwing citywide celebrations and keeping their memories alive. It seems like a pretty nice place to spend an afterlife.

LIGURIAN FOCACCIA

Triora is famous for its particular round-shaped bread, Il Pane di Triora, the recipe for which isn't known outside the village. Bread has historically been so important to the village that there's an "oven alley" (Vicolo Forno) with an ancient bread-making oven, one of four public ovens once present in the city. In addition to Triora's famous round bread, there's plenty of focaccia, a signature bread of Liguria and one that's relatively easy to make, even with the various rises. The quality of the olive oil makes all the difference in this recipe, so splurge on something really good when you're ready to bake.

Prep Time: 45 minutes, plus rising time | Cook Time: 18 minutes | Yield: 2 large sheets

INGREDIENTS

4 1/2 cups all-purpose flour, divided, plus more for dusting

3 cups lukewarm water, divided

2 1/2 teaspoons active dry yeast, divided

2 1/2 teaspoons salt, divided

1 tablespoon sugar

1 1/4 cups extra virgin olive oil, divided, plus more for brushing

INSTRUCTIONS

1. Prepare the "sponge" (similar to a sourdough starter). In a small container with a lid, such as a mason jar, combine 1 cup of the flour, 1/2 cup of the lukewarm water, and 1/4 teaspoon of the yeast. Cover and leave at room temperature for about 12 hours.

2. Prepare the focaccia dough. Combine 1/2 cup of the lukewarm water and the remaining 2 1/4 teaspoons yeast. Let sit for 5 minutes to activate. In the bowl of a stand mixer fitted with a dough hook, combine the sponge mixture, 1 cup of the lukewarm water, the remaining 3 1/2 cups flour, 1 teaspoon of the salt, and the sugar. Knead for about 5 minutes on medium, then add the water and yeast mixture and 1/4 cup of the olive oil. Increase the kneading speed to medium-high and mix for about 10 minutes. Test its readiness by trying to tear a piece away. If it's too elastic to easily tear, it's ready. If not, knead for a few minutes more.

3. Remove the dough from the mixing bowl and turn it out onto a floured surface. Stretch the dough into a large rectangle, then fold it into thirds like you're folding a piece of paper to fit in an envelope. Make sure the seam side is down, then cover the dough with a kitchen towel and let rise on the counter for 30 minutes.

(recipe continues)

(recipe continued from page 27)

4. Divide 1/2 cup of the olive oil between two 15 x 13-inch rimmed baking sheets, spreading it evenly. Divide the dough in half, and flatten each portion of dough to roughly the size of the baking sheet, leaving 1–2 inches of space all around the dough. Transfer to the pans and let rest another 30 minutes, covered.

5. Uncover the dough, dust it with flour, and stretch the dough to the edges of the pan. (If it springs back into its original shape, let it rest for another 15–20 minutes, then try again.) Cover and let rise for another 60 minutes.

6. In a measuring cup, combine the remaining 1 cup lukewarm water and the remaining 1 1/2 teaspoons salt. Set aside.

7. Uncover the dough and make dimples with your fingers throughout—be generous with how many indentations you make. Make sure the dough stretches all the way to the lip of the pan so no liquid can get underneath in the next step.

8. Pour the remaining olive oil over the dough, 1/4 cup on each pan, spreading liberally, then divide the salted water evenly between the pans. Mix with your fingertips, making sure the entire surface is covered in liquid.

9. Let rise another 60 minutes.

10. Preheat the oven to 450°F. Bake for 16–18 minutes until lightly golden brown, then remove from the oven and immediately invert onto a wire rack. Brush with additional olive oil on the top and bottom, if desired.

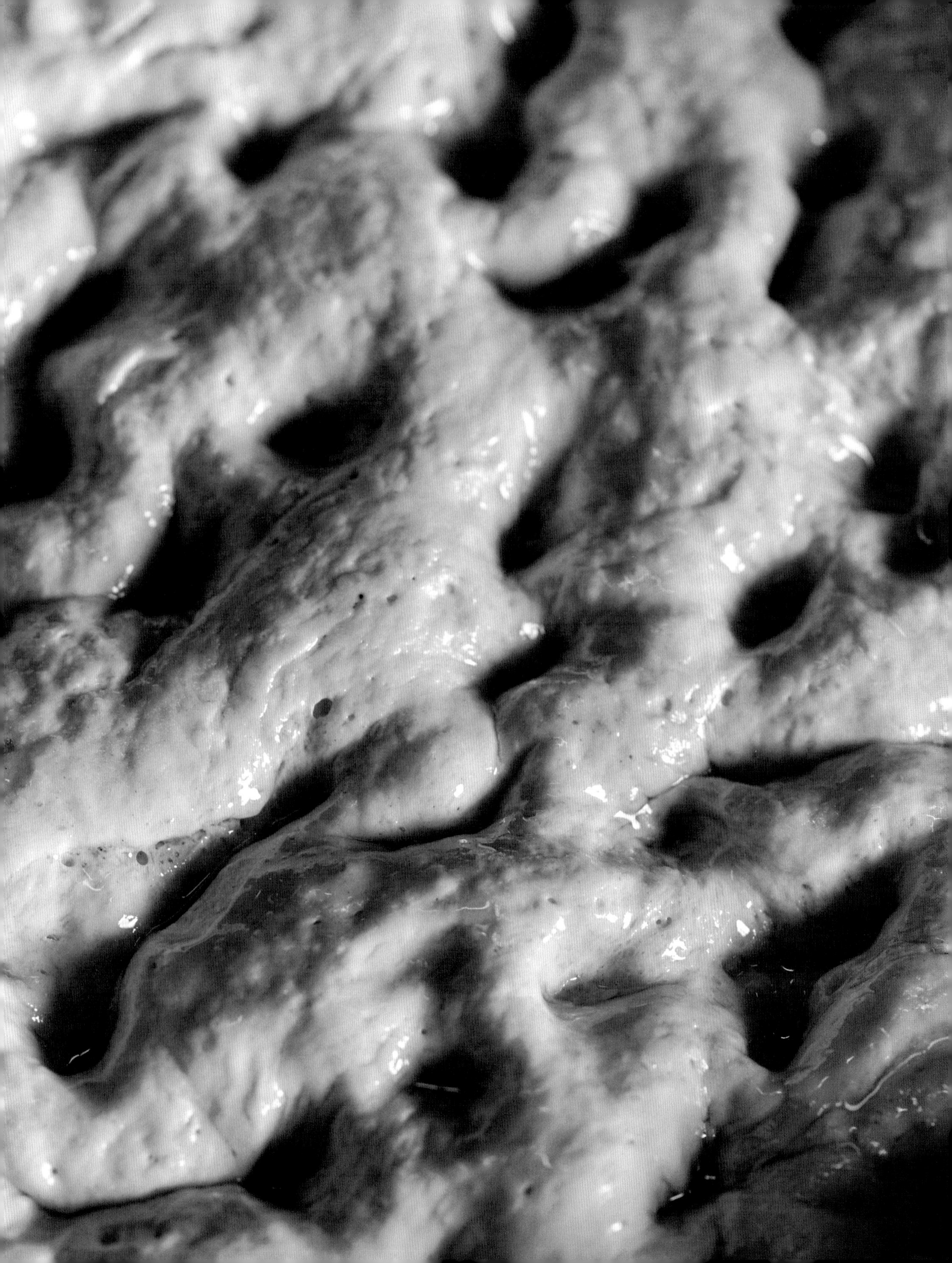

THE SPANIARDS INN

LONDON, ENGLAND, UK

Even if it weren't full of ghosts, the Spaniards Inn would be a historically significant location in London. In its more than four centuries of operation, the inn has seen many important moments—and collected plenty of spirits along the way.

Often referred to as the most haunted pub in London, the Spaniards was originally built in 1585 as a tollgate inn, a stopping place on a road where travelers once paid a toll to pass. Some of its earliest landlords were two brothers from Spain, Francesco and Juan Porero, likely the source of the inn's name. According to legend, the brothers fell in love with the same woman and dueled for her affection. Francesco won, and Juan died. Juan's body is buried nearby, and he's now one of the Spaniards' most famous ghosts—but far from the only one.

Notorious eighteenth-century thief and murderer Dick Turpin is also believed to haunt the property. Turpin's father, John, was the innkeeper at the Spaniards. His presence was a welcome one for the coach robbers known as highwaymen, who would use the quiet inn as a hideout between jobs. The Spaniards' staff told me that Dick is believed to haunt the upstairs rooms where he once hid and even the road outside. Also outside is the ghost of a horse, possibly Turpin's beloved Black Bess, that still trots through the car park.

Vintage engraving of a highwayman robbing a traveler

Downstairs, a spirit known as "Black Dick"—a *different* Dick than Turpin—is said to reach out to patrons he believes have had too much to drink, tugging their sleeves when it's time to go home. When he walked the earth in his mortal body, Black Dick was a moneylender. But one day, when he was on the road outside the inn, he was struck by a coach and killed. There's also a mysterious woman in white who is often spotted roaming the gardens; however, her identity is unknown. Staff have reported hearing their names whispered when no one living is around and witnessing objects falling and landing gently on the floor.

The Spaniards has a significant place in literary history, too. It was a frequent haunt of renowned authors and poets like William Blake, Robert Louis Stevenson, Mary Shelley, and Lord Byron. John Keats is believed to have written his famous "Ode to a Nightingale" in the pub's garden. The inn has even been inked into the pages of classic literature. Charles Dickens mentioned the Spaniards in *The Pickwick Papers*, and Bram Stoker wove the hotel into *Dracula* (we'll get deeper into Dracula lore later in chapter 2).

As part of his investigation of the Spaniards, British paranormal researcher David Farrant stayed overnight in one of the inn's upstairs rooms, once used as housing for staff. According to Farrant, staff in the pub often reported footsteps in those rooms, objects ending up in unusual places, and cold spots. "It was at 3:23 that an event occurred that seemed to defy any plausible explanation," he wrote in his 2004 book, *Dark Journey: True cases of Ghostly Phenomena from the Files of the British Psychic and Occult Society.* Farrant said that a light in the hallway shone through the gap under the door to his room. Then he saw the light change, assuming it was someone moving across the hallway. But when he got up from bed and poked out his head to look, no one was there. He went downstairs the next morning to ask guests and staff if they'd been in the hallway—and no one had. There were no pet dogs or cats at the hotel that would've been walking the halls either. "Casual coincidence, or the possible continuation of some ghostly activity?" Farrant wondered. He'll never be sure. But in the inn's nearly 450-year history, a few unsettled spirits are bound to still be swalking the halls.

STEWET BEEF

Centuries ago, pub fare largely consisted of roasted meat and poultry. But it was also common to find recipes like this stew, adapted from *Medieval Cookery*'s version of a fifteenth-century English recipe, fare likely served on the Spaniards' tables when it opened in 1585. The original ingredient list called for now-endangered red sandalwood and hyssop, though sage works nicely as a substitute.

Prep Time: 20 minutes	Cook Time: 1 hour 30 minutes	Yield: 4 servings

INGREDIENTS

1 pound stew beef, cubed

1 medium onion, chopped

1 cup water

2 cups medium-bodied red wine like Syrah or Zinfandel

1 tablespoon dried parsley

1 teaspoon dried sage

2 teaspoons salt

3 slices sandwich bread

1 1/2 cups beef broth

1/2 teaspoon ground cinnamon

1/8 teaspoon ground cloves

1/8 teaspoon ground mace

1 tablespoon red wine vinegar

2 tablespoons dried currants (see Note below)

Crusty bread, for serving

INSTRUCTIONS

1. In a large pot or Dutch oven over medium-high heat, add the beef, onion, water, wine, parsley, sage, and salt. Bring the mixture to a boil, then reduce the heat to a simmer.
2. While the stew is simmering, tear the bread into small pieces, discarding the crusts, and place the pieces in a medium bowl. Add the beef broth. Stir and mash the bread in the broth, making sure to break it down. Add the bread mixture into the stew. Cover the pot and simmer for 1 hour.
3. Combine the cinnamon, cloves, and mace in a small mixing bowl, then stir in the vinegar. Add the vinegar mixture to the stew, then add the currants. Simmer uncovered for another 20 minutes. Serve with crusty bread.

Note: If you can't find currants, dried cranberries could work in a pinch.

FENESTRELLE FORT

TURIN, ITALY

Depending on who you ask, the Fenestrelle Fort is famous for one of two reasons. Some would say the abandoned fort's biggest claim to fame is its architecture. Snaking down the alpine mountains is an enormous stone fortification that took more than one hundred years to build. Others would say the fort is best known for the prisoners who were once trapped there—some of whom are allegedly still there to this day.

Sometimes called the Great Wall of the Alps, the Fenestrelle Fort is located in the northwestern Piedmont region of Italy, about fifty miles from the region's capital city, Turin. The fort's scale would be impressive by modern standards, but given that construction on Fenestrelle began in 1728, its size is a marvel. The series of military and civilian buildings were built to protect Piedmont, producer of some of the world's best wines, from French invaders to the north. Fortifications stretch two miles along a mountainous ridge of the Chisone and are connected by a tunnel staircase that has four thousand steps.

Inside the heavily protected fortification are military barracks, munitions storehouses, a governor's palace, a church, parade grounds, and "a drawbridge of astonishing elevation," as described in an 1852 article in London's *Morning Chronicle*. But the enormous fort, completed in 1850, never saw military conflict. Instead, Fenestrelle became a prison, used to hold enemies of whoever was in power over the hotly contested border region—sometimes the northern Italian kingdom of Piedmont-Sardinia but sometimes the French.

Fenestrelle's original prisoners were misbehaving military officers who had been sent there after engaging in duels. Napoleon also sent political dissidents and conspirators to the alpine fort (though let me debunk a rumor: Some say the Man in the Iron Mask was imprisoned at Fenestrelle, but he was actually held in the Fort of Pignerol).

In 1861, a monumental change occurred: The city-states that had made up the Italian peninsula for centuries united into one nation state, the Italy we know today. This movement was driven by powerful rulers like Victor Emmanuel II, the king of Piedmont-Sardinia, who became the first king of Italy. Many people in the south of the country resisted the change, and hordes of soldiers who had fought against unification were imprisoned in Fenestrelle.

That same year, a group of a few hundred Neapolitan prisoners attempted a coup in the fort but were thwarted. Many prisoners died in the harsh mountain climate. In the 1800s, the Catholic journal *The Rambler* called Fenestrelle "the Siberia of Italy," referring to its frozen climate much of the year. In 2008, the Two Sicilies Committee installed a plaque at the Fenestrelle Fort, reading, "Between 1860 and 1861, thousands of soldiers from the army of the Two Sicilies who had refused to renounce the king and their ancient homeland were segregated in the fortress of Fenestrelle. Few returned home. Most died of starvation." Some contest this claim, citing the lack of mass graves at Fenestrelle as evidence. According to the fort's website, those soldiers were briefly imprisoned there before being conscripted into the newly formed Army of the Kingdom of Italy.

After World War II, the fort was largely abandoned, falling into disrepair as it was looted over the decades. "This is not simply a fortification," *Observer* travel editor Eric Newby wrote in 1967, "but a whole forgotten and ruined world. . . . It is an untenanted, nightmare place, which seems to go on for ever and ever and one in which utter silence prevails."

Well, sometimes it's silent. Sometimes there's a ghost shooting off a musket in the middle of the night, which is what travel journalist Nino Lo Bello went in search of in 1985. "You don't have to be a nut to do the 'ghost fortress,'" he wrote afterward. "All you need is a nimble pair of sneakers or rubber-soled shoes and a disbelief in ghosts." At that time, the fort was still abandoned, so Lo Bello hired a "willing Fenestrelle youth" who showed him "how to go up, what to look for once up there, and where to avoid the ghost." On his visit, he did witness the majesty of the old fort but didn't report any ghostly encounters.

Today, the fort is a historic site where many visitors report experiencing things they can't explain, like shadows moving around the crypt in the chapel, hearing disembodied screams and moans, seeing tables and chairs move on their own, being touched by invisible icy hands, and hearing footsteps, including marching feet, after hours.

But according to Lo Bello, those ghosts are friendly. That phantom shooter, he wrote, is "not likely to give rubberneckers much trouble inasmuch as he usually lets off with an authoritative musket shot in the middle of the night when no one is there poking around," he said. "Besides, the ghost is a good guy."

BAGNA CAUDA

A Piedmontese recipe that hails from the medieval period, bagna cauda is northern Italy's answer to fondue. Bagna cauda, which translates to "hot bath," is a simple, garlic-forward dip kept warm over a burner, served with vegetables and bread. If you don't want to invest in a specialty bagna cauda serving dish, any fondue-style warming dish with a gentle heat source underneath will work. (A warning: Don't serve this dish to any vampire friends.)

Prep Time: 10 minutes | Cook Time: 40 minutes | Yield: 6 to 8 servings

INGREDIENTS

6 heads garlic (about 12 cloves per head)

1 1/2 cups good-quality olive oil, divided

3 ounces good-quality anchovy fillets, drained

1–2 tablespoons unsalted butter, optional

An assortment of bite-sized raw and cooked vegetables, for dipping (try a mix of small potatoes, bell peppers, celery, fresh fennel, Romanesco or cauliflower, and endive or radicchio leaves)

Crusty bread, for dipping

INSTRUCTIONS

1. Peel the garlic cloves. Slice each clove in half lengthwise.
2. In a medium skillet over low heat, combine the garlic and 1/2 cup of the olive oil. Cook the garlic low and slow for 10 minutes, stirring occasionally with a wooden spoon. (It's very important to keep your temperature low and not burn the garlic.)
3. Add the anchovies. Cook for another 10 minutes, stirring often and mashing the fillets gently with the wooden spoon to help dissolve them into the oil.
4. Add the remaining 1 cup olive oil and cover the pan. Simmer on low for 30 minutes until the flavors have fully melded.
5. Remove the pan from the heat. If using the butter, swirl in a pat (the most traditional bagna cauda recipes don't include butter, but I like the silky texture and flavor it adds to the dip).
6. Transfer the dip to a warming dish and serve immediately with the vegetables and bread.

WINCHESTER MYSTERY HOUSE

SAN JOSE, CALIFORNIA, USA

The legends of Winchester Mystery House reach into every corner of the spooky American psyche. A solitary widow spending her money on whims because she had no one left to spend it on. A sprawling estate that makes no logical sense, even after a century of study. A legacy of loneliness and sorrow. An American dream gone wrong.

From the outside, Sarah Winchester's life was charmed. In 1862, she married William Winchester, son of the founder of the Winchester Repeating Arms Company, and the two lived well in New Haven, Connecticut, on the company's earnings (especially after 1873, when the company released the Winchester Model 73, called "the gun that won the West").

But on the inside, Sarah's life was filled with loss. She and William welcomed a baby, Annie Pardee Winchester, in 1866, but the infant died at only five weeks old. The loss of their only child devastated the couple, who never had more children. Three years later, Sarah's father, Leonard Pardee, died. In an eight-month span between 1880 and 1881, Sarah lost three more people who were very important to her: her father-in-law, Oliver Winchester, her mother, Sarah Pardee, and finally, her husband, William, who died of tuberculosis three months after inheriting the rifle company from his father.

Forty years old and an unimaginably wealthy widow, Sarah was looking for a fresh start—so she headed west, landing in San Jose, California, just south of San Francisco. She purchased a modest farmhouse called Llanada Villa in 1886, and she got to work on construction and renovations. Once the building started, it didn't stop until her death in 1922.

The end result of her work: 160 rooms across 24,000 square feet, with 10,000 windows, 2,000 doors, and 6 kitchens. Sarah definitely imbued the house with peculiarities, using the number thirteen often and working mostly without blueprints or a professional architect. Some of the windows are embedded into floors; some of those doorways open into nothing but a drop down to the room below; some of the staircases dead-end at a ceiling. One room even has a one-way door leading into the room and an exit that, once you've gone through, you can't open again.

The Winchester rifle, the first to fire repeat rounds without stopping to reload, revolutionized the world. It also fueled wars and colonization, enabling the killing of countless people, many of them innocent of any crime. Writing of her family's legacy in *The Guardian* in 2016, Winchester descendant Laura Trevelyan said, "The company's officials were always wary of having a history of their beloved rifles written—we don't want dead buffalo and Indians on every page, observed my great-great-uncle Ed Pugsley, the chief engineer." Famous criminals also favored the guns, including, in more modern times, the Zodiac Killer, who used Winchester Western Super X ammunition to shoot two of his victims.

People claimed that Sarah was crazed with grief and kept building to escape the ghosts of those people who died by Winchester guns. (If she kept building, the logic went, the restless spirits would be confused and not find her.) Others said she was obsessed with spiritualism and conducted séances inside, that Sarah had enlisted a spiritualist who told her that she had to build twenty-four hours a day to appease ghosts who had placed a curse on her.

In reality, Sarah enjoyed architecture, and it's likely that she just kept building because it was a way to keep staff employed during times when there wasn't much other work to be done.

One room even has a one-way door leading into the room and an exit that, once you've gone through, you can't open again.

After Sarah's death, John and Mayme Brown bought the house in 1923, with the intention of building an amusement park on the grounds. But the curiosity factor was so strong that people came in droves to see the house—no need for any other attractions. The Browns started giving tours, and it even attracted the attention of Harry Houdini in 1924, who gave it the nickname "the mystery house."

Take a tour today, and you'll almost definitely hear tales of staff members' paranormal experiences in the home. In the basement, people see a "wheelbarrow ghost" pushing a cart to gather coal or lumber. In a room used for linen storage, people feel tugs at their skirts or their hair. Shadow figures appear frequently, even allegedly showing up in a photo taken by a former marketing employee.

The house definitely embraces its spooky reputation. Every Halloween, it hosts a major haunted house event and offers flashlight tours after dark. Sometimes you can even go on paranormal investigations there. Who knows? You might be the one to get answers from Sarah after all these years.

CHERRY ICE

San Jose's Santa Clara Valley has a year-round growing season, which allows for excellent fresh produce in any month. This recipe, adapted from an April 1900 recipe in the *San Jose Herald*, makes the most of that seasonal bounty. We don't know whether Sarah Winchester would have enjoyed a cherry ice, but we do know that she grew cherries on her property. So it's possible that, when you enjoy this, you're tasting something exactly Sarah she would have.

Prep Time: 15 minutes, plus at least 2 hours freezing time — Yield: 4 servings

INGREDIENTS

2 cups granulated sugar

2 cups water

1 quart (about 1 1/2 pounds) ripe fresh cherries, plus more for garnish

1/2 cup brandy

Juice of 10 lemons

Lemon twist for garnish

INSTRUCTIONS

1. In a medium glass bowl with a lid, dissolve the sugar into the water.
2. In a large mortar or a large mixing bowl, pound the cherries with a pestle until they're fully mashed. Don't mind the pits. Remove the fruit to a cheesecloth and strain the juice into the sugar mixture (squeeze tightly to get as much liquid as you can from the fruit). Discard the solids.
3. Stir in the brandy and lemon juice, then cover and freeze until solid.
4. To serve, scrape the top of the ice mixture with a large spoon to create a slushy texture, then scoop into small serving dishes. Garnish with a cherry or a lemon twist.

ORANGE VALLEY

DEVONSHIRE, BERMUDA, UK

When the *Sea Venture* shipwrecked on an uninhabited island in 1609, not all the passengers were unhappy about the unintended stop. Rather than press on to the Jamestown Colony, where famine and conflicts with Native Americans awaited them, some wanted to stay behind in Bermuda, where food was plentiful. In fact, two of them, Edward Waters and Christopher Carter, so desperately wanted to stay that they attempted to murder governor Sir Thomas Gates to thwart their departure. When the party set sail for the colony (where they ended up saving the starving colonists with wild pigs from the island) Waters and Carter were left behind. Two attempted murderers became the island's first permanent inhabitants.

The wreck of the *Sea Venture* became so legendary that it inspired William Shakespeare to write *The Tempest,* but it was only one of the hundreds upon hundreds of incidents that gave the mythic Bermuda Triangle its reputation for causing an inexplicably high number of downed ships and strange disappearances. That stretch of sea has claimed countless lives. Maybe that's why the island has so many ghost stories. When I visited, I could immediately feel something uncanny about the island, especially at Orange Valley.

Orange Valley, the historic estate in Devonshire, Bermuda, embraces that spooky reputation. When you approach today, you'll notice something striking before you reach the stately home: a sign on the gatepost that reads, "Orange Valley, circa 1802. Beware of Ghost."

It's not exactly accurate. According to Orange Valley owner John Cox, more than one ghost has been spotted on the property. And none of them are anything to be wary of.

"Looking up at Orange Valley from the old pedestrian gate off Parsons Lane, one would never guess that as many as three ghosts inhabit the old house," John wrote in his latest book, *Ghosts and Other Bermuda Tales.*

Part of the sixth generation of Coxes to live at Orange Valley, John is a historian and author preserving the history of the estate named after the orange groves that grew when his great-great-great-great-grandfather, Captain William Cox, purchased the land in 1796. Today, the home is open for tours, where many people report seeing apparitions of spirits who lived in the house in ages past.

Two attempted murderers became the island's first permanent inhabitants.

One woman, as John wrote in his book, reported seeing "a middle-aged woman dressed in beautiful but strikingly early period costume." Others have witnessed candles blowing out on their own and then reigniting.

Although he lives in a house many people—including himself—believe is haunted, John says he hasn't had an encounter in many years (unlike the visitors who frequently claim to experience ghostly activity there). As he wrote in *Ghosts and Other Bermuda Tales*, John had an intense experience in his early teens. "At the time, I was occupying the west bedroom upstairs," he wrote. "Night after night I would be shaken awake—someone or something intentionally disturbed my sleep. Turning on the bedside lamp and looking about me, there was nobody but myself in the room. Then the sound of footsteps would begin, pacing back-and-forth across the room. An orb of light would also pass by the unopened door, which led into the day room.

"Finally, one blustery night, I had had enough. I sat up and spoke out loud, 'Please stop this. You are scaring me!' In the next instant, I felt a warm hand touch my neck. It was as real as if my own mother had touched me. Again, no one else was in the room. After that night, I was never again troubled by the ghost."

Sea Venture depicted on a 1910 Bermuda postage stamp

John believes that the ghost in that bedroom is Mary Robinson Cox, wife of the original owner, Captain William Cox, who died in 1806 while her husband was away at sea. She has appeared to other family members wearing a long white dress with her hair in ringlets. "The mysterious woman stood by the chimney and seemed to want to communicate with me, but she said nothing," John quoted his cousin as saying in *Ghosts and Other Bermuda Tales*. "She just gazed at me and then beckoned me towards the rose garden." The cousin looked away, and when she looked back, the woman had vanished. Other family members have seen departed relatives as well, like John's brother Donald seeing a man that the brothers believe is their great-uncle Aubrey Cox in an upstairs window.

ORANGE VALLEY SPONGE CAKE

In his vast archives of the Cox family history (and the Cox family ghosts), John Cox has a handwritten recipe from Aubrey Cox for Orange Valley sponge cake, which he shared with me for this book. Aubrey Cox lived from 1861 to 1929 and, according to John, could very well be a ghost whose presence is still at Orange Valley today.

Prep Time: 15 minutes	Cook Time: 60 minutes	Yield: 12 servings

INGREDIENTS

Butter, for greasing

1¾ cups all-purpose flour, sifted, plus more for the pan

10 eggs

2 cups granulated sugar

Powdered sugar, for dusting, optional

INSTRUCTIONS

1. Preheat the oven to 325°F. Butter and flour a 12-inch Bundt pan.
2. In a medium mixing bowl, combine 4 of the eggs with the sugar. Mix well, then add the flour and stir to incorporate well.
3. Separate the remaining 6 eggs. Add the yolks into the batter, mixing well, and place the 6 egg whites into a separate mixing bowl.
4. Using a hand mixer or a stand mixer, beat the egg whites on high until stiff peaks form.
5. Gently fold one third of the whites into the batter, incorporating fully, as gently as you can. Repeat with another third, incorporating fully, then the final third.
6. Transfer the batter to the prepared pan and bake for about 60 minutes, until a knife comes out clean. Take care not to disturb the pan while baking or the cake will fall. Remove to a rack to cool until just warm to the touch, then turn the cake out onto a platter. Dust with powdered sugar before serving, if using.

CAVE OF WITCHES

ZUGARRAMURDI, NAVARRE, SPAIN

Deep within the maw of a cave in northern Spain, a dark ritual ensues. Feet pound on the dirt below, flames create flickering shadows on the walls, sweat and smoke fill the air—and in the midst of it all, the Devil appears, standing on the banks of a river flowing straight from hell.

The legends of the *akelarre*, the pagan observance of the witches' sabbath, have spread throughout northern Spain's Basque countryside for centuries. The folktales—of events that likely didn't happen, like salacious dances, animal sacrifices, and Devil worship—are so ubiquitous that master painter Francisco Goya portrayed the rituals in his works *Aquelarre* and *Witches' Sabbath*, which depict reverential women encircling a demonic goat-man.

During a dark time ruled by superstition and fear, those legends led to innocent people's deaths.

Zugarramurdi may be a tiny village in northern Spain, but it was the site of the largest witch trial in all of history. At its peak, more than seven thousand people stood accused of witchcraft, many of them accused by children, based on their dreams. The "witches" were accused of participating in akelarre in Zugarramurdi's Cave of Witches, an enormous cave carved by the flow of the Olabidea stream, said in local lore to flow directly from hell itself.

Witchcraft—or at least the practice of making medicinal "potions" from plants—had been around for centuries. But in 1608, a local woman named María de Ximildegui made some eyebrow-raising claims that she had taken part in demonic rituals at the cave and named other Zugarramurdi residents as participants. In 1609, the Spanish Inquisition came to the tiny village at the French border, undertaking an enormous investigation that became known as the Basque Witch Trials, the largest witch hunt in history. Inquisitors extracted confessions from more than eighteen hundred people—the vast majority of them were children who claimed to have unwillingly participated in the rituals while they were asleep—but almost every person later recanted their stories. Of those tried, fifty-three were found guilty. Some were burned at the stake, while others died while being marched long distances to prisons. Many people believe that their spirits linger in the village where they were wrongfully accused of and cruelly executed for those crimes.

At the peak of the witch trial, more than seven thousand people stood accused of witchcraft, many of them accused by children, based on their dreams.

Today, Zugarramurdi honors that era and those who were killed at the Witches Museum, explaining the Basque myths and legends that fueled the panic in the seventeenth century.

Festivalgoers in Zugarramurdi

Locals also hold a huge unofficial party at the cave every year around the summer solstice in tribute to those witches. Local photographer Pablo S. Quiza has written about his experience covering the festival, saying, "This was not the typical festival. It wasn't advertised in media and most information you could get about it was mouth to mouth. It used to be celebrated in the Saturday closest to June 21, the summer solstice, but you never knew if you were going on the correct Saturday until you were there!

"The festival used to happen very late in this remote location," he added. "Rivers of alcohol, drugs of all kind, and fights became too common and at one point the organizers decided to halt the rave. Attending revelers would usually sleep at the site, in the fields, inside cars, or wherever they collapse."

Maybe if you're visiting Navarre around the summer solstice, you'll be lucky enough to stumble onto the revelry. If not, there are other ways to experience it. The Basque Witch Trials were a plotline in season 4 of *True Blood*, and were the subject of a 2013 movie, *Witching and Bitching*.

SALT COD–STUFFED PIQUILLO PEPPERS

The sweet, slightly spicy piquillo pepper is native to Navarre and is so exceptional that it's a protected food with a Designation of Origin, like Champagne. Because it holds its shape well, the piquillo is ideal to use as a vessel for other foods—like the unbelievably delicious salt cod so common in Basque cuisine.

Prep Time: 10 minutes | Cook Time: 40 minutes | Yield: 4 servings

INGREDIENTS

4 tablespoons olive oil, divided

1 1/2 small white onions, chopped, divided

2 cloves garlic, minced

1 pound salted cod, soaked and drained, or fresh cod (see Notes below)

2 tablespoons all-purpose flour

2 3/4 cups milk, divided

20–24 jarred piquillo peppers, drained, divided (see Notes below)

1/4 cup dry white wine

Salt and pepper, to taste

INSTRUCTIONS

1. In a large skillet over medium heat, heat 2 tablespoons of the olive oil. Add half a chopped onion and the garlic, and cook until translucent, about 8 minutes.
2. Add the cod, breaking it up as it cooks. Cook about 6–8 more minutes until opaque, depending on whether you're using salted cod or fresh.
3. Stir in the flour and cook 1 more minute, stirring often. Slowly stir in 1 1/2 cups of the milk, and cook 2–3 more minutes, until the mixture has thickened.
4. When the mixture is cool enough to handle, stuff 12–14 piquillo peppers with the mixture, and lay them in a single layer in a baking dish. Set aside.
5. Preheat the oven to 375°F.
6. Roughly chop the remaining peppers.
7. In a large skillet over medium heat, heat the remaining olive oil and add the remaining onions. Cook until translucent, about 8 minutes. Add the chopped peppers and cook 2 more minutes, followed by the wine, cooking another 2–3 minutes. Add the remaining 1 1/4 cups milk and stir everything together.
8. Remove from the heat and blend the sauce in the pan using an immersion blender (or transfer to a blender). Taste the sauce and adjust the seasonings if desired.
9. Pour the sauce over the peppers, then bake for 10 minutes. Serve hot.

Notes: Salted cod should be soaked in water and drained to remove some of the salt, but you could also use fresh cod and add 1/2 teaspoon salt.

You should be able to find jarred piquillo peppers, but if you can't, whole roasted red peppers could work in a pinch.

CHAPTER 2

NOBLE CRIMES

Growing up as an American kid in a country that's fairly new to the game of, well, being a country, I found the idea of castles and ruins felt like it was a world away. The ghosts—which I imagined as apparitions of bloodthirsty royalty, ghostly knights in shining armor, and transparent moaning monks, to name a few—who made those places home seemed out of reach in my younger years. Today, not only have I become more familiar with the real stories of these spaces, but I've also even investigated a few myself. Their haunts are the type that locals speak of in whispers, generation after generation. And as legendary as these supernatural stories may be, the foods associated with some of these jaw-dropping locations will give you the opportunity to fix a hauntingly royal feast of your own, moaning monk not included.

CHÂTEAU DE BRISSAC

BRISSAC LOIRE AUBANCE, FRANCE

At seven stories tall and containing more than two hundred rooms, the Château de Brissac is the tallest castle in France, locally described as the "giant of the Loire Valley." It's in remarkably good condition for a fifteenth-century structure, which was built by the first Duke of Brissac, with stunning stonework and turrets reaching into the sky. Today, it's still an aristocratic family home, owned by the fourteenth Duke of Brissac, and is home to the Château de Brissac winery. It's an idyllic place to visit on a wine-tasting tour of the French countryside, especially because of the château's lush grounds and underground river. It's also an ideal place to visit if you're looking for a resident ghost.

In the late-fifteenth century, the castle belonged to the second Duke of Brissac, Jacques de Brézé, and his wife, Charlotte, who was believed to be the daughter of King Charles VII and his mistress, Agnes Sorel. Jacques and Charlotte didn't exactly have a happy marriage. According to legend, Charlotte began an affair with huntsman Pierre de Lavergne. De Brézé caught the couple together—and murdered them both in one of the castle's tower rooms.

As the story goes, the spirits of the murdered lovers drove de Brézé away from his ancestral home, haunting him with their ghostly moans.

In the centuries since the crime, Pierre's spirit is believed to have moved on. Charlotte, though, is still a regular presence in the château. Today, she's known as La Dame Verte—the "Green Lady"—who appears as an eyeless specter in a green dress. The Green Lady is known to moan in the night and to prefer the tower room, where her life ended.

Despite Jacques fleeing the castle, the de Brézé family has continued to live there. Château de Brissac is now open to visitors, including overnight stays in two guest rooms. That's where visitors may or may not encounter Charlotte—"A troubled soul," as the castle's website describes her, who "wander[s] through feverish nights." Some might be discouraged by the promise of the Green Lady. I (and probably you) consider it an overt enticement.

"I'll stop there," the twelfth Duke of Brissac, Pierre de Cossé, wrote of the home in 1954, as quoted on the château's website. "You have to know how not to say everything. May this work inspire in the reader the temptation to visit, in Anjou, one of the jewels in its crown, Brissac, this great vessel sometimes harshly tormented in the gusts of our history, but fortunately piloted by the same hands for nearly half a millennium."

"May the visitor discover, in the gentleness of Anjou, what I have not described," he added, "may he know how to compose an emotion from his impressions, and under the sky of the Loire Valley, from his emotions, a memory."

Guest bedroom in Château de Brissac

PORK RILLETTES

The French affectionately call this appetizer *confiture de cochon* (which literally translates to "pig jam"), but don't be fooled: Pork rillettes (ree-yet) are something truly special. Similar to a pâté, this rich, slow-cooked spread is a perfect addition to a charcuterie board, along with cheese, bread, and cornichons. The recipe originated in the Loire Valley and dates back to the medieval period—the château even celebrates a "Rillauds Fair" every year in homage to the village's signature dish. Like many French foods prized today, rillettes evolved from the need to take the least usable food scraps and transform them into something edible. It takes some time to make, but once you taste the results, you won't mind at all.

Prep Time: 30 minutes, plus marinating time | Cook Time: 3 hours | Yield: 8 servings

INGREDIENTS

1 pound boneless pork shoulder, cut into 1-inch cubes, skin-on

1 pound pork belly, cut into 1-inch cubes, skin-on

1 tablespoon salt, plus more to taste

1 teaspoon black pepper, plus more, to taste

10 sprigs fresh thyme

1 cup dry white wine, such as Sauvignon Blanc or Chenin Blanc

1 cup water

3 cloves garlic, crushed but still whole

3 bay leaves

2 shallots, quartered

INSTRUCTIONS

1. Place the cubed pork shoulder and pork belly in a mixing bowl. Coat well with salt and pepper. Toss in the sprigs of thyme and mix everything together. Cover and refrigerate overnight.
2. Preheat the oven to 275°F.
3. In a large Dutch oven over medium heat, combine the marinated pork, wine, water, garlic, bay leaves, and shallots. Bring to a simmer, then cover the pot and transfer it to the oven.
4. Cook for 1 hour, then stir the mixture. Press on the pork to encourage it to break up and release its fats. Replace the lid, then place the pot back in the oven. Cook for another hour.
5. At the 2-hour mark, stir the mixture again. Leave the lid off to encourage the liquids to evaporate. Cook another 30 minutes to 1 hour, until there's mostly only fat at the bottom of the pot and the pork is very tender and easily falling apart.
6. Remove the pork from the oven. Discard the thyme, garlic, bay leaves, and shallots. Remove any large chunks of fat or skin and discard.

(recipe continues)

(recipe continued from page 55)

7. Separate the pork from the fat either by removing the meat using a skimmer or by straining the mixture through a colander. Make sure to reserve the fat—you will use it again later.

8. Place the pork in a large mixing bowl and shred it with a fork (you want the pork to be in small, fine pieces). Add 3–4 tablespoons of the fat back to the pork to make a smooth mixture that will spread easily on a cracker or slice of baguette. Taste the rillettes and adjust the seasonings if necessary.

9. Transfer the rillettes to a lidded jar (or several small ones). Pour additional fat (or oil, see Note below) over the mixture. This will seal the rillettes from the air and allow the mixture to last several days before consuming—if you can wait that long. Cover and refrigerate.

10. Once you're ready to eat, scrape off the fat (or oil) layer. At that point, eat the whole jar of rilletes within a few days. Serve as an appetizer with bread and cornichons, or as part of a charcuterie spread.

Note: If you don't have enough rendered fat from the pork, you can use olive oil to cover the meat.

ČACHTICE CASTLE

ČACHTICE, SLOVAKIA

Elizabeth Báthory—or as you may know her, the "Blood Countess"—was born in 1560, into a wealthy and powerful Hungarian family that, well, had a bit of a reputation. The Báthorys, possibly because they often married within their own family, were predisposed to mental illness and excessive violence: Her cousin, King Stephen Báthory of Poland, punished peasants for speaking out against him by cutting off their ears and noses.

"Elizabeth had a slender body, gorgeous cream complexion, and beautiful raven-black hair," University of Lodz professor Aleksandra Bartosiewicz wrote in *Review of Historical Sciences* in 2018. "From an early age she distinguished herself by not only her extraordinary beauty but also enormous intelligence." Báthory spoke five languages and unfortunately suffered from her family's epileptic seizures.

When she married nobleman Ferenc Nádasdy in 1575, he gifted his young bride Čachtice Castle (in Slovakia) as a wedding present. Nádasdy was cruel; there are reports of him torturing his prisoners for fun while out fighting wars, and of him entertaining himself at home by physically abusing his servants. "Once he ordered to smear a young girl with honey so that she was constantly bitten by insects," Bartosiewicz wrote. "Apparently, it was Ferenc who taught his wife a trick called 'kicking the stars' which consisted of putting a piece of oil-soaked paper between the fingers of a disobedient servant and setting it on fire."

While Nádasdy was away fighting, Báthory devoted herself to herbalism, learning which plants most effectively worked as medicine—and this is likely how legends of her making potions and poisons grew, which became part of the crimes she was accused of. Those same legends had her consorting with a pale, sharp-toothed man who was allegedly a vampire and had her torturing servants by sticking needles under their fingernails or pouring water on them and sending them outside to freeze. She didn't just torture her servants in these stories; she murdered them and bathed in their blood for her own selfish gains and relied on her closest confidants to remove the bodies.

According to Bartosiewicz and other contemporary scholars, the stories just don't add up. Disease and early mortality rates meant that staffing the castle would have been a challenge, never mind treating that staff as disposable and replacing them after a murderous whim. Bartosiewicz also pointed out that it would take the blood of thirty people to fill a bath, and that "the bloody custom" wasn't mentioned until one hundred years after Báthory's death.

What scholars can verify is that Elizabeth's husband died in 1604, and her cousin Stephen Báthory died in 1605, leaving Elizabeth enormously wealthy. At the time, it was customary for the crown to seize assets from those convicted of crimes. Hungarian King Matthias II just so happened to owe Báthory a substantial sum; if Elizabeth turned out to be a criminal, the Hungarian king could not only fill the royal coffers, but he could also remove the head of a powerful family. King Matthias II ordered investigations into her alleged tortures, which were likely exaggerated. The findings, provided by Elizabeth's own cousin, stated that she had tortured and murdered more than six hundred women. She was accused and imprisoned in Čachtice Castle in 1610 but was never actually tried. But her extended family agreed to cancel the king's debt in exchange for managing Elizabeth's imprisonment, likely as a means to seize her lands. Three servants who were accused with Báthory were found guilty and executed in 1611. She died in 1614, a prisoner in her own home.

Čachtice Castle burned to ruins in 1799 and didn't open to the public as a tourist attraction until 2014, centuries after Báthory's reputation as a notorious serial killer had been cemented in the public imagination.

"I'm very convinced that it is, as we put it in England, a stitch-up job," Cambridge professor Annouchka Bayley told the *Associated Press* in 2024. Among Bayley's concerns: that Báthory was educating young women in the castle, not just in folk medicine but also in literacy, and that she owned a printing press. "You have to remember, these are the years of the Reformation and the Counter-Reformation where people were being burned at the stake for their heretical beliefs. The printing presses, which had started flourishing across Europe, were giving people much wider access to information, and this was seen as very dangerous," Bayley said. Essentially, Báthory was the first female self-publisher on record. "And that's arguably why she needed not only to be shut up," Bayley told the BBC, "but erased from the history books and, where not erased, turned into a bogeyman."

Bayley wasn't talking about ghosts when she likened Báthory to a bogeyman, but she could have—according to legends, the countess's ghost still roams the castle today.

BRYNDZOVÉ HALUŠKY

Not much is known about what Elizabeth Báthory liked to eat in the castle—except, as we now know, it almost definitely wasn't the blood of her servants. She likely would have eaten this traditional Slovakian meal, which dates back to about the thirteenth century and is widely considered the national dish of Slovakia.

Prep Time: 20 minutes | Cook Time: 15 minutes | Yield: 4 servings

INGREDIENTS

6 slices thick-cut bacon, cut crosswise into 1/2-inch pieces

1/2–1 teaspoon salt, plus more for salting the cooking water

4 medium-size starchy potatoes (such as Russet or Yukon Gold), peeled and grated (see Notes below)

1 cup all-purpose flour

1 1/2 cups bryndza, or sheep's milk feta (see Notes below)

2 tablespoons milk (if using feta)

Fresh chives, chopped, for garnish

INSTRUCTIONS

1. In a large skillet over medium heat, cook the bacon until crispy, about 4 minutes. Scoop out the bacon with a slotted spoon and drain on a paper towel–lined plate.
2. Fill a large pot with water, salt well, and bring to a boil.
3. While the water heats to a boil, place the grated potatoes in a medium mixing bowl. Add the flour and salt and mix well. (If you are using bryndza, use 1 teaspoon salt. With feta, you'll likely want 1/2 teaspoon salt as the cheese is naturally saltier.)
4. If using feta, blend the cheese and milk in a food processor to create a smooth texture, then transfer it to a large mixing bowl. If using bryndza, place it directly in a large mixing bowl.
5. When the water is boiling, set a metal colander over the boiling water, ensuring that the water doesn't touch the bottom of the colander. Place about a third of the potato dough in the colander, and press it through the holes to create small dumplings, which will drop through the holes into the water.
6. Boil the dumplings until they float, about 3 minutes. Remove with a slotted spoon, drain well, and transfer to the bowl with the cheese. Repeat with the remaining dough, and toss the hot dumplings in the cheese to create a rich, melty sauce. Season to taste, if desired.
7. Transfer the mixture to a serving dish, then top with bacon and chives. Serve hot.

Notes: You want to grate the potatoes as finely as possible for the best texture. If your pieces are large, the dumplings won't cohere as well.

Bryndza is a regional Slovakian cheese, which might be hard to find. If the cheesemonger at your local specialty shop can't help you, try an Eastern European grocery store. If you still can't find it, I've included a workaround that's just as delicious—just make sure you buy good-quality sheep's milk feta in brine as a substitute.

THE RED LION

SOUTHAMPTON, ENGLAND, UK

I didn't see any of the twenty-one ghosts said to haunt the Red Lion when I visited in 2022. But I was there for dinner, not an investigation, and the pub's perfect fish and chips were taking up all my attention. I have it on good authority, though, that the place is full of active spirits. With nearly a millennium of history in the space, how could it not?

The Red Lion in located in Southampton, on the southern edge of England, where the Pilgrims boarded the *Mayflower* to start the Massachusetts Bay Colony that became New England, my adopted home. Southampton is an ancient city, with settlements dating back to the Stone Age, and you can't step foot into its Old Town without sensing that history.

The pub itself dates back to the High Middle Ages—its original structure was built in 1148 and was once called "the court room." It's now the basement of the pub. When I visited, the bartender took some of us down there and explained how it used to be a holding place for convicted criminals before they were put on ships and sent off to the Americas. The space was absolutely fascinating—and absolutely creepy.

The building became a pub in 1552 and was possibly called the Nag's Head before 1740. But despite any name changes, the spirit of the place has always been the same: a stately gathering place organized around a main hall, with half-timbered walls of dark wood and white plaster, decorated with what today are antiques but were once just decorations.

In addition to its reputation for great food and drink, the Red Lion is believed to have played a central role in one of the most notorious treason plots in all of England's history. In 1415, a group of noblemen conspired to depose King Henry V, believing that Edmund Mortimer, fifth Earl of March, had a stronger claim to the throne. (It quickly gets complicated with the British monarchy, but here's the short version: Mortimer was descended from the second surviving son of King Edward III, and King Henry was descended from the third. When Mortimer's father Roger was alive, he was considered the heir apparent to his uncle, Richard II, but Roger was not coronated.)

Henry V of England

In a shocking turn of events, it was Mortimer himself who turned in the men trying to get him the crown. Richard of Conisburgh, third Earl of Cambridge; Henry Scrope, third Baron of Masham; and Sir Thomas Grey were all arrested for what became known as the Southampton Plot. They were tried in the very courtroom that's the cellar of the Red Lion today, and on the committee that convicted them . . . was Mortimer. (Some say the location of the trial is a local legend, that there were other buildings that would have made more sense, but the pub believes the location is accurate.) The three were beheaded outside the city's Bargate in August 1415, and the Earl of Cambridge's head was displayed on a pike outside the city gates. The impulse behind the crime was apparently genetic: Decades later, the earl's son, Richard Plantagenet, used his own titles to try to depose King Henry VI—and was also unsuccessful.

But about those ghosts. The three conspirators of the Southampton Plot are believed to haunt the place, leaving in a ghostly procession from the pub to meet their fate. Another frequent sighting: a former barmaid, who died in her sixties after falling down the stairs, appears only from the knees up when people report seeing her. Other spirits looming around include that of Michael Carstairs, said to have died by suicide in the pub in 1932, and a group of male spirits seen sitting by the fire, enjoying a pint. Staff also report hearing heavy boots overhead and seeing a glass explode unprompted. Keep an eye on the Red Lion's socials: They've been known to post footage of paranormal activity in the past.

BUTTERED BEERE

It's not just a certain wizard's favorite beverage—buttered "beere" is a real drink that's been served in English pubs for centuries. The earliest written recipe dates back to 1594, in Thomas Dawson's *The Good Huswifes Handmaide*, and this version is adapted from Max Miller's Tasting History site, based on that first recipe. Think of this warm libation like a beer lover's version of mulled wine: warm, comforting, and perfect for chilly nights.

Prep Time: 5 minutes | Cook Time: 20 minutes | Yield: 4 servings

INGREDIENTS

4 egg yolks

1 cup firmly packed light brown sugar

48 ounces dark ale, preferably British

1/2 teaspoon ground ginger

3/4 teaspoon ground cloves

3/4 teaspoon ground nutmeg, plus more for garnish

1/2 cup (1 stick) unsalted butter, cubed

INSTRUCTIONS

1. In a small mixing bowl, whisk together the egg yolks and brown sugar. Set aside.
2. In a large saucepan, combine the ale, ginger, cloves, and nutmeg. Cook the mixture over medium heat until just boiling. Reduce heat to a simmer and cook for 2–3 minutes (for a nonalcoholic version, simmer for 20 minutes to burn off the alcohol). Remove the pan from the heat.
3. Temper the yolk mixture: Slowly stream in about 1/4 cup of the hot ale mixture into the egg mixture, whisking constantly, to raise the temperature of the eggs. Be careful to add the hot liquid gradually so as to not scramble the yolks. Then, slowly whisk the tempered egg mixture into the pan of hot ale.
4. Cook the mixture over low heat for an additional 5–7 minutes, whisking often, until it has a slightly thicker texture. Stir in the butter and whisk until melted. Simmer on low for a few minutes more.
5. Remove the buttered beere from the heat and whisk vigorously to froth before serving. Pour into mugs and finish each with a pinch of nutmeg on top.

KYTELER'S INN

KILKENNY, IRELAND

Alice Kyteler was self-possessed, financially independent, and unbothered by what other people thought she owed them. It's women like that who, historically, have been accused of witchcraft.

When men in power want to take away something from a woman who has it on her own terms, they accuse her of being a witch, or a devil worshipper, or a murderess. It happened to Bridget Bishop, a wealthy widow in Salem, Massachusetts, who was hanged as a witch. It happened to Mary, Queen of Scots, seen as a threat to Elizabeth I's throne and beheaded for her power. It happened to countless women throughout history. All we can do today is tell their stories, keep their names alive, and pay our respects to their memories.

Kyteler was—you guessed it—a well-to-do woman who opened Kyteler's Inn in Kilkenny sometime around 1323. She had buried three husbands, inherited their estates, and married a fourth. He also died, but not before changing his will to benefit Kyteler rather than his children from previous marriages. When she was accused of witchcraft in 1324, it was by those stepchildren, who felt entitled to their late father's riches.

"The wealth that Alice had accumulated at the expense of her stepchildren had made them angry and suspicious; they came to the conclusion that she was practising witchcraft and accused her to the ecclesiastical authorities of *maleficium* or witchcraft, a fairly commonplace accusation, and one usually treated by English law as a petty criminal offence," Bernadette Williams wrote in a 1994 article in *History Ireland.* "Witchcraft was a form of magic, and magic had always existed in one form or another. Popular medicine was often based on herbal preparations made by good witches."

Today, the charges against Kyteler and members of her household are so ridiculous that they almost sound funny. Among the accusations, according to Williams, was that they "cut up living animals and scattered the pieces at cross roads as offerings to a demon called the son of Art;" and using the hollowed-out skull of a thief as a cauldron, "they placed the intestines and internal organs of cocks, worms, nails cut from dead bodies, hairs from the buttocks and clothes from boys who had died before being baptised" to make potions to influence people's behavior. Oh, and Kyteler "permitted herself to be known carnally" by a demon in the form of a shaggy black dog.

Even in the earlier Middle Ages, these accusations might have been dismissed as a little silly, but the Catholic Church had been taking an increasingly harsh view of witchcraft, likening it to devil worship, not just as knowing which herbs worked best to treat illness. Kyteler became the first woman to be tried for witchcraft in Ireland and the first to be convicted. She fled to England and lost her property, including Kyteler's Inn. Her only biological son, and the rest of the accused, were essentially able to pay their way out of prosecution—but Kyteler's maid Petronilla de Midia was not so lucky. She was tortured (in a legal interrogation by the Church) and burned at the stake, the first time a person was executed by fire anywhere in Great Britain for the crime of heresy. Even at the time, this was considered cruel. When chronicler John Clyn reported her death, he wrote, "before her even in olden days it was neither seen nor heard of that anyone suffered the death penalty for heresy in Ireland."

Kyteler became the first woman to be tried for witchcraft in Ireland and the first to be convicted.

What is worth noting, though, is that while Kyteler likely wasn't a witch, that doesn't mean she wasn't a murderer. All four of her deceased husbands died unusually young, and her fourth husband showed ailments consistent with arsenic poisoning before his death.

Alice Kyteler lost Kyteler's Inn when she fled to England, but it remained in periodic operation throughout the centuries. Today, it's still in the same location; a massive renovation in the 1980s removed centuries of remodels and restored the place to its original Medieval architecture. What the renovation didn't remove, though, were the ghosts. Kyteler is believed to haunt the place, as is her unfortunate maid who died in the crossfire. But even if Kyteler's ghost isn't there, she's still there in spirit. The restaurant tells her story on its walls and has a statue in tribute to her. Dressed as a witch, of course.

IRISH LAMB STEW

Likely originating in the seventeenth century, Irish stew has become a staple in home kitchens and restaurants throughout Ireland—so much so that it's now the national dish. Kyteler's Inn serves a traditional Irish lamb stew that draws rave reviews from visitors all over the world. This version is inspired by theirs.

Prep Time: 20 minutes | Cook Time: 3 hours, plus resting time | Yield: 4 to 6 servings

INGREDIENTS

1 tablespoon neutral cooking oil

1½ pounds boneless lamb shoulder or neck, cubed into 2-inch chunks

4 tablespoons unsalted butter, divided

2 tablespoons all-purpose flour

4 cups chicken broth

2 large carrots, chopped

2 celery stalks, sliced

1 medium yellow onion, diced

2 pounds Russet potatoes, peeled and cubed

1 teaspoon sea salt, plus more, to taste

½ teaspoon black pepper, plus more, to taste

1 bay leaf

2 tablespoons chopped fresh Italian parsley, plus more for garnish

Crusty bread, for serving

INSTRUCTIONS

1. Preheat the oven to 250°F.
2. In a large skillet over medium-high heat, heat the oil until hot and shimmering. Add the lamb chunks and brown them on all sides, about 2 minutes per side (you may need to work in batches so as not to overcrowd the pan). Remove the lamb from the pan and set aside.
3. In the same skillet, make a roux. Lower the heat to medium, then add 2 tablespoons of the butter and the flour. Whisk constantly to avoid burning. Cook for about 5 minutes, until the roux turns a deep golden brown. Add the broth and whisk until incorporated. Take the skillet off the heat and set aside.
4. In a large Dutch oven over medium-high heat, melt the remaining 2 tablespoons butter. Add the carrots, celery, and onion. Cook until the vegetables start to soften, about 8 minutes. Add the lamb, potatoes, salt, pepper, bay leaf, and parsley. Add the broth mixture and stir to combine.
5. Cover the pot and place in the oven. Braise for about 2½ hours, until the lamb is tender and shreds with a fork.
6. Remove the stew from the oven and season to taste with salt and pepper. The stew is best enjoyed if left to rest for about 30 minutes after cooking. Serve garnished with more fresh parsley and crusty bread on the side.

BRAN CASTLE

BRAN, TRANSYLVANIA, ROMANIA

"Suddenly, I became conscious of the fact that the driver was in the act of pulling up the horses in the courtyard of a vast ruined castle, from whose tall black windows came no ray of light, and whose broken battlements showed a jagged line against the sky."

As he arrived at Castle Dracula for the first time in Bram Stoker's *Dracula*, the character Jonathan Harker had a *very* different first impression than most visitors have as they arrive at Bran Castle, located in Transylvania, a central region of Romania. While Castle Dracula is a fictional hellscape filled with vampires and familiars, Bran Castle is a gleaming royal fortress beautifully preserved by Queen Marie of Romania. The medieval structure is full of exhibits, interactive experiences, and—yes—almost certainly ghosts.

Bran Castle is associated with Stoker's masterwork because so many of its architectural details match the fictional one. It's the only castle in the country that fits Stoker's description, so it became known informally as Dracula's Castle, despite its distinct lack of vampires. "Visitors to Bran Castle should make the distinction between the historic reality of Bran and the character of the Count in Bram Stoker's novel," the castle's website warns. "Dracula exists in the imagination."

I find it endlessly fascinating that a real place has fixed itself in the world's imagination as the location of fictional crimes—but it happened because the inspiration for the literary monster came from a real-life one, a person who may or may not have ties to Bran Castle. Vlad Dracula, also known as Vlad the Impaler for his penchant for impaling the bodies of his slain enemies on stakes and displaying them in horrifying fields of bodies, was a fifteenth-century ruler of neighboring Wallachia. It's unclear whether Vlad Dracula ever occupied Bran Castle, but it's possible, as the castle was on a main route between Wallachia and Transylvania.

(Those horrifying fields of bodies, one of which was called the Forest of the Impaled, were in places like Tirgoviste, Brașov, and Sibiu, Romania.)

> If you're looking for the lair of Vlad Dracula—also known as Vlad the Impaler and the inspiration for Stoker's monster—that's Poenari Castle in Arefu, Romania.

Bran Castle was built in 1388, a military fortification occupied by a lord of the castle who was appointed by the king (Transylvania was then part of the Kingdom of Hungary). The castle was an important location occupied by local royalty for centuries but became less vital in the 1830s when the dividing line between Transylvania and Wallachia was changed and the castle was no longer in a prime border location. In 1920, shortly after Transylvania became part of Romania, the city of Bran gifted Bran Castle to Queen Marie of Romania, writing in the deed that she was "the great queen who . . . spreads her blessing everywhere she walked, thus winning, with an irresistible momentum, the hearts of the entire country's population." The castle had fallen into disrepair, but Queen Marie restored it. She used the castle as a summer royal residence for more than a decade before her death. (The castle briefly housed a marble sarcophagus containing her heart, as a tribute to her.)

There might not be any vampires *in* Bran Castle, but for generations, locals have warned against the *strigoi* who live in the surrounding area. According to legend, strigoi are evil spirits who lead normal lives during the day, walking among humans. At night, however, the spirits of the strigoi leave their bodies to torment their victims by slowly draining their life force (not a far leap between them and vampires, right?). An exhibit at the castle, *A History of Dreads in Transylvania*, digs into the folklore of the area.

Inside the castle, people report experiencing quite a bit of unexplained phenomena. A woman in white is said to roam the grounds, possibly the ghost of a noblewoman who, some say, was wrongly accused of treason and died in the castle. A phantom monk is also believed to haunt the halls, allegedly bricked up within the walls because he broke his sacred vows.

Even if those stories are exaggerated, there are so many centuries-old items in the castle that it only makes sense that some spirits could be attached to them—especially in the torture chamber, a place of intensely concentrated negative energy. Some people report seeing green mists or having a sudden feeling of malaise. Others claim to have had rocks thrown at them, especially in the tunnels underneath the castle.

Torture chamber at Bran Castle

MEAT STEW WITH POLENTA AND EGG

As its website says, "Most of the visitors arrive at Bran Castle with a certain hunger, from the long journey through the country." Whether that hunger is for food or . . . something else is for you to decide. This recipe comes from Queen Marie's Tea House, housed in a quaint little cottage in the castle's Royal Park. If you can't find *kabanos*, a regional smoked sausage, substitute with another smoked sausage like chorizo or hard pepperoni.

Prep Time: 10 minutes | Cook Time: 40 minutes | Yield: 4 servings

INGREDIENTS

2 tablespoons neutral cooking oil

1 pound boneless pork chops, cubed into 1-inch pieces

4 ounces kabanos, or other smoked sausage, sliced into 1/2-inch coins

2 cloves garlic, peeled and crushed

1 tablespoon red wine

1 tablespoon tomato paste

1 tablespoon fresh thyme, or 1 teaspoon dried thyme

1 teaspoon salt

1/2 teaspoon black pepper

1/2 teaspoon sweet paprika

4 cups chicken or vegetable broth

3 1/2 cups cooked polenta

4 fried eggs

1/4 cup chopped fresh Italian parsley

INSTRUCTIONS

1. In a large skillet over medium heat, heat the oil and brown the pork chops and sausage, about 2 minutes per side.
2. Add the garlic, wine, and tomato paste. Stir to combine. Add the thyme, salt, pepper, and paprika. Stir the meat until coated with the spices.
3. Add the broth and stir to combine. Simmer, uncovered, for about 40 minutes.
4. To serve, portion out the cooked polenta into four bowls. Pour some stew over the polenta, top with a fried egg, and garnish with the parsley.

PALACE OF VERSAILLES

VERSAILLES, FRANCE

As Marie Antoinette and her husband, King Louis XVI, enjoyed the riches of their royal lives, most of their subjects lived in starvation so extreme that those subjects were prompted to overthrow the monarchy. "Let them eat cake," they imagined her saying when confronted with the fact that most did not have bread to eat.

The last queen of France never actually said that. It turns out, no one actually said "let them eat cake" at all (but some out-of-touch, privileged women at the time suggested that the starving should "eat the crust of the pâté" if they were still hungry).

The Palace of Versailles is where Marie Antoinette and Louis XVI lived happily until the French Revolution, when they became the most reviled symbols of the excesses of the French monarchy and were beheaded in 1793. But long before the palace housed royalty accused of crimes against the French people, it was the site of scandals so notorious that the spirits touched by those heinous actions still linger in its halls.

For as much as Versailles is an outsized historic monument, known the world over for its beauty and role in French history, it had a relatively short lifespan as a royal residence. King Louis XIII first built a small hunting lodge on the property in 1623, which his son Louis XIV expanded into a proper royal residence starting in 1661. The Sun King was so obsessed with citrus fruit, a rarity at the time, that he installed an Orangerie at the palace in 1684, a greenhouse housing more than one thousand orange trees.

During Louis XIV's reign, the poverty that later pushed the commoners to revolt was already widespread, but the aristocracy continued to relish in excess—gambling, spending lavishly on clothing, and consulting the palm readers and fortune tellers who were increasingly present at court. Maybe if the supernatural weren't so fashionable at the time, the discovery of a single pair of poisoners wouldn't have resulted in a full-blown witchhunt. But as it happened, hundreds of people were implicated, and dozens of them died in what became known as "The Affair of the Poisons."

In 1672, Marie de Brinvilliers and Gaudin de Sainte-Croix were discovered to be master poisoners who had not only been feeding poison-laced cakes to hospital patients for the thrill of it, but had also allegedly been teaching their arts to others. Sainte-Croix died before he was tried, but de Brinvilliers was tortured to extract the names of others before being beheaded, her ashes scattered in the wind. "Never has Paris seen such crowds of people," a witness wrote on the day of her execution. "Never has the city been so aroused, so intent on a spectacle."

The king, who was paranoid about being assassinated (especially through poison), launched an investigation into other potential poisoners. The next to be arrested was poisoner Marie Bosse, who implicated Catherine Monvoisin. Nicknamed La Voisin, she was called a "divineress" for her abilities to brew powerful potions for everything from health concerns to unwanted pregnancies to, yes, death.

Illustrated depiction of Marie Antoinette's beheading

Aristocrats were frequently her customers. Once La Voisin was arrested, hundreds of others were implicated—not just the rich who used her potions to solve their problems, but servants who had accompanied them and any number of helpless people guilty by association. The targets were largely wealthy women of influence. While La Voisin's business was primarily in Paris, the same people who were her customers were also frequently guests at court in Versailles. The affair was about witchcraft as much as it was about murder, and it was a scandal that led to 442 people being accused of crimes and 218 being arrested. Thirty-four of them were executed, and another twenty-three were banished, all because one murderous couple created a citywide moral panic. Louis XIV didn't die by poisoning after all but from a gangrenous wound in 1715.

It was his son Louis XV who turned Versailles into what it is today, a palace that draws more than fifteen million visitors annually. His son Louis XVI and his wife, Marie Antoinette, were the last royalty to live at the palace. You can probably already guess why Versailles is said to be haunted, with visitors claiming to see full-bodied apparitions of Marie Antoinette and Louis XVI and hearing disembodied voices and unexplained footsteps. But they're far from the only ghosts in the palace. In 1901, two Englishwomen visited the palace and had such an intense encounter at the Trianon (a smaller home on the grounds of the estate) that they published a book about it. In the 1911 *An Adventure*, the women wrote that they encountered men speaking a strange language; decades later, unearthed plans confirmed that there was a "Chinese kiosk" in that location in 1774, during the reign of Louis XV.

LOUIS XV'S DRINKING CHOCOLATE

Long before chocolate was in every home, it was a rarified treat reserved for the rich and royal. At the Palace of Versailles, chocolate was especially beloved. After its introduction to France in 1615, drinking chocolate became a favorite royal indulgence. Louis XV loved it so much that he would sometimes prepare it himself in his private apartment. In 1770, when Marie Antoinette arrived at court, she brought her personal chocolate maker with her from Austria; he was named Chocolate Maker to the Queen after she married Louis XVI. Even if you don't have your own royal chocolatier, you can enjoy Louis XV's favorite preparation, adapted from prolific French food writer Menon's 1755 cookbook, *Dinners of the Court or the Art of working with all sorts of foods for serving the best tables following the four seasons*.

Prep Time: 5 minutes	Cook Time: 10 minutes	Yield: 4 servings

INGREDIENTS

4 (3.5-ounce) bars good-quality dark chocolate, such as Godiva or Guittard

4 cups water

1 egg yolk

INSTRUCTIONS

1. In a medium saucepan over medium-low heat, heat the chocolate and water until simmering, whisking often to incorporate.
2. According to Menon, the treat tastes better if this step is done a day in advance. Just make sure to store your chocolate mixture in the refrigerator and bring to a simmer before proceeding.
3. In a small mixing bowl, whisk the egg yolk until frothy. Then temper the egg: Slowly pour a small amount of the chocolate mixture into the bowl, whisking constantly to gently raise the temperature of the egg. Whisk the tempered egg mixture back into the pan with the chocolate—the end result is a very thick, smooth mixture.
4. Divide into 4 small mugs and enjoy.

HOUSKA CASTLE

BLATCE, CZECH REPUBLIC

As you've already seen in this chapter, it's pretty much a given that castles that have survived into modern times will have ghost stories. It only makes sense that after surviving centuries of wars and housing generations of power struggles, these larger-than-life structures would have some stories to tell.

But Houska Castle, about an hour north of Prague in the Czech Republic, is different. That castle didn't earn its ghosts over the centuries. It was built to capture and contain demons coming up from inside the earth. Did it? Does it still? Well, let's find out.

From the very start, there was something strange about Houska Castle. Built in the latter thirteenth century, the structure didn't match traditional castle architecture of the day. Built on mountainous terrain and forested land, Houska didn't have any fortifications around it, and it was missing key elements of living space. There was no water source supplying the castle with drinking or bathing water. There was no kitchen. There was no main road nearby. And when it was completed, no one moved in.

There is, though, one very curious architectural feature. Underneath the castle's two-story chapel, there's an enormous pit reaching into the ground, one that some believe is bottomless. The castle itself is said to have been built to conceal this hole. Of course, there's no real way to verify that—just like there's no real way to verify the story of the prisoner who volunteered to be lowered into the portal in exchange for a pardon.

"When the first prisoner was lowered, he started screaming after a few seconds," *Condé Nast Traveler* wrote. "When he was raised back up, he appeared to have aged thirty years. Or so they say."

The castle was built to capture and contain demons coming up from inside the earth.

When the castle was built, according to German travel magazine *Travel Book*, villagers would report seeing flying half-human, half-animal creatures and unexplained trails of blood on the ground. They believed the monsters were coming from that hole, which they said was a portal to the underworld, to hell itself. Allegedly, after the castle's completion, appearances from those creatures stopped—but not the connections to dark legends. According to Discovery UK, a "Swedish black magic practitioner named Oronto" lived in the castle. He's believed to have been working on a potion to grant immortality, working sometime during the seventeenth century, and to have carried out terrible experiments tantamount to torture in his research. Locals discovered his misdeeds, and two hunters are said to have broken into the castle and murdered Oronto to put an end to them. During World War II, Nazis occupied the fortress and were rumored to have conducted occult experiments there (there's no real documentation of this experimentation, only myths).

Today, you can visit the castle and decide for yourself what its real purpose was. Historians say it was merely a place from which to manage local lands. But that doesn't explain the murals in the chapel, which is said to cover the portal itself: Those artworks depict strangely pagan imagery, like a half-woman, half-horse figure. And the historians' theories don't explain the "chorus of screams" a visitor heard coming from underneath that space or the scratching of claws, according to Discovery UK. Maybe it's totally normal for a castle to have a "hand-carved linden mechanical hell," a huge carved piece of art with moving elements depicting "hellish punishments for earthly sins," as Houska's website describes. Other castles choose unicorn tapestries as decor, but okay, cool, that seems fine.

Inside the chapel at Houska Castle

"The Hell gateway is allegedly [guarded] by a terrible faceless black monk, but no one knows where exactly it is," *Visit Czechia* wrote about Houska. "Some look for it in the local chapel, others in the castle well; whatever your fantasy tells you."

BLACK KUBA

In the Czech Republic, Christmas Eve is a day of celebration—but also, as in times past, a day of fasting. Legend has it that if you fast all day, you'll catch a glimpse of the little golden pig as night falls, a sign of luck for the coming year. In modern times, many simply choose to abstain from meat during the daytime on Christmas Eve and opt for this hearty mushroom casserole instead.

Prep Time: 15 minutes | Cook Time: 1 hour | Yield: 4 servings

INGREDIENTS

1½ ounces dried mushrooms

1½ cups pearl barley

2 tablespoons unsalted butter, plus more for greasing

1 large yellow onion, minced

4 cloves garlic, minced

1 tablespoon dried marjoram

1½ teaspoons salt

1½ tablespoons chopped Italian parsley

INSTRUCTIONS

1. In a medium saucepan add the mushrooms and cover them with water by 2 inches. Bring the water to a boil, then reduce to a simmer. Cook the mushrooms until they're soft and reconstituted, about 10–15 minutes.
2. Remove the mushrooms from the heat and allow them to rest for 10 minutes. Drain, reserving the mushroom broth. When the mushrooms are cool enough to handle, coarsely chop.
3. Cook the pearl barley according to the package instructions, using half water and half reserved mushroom broth. If any excess water remains in the pot after the barley is fully cooked, drain it off.
4. Preheat the oven to 350°F.
5. In a large skillet over medium heat, melt the butter. Add the onions and cook until golden, about 10–12 minutes. Add the garlic and cook 1 minute more. Stir in the marjoram, salt, and mushrooms, followed by the cooked barley.
6. Grease a casserole dish with butter, then transfer the mixture to the dish. Bake, uncovered, for 20 minutes, until the top is golden and crisped.
7. Garnish with the parsley and serve.

TOWER OF LONDON

LONDON, ENGLAND, UK

A signature landmark of Britain's premier city, the Tower of London dates back to 1066. While it's one of the most infamous jails of all time, it wasn't originally designed to house prisoners.

"It was in the 150 years following the 1480s that the Tower earned its reputation as a political prison," Bill Newcott wrote for *National Geographic* in 1993. "During these dark years a melancholy list of prisoners entered its gates en route to execution on Tower Green: Anne Boleyn, who failed to give Henry VIII a son; The Countess of Salisbury, whose only crime was to give birth to one of Henry's enemies; Teenaged Lady Jane Gray, perhaps the most pitiful victim of the Tower, who was Queen for ten days before her cousin Mary removed Jane's crown and head."

The Tower of London was originally built as a royal residence. Over the years it has been an armory; a zoo for the crown's "wild beasts," as the UK government puts it; and the Royal Mint. Today, it's still home to the lavish collection of crown jewels, which people can see on display.

Today, nearly a thousand years into its history, the Tower of London is primarily remembered as a place where enemies of the throne were executed, many of them capriciously at the whim of the crown. Henry VIII ordered two of his wives' executions there, the aforementioned Anne Boleyn for not providing the king an heir; and also Catherine Howard, for allegedly having an affair.

In 1483, two princes were sent to the tower by their uncle, the Duke of Gloucester, for safekeeping during the War of the Roses, but they never reemerged. The duke ascended the throne as Richard III, while nearly two hundred years later, the skeletons of two children now known as "the Princes in the Tower" were discovered, likely the remains of the boys.

England was rocked by its share of religious wars, which the Tower was privy to. In the sixteenth century, writer and poet Anne Askew was tortured for being a Protestant at a time when England was a Catholic nation, and she was interrogated to reveal names of others who shared her faith. Those "interrogations" often took place in the torture chamber and included being tied to a "rack" with shackles at either end for a person's hands and feet. Once a person was fastened to the table, an operator would crank a lever, separating the sections of the rack—and therefore a person's body—farther and farther apart, causing dislocation of joints, tearing of ligaments, and excruciating pain. "Because I lay still and did not cry, my Lord Chancellor and Master Rich took pains to rack me with their own hands till I was nigh dead. . . ." Askew wrote in 1546. "The Lieutenant caused me to be loosed from the rack: incontinently I swooned, and they recovered me again." She was injured so badly that she could no longer walk and was eventually burned at the stake.

Others were imprisoned and not killed. After Anne Boleyn's execution, her youngest daughter, Elizabeth, was imprisoned in the tower in 1554. She was put there by her own half-sister, Queen Mary I, as she feared the princess was plotting against her. Five years later, that prisoner became Queen Elizabeth I at the same location. In 1592, Elizabeth imprisoned famed explorer and writer Sir Walter Raleigh, angry that he had married one of her ladies-in-waiting without her permission. He was released but was imprisoned again after her death, when King James I incorrectly believed that Raleigh was involved in a treasonous plot to overthrow him. He spent twelve years in what is now called the "Bloody Tower."

A thousand years of imprisonments, tortures, and deaths has certainly accrued a level of spectral unrest. In 1789, the *Hereford Journal* wrote that locations in the tower had "long been disturbed with noises, and spectres in various fearful shapes." Stories of hauntings are so prevalent that even the UK government, on its Historic Royal Palaces website, acknowledges the activity. "Anne Boleyn is said to stalk the site of her execution on Tower Green," the Tower's official website reads. "Arbella Stuart, the cousin of Elizabeth I who starved while under arrest for marrying without royal permission, is said to frequent the King's House still." Henry VI, deposed by his nephew, Edward IV, was imprisoned in the Tower and eventually murdered there. He's said to appear in the Wakefield Tower at midnight.

But interestingly, the spirits that roam the Tower don't all belong to humans. Dr. Alden Gregory, curator of the Tower, has written of its phantom polar bear, once owned by King Henry III. It's rumored to be "a sight so fearsome that those unfortunate enough to see it, suffer fatal consequences," he wrote, adding, "It is, without doubt, one of the more unusual workplace risks."

PAUPER'S BREAD

Impoverished prisoners in the Tower of London were fed only stale bread and scraps. In medieval England, wheat was a luxury many couldn't afford, so peasants would supplement their loaves with other grains, or even peas and lentils. This rye bread was adapted by Holden Wilson on AnthroChef from a historic recipe. Poor laborers would have considered this loaf a treat—and so do I.

Prep Time: 15 minutes, plus rising time	Cook Time: 40 minutes	Yield: 1 loaf

INGREDIENTS

3½ cups rye flour, plus more for dusting

1 cup barley or whole wheat flour

1 cup plus 2 tablespoons rolled oats

2 tablespoons fennel seeds

2 teaspoons salt

1¾ cups water, divided

2¼ teaspoons (1 packet) instant yeast

¼ cup barley malt syrup or molasses

INSTRUCTIONS

1. In a large mixing bowl, combine the rye flour, barley or wheat flour, oats, fennel seeds, and salt. Set aside.
2. In a microwave safe bowl or liquid measuring cup, warm ¼ cup of the water. Stir the yeast into the warm water and add the barley malt syrup or molasses. Stir again and let the mixture sit for 15 minutes. Stir in the remaining 1½ cups room temperature water. Combine the yeast mixture with the dry ingredients and mix until a dough forms.
3. Turn the dough onto a floured surface and knead for 5–7 minutes.
4. Cover the dough with a damp kitchen towel and let rise at room temperature for about 2 hours.
5. Flour a work surface, then turn out the dough. Shape it into a round loaf, then cover and let proof 1 hour. Flour the loaf, then score the top with a few light cuts for air vents.
6. Preheat the oven to 475°F. In the oven, place a large Dutch oven and allow it to preheat, uncovered, for about 45 minutes before baking.
7. When the Dutch oven is hot, flour the interior, then place the loaf inside and cover with the lid. Bake for 20 minutes, then uncover and bake for another 15–20 minutes, until the crust is a deep golden brown.

EDINBURGH CASTLE

EDINBURGH, SCOTLAND, UK

Rising up on Castle Rock, towering over the city below, Edinburgh Castle is one of Europe's great castles and one of the most recognizable landmarks in the United Kingdom. It's also one of the most attacked, having been besieged more than two dozen times in its eleven-hundred-year history.

"Edinburgh Castle has always been a royal castle, one of the chief fortresses of the kingdom, and one generally considered impregnable," archaeologist and president of the Society of Antiquaries of Scotland, Dr. David Caldwell, wrote. "A weakness, however, that more than one keeper had to deal with was the proximity of the town of Edinburgh, not because it and its residents were a threat to the castle defences but because the keepers felt constraint not to fire their guns and threaten the lives and well-being of the townsfolk." Because of that, the castle once fell in thirty minutes in a 1639 siege led by the Covenanters, a group of Scottish Presbyterians disgruntled by King Charles I's insistence that they practice an Anglican liturgy. But in 1715, the castle's fortifications held—because the ladder brought by the rebelling Jacobites was too short to allow their forces inside.

Like the Tower of London, Edinburgh Castle has served many roles over the centuries. It has been a royal residence, an armory, a treasury, and keeper of the Honours of Scotland, the country's crown jewels.

"Not everyone who came to the castle enjoyed their stay," the castle's history reads on its website. "Even royals were sometimes known to complain about the draughts. But life was truly grim for many of the prisoners who were locked up in the vaults below Crown Square." A formidable stronghold, the castle was the most secure lockup in Scotland. Between 1757 and 1814, the vaults became home to hundreds of prisoners of war—including Americans, who had been fighting in what the British called "The War of Independence." In 1811, forty-nine prisoners escaped by digging a hole through a fortress wall and scaling down Castle Rock. One man didn't make it, but the other forty-eight escaped.

Today, Edinburgh Castle is home to the country's National War Museum. The enormous cannon, Mons Meg, which could shoot a cannonball for up to two miles, is still on display, as are the five-century-old Seven Sisters guns used to defend the castle's Half Moon Battery.

Though primarily a museum and tourist attraction, Edinburgh Castle still keeps many of its traditions alive, including military maneuvers. At precisely 1 p.m. each day—except Sundays, Good Friday, and Christmas Day—the castle sets off the One O'Clock Gun. The tradition dates back to 1861, when docked ships relied on the gun to set their clocks. (If you've seen *Mary Poppins*, you've seen this in action.) And every August, the Royal Edinburgh Military Tattoo is a monthlong celebration of military prowess and performance.

So much of what happens at the castle today resembles its past; perhaps that's why there's a high level of paranormal activity. Many people report strange occurrences in the castle's dungeons, especially the appearance of blue orbs in the areas still littered with the graffiti of French and American prisoners.

As early as 1650, people reported seeing an apparition of a headless boy beating a Scottish war drum. According to legend, the boy was playing the same song the English used as a warning to Scottish troops as Oliver Cromwell attacked and overtook the castle that same year. Sometimes the staff still hear the drumming today.

The Lost Piper Boy, with his phantom bagpipe music, is said to be the ghost of a young boy sent into the castle's small, tight tunnels with his bagpipes, tasked with blowing into the pipes to help map the spaces. He was heard for a time and then abruptly went silent—never seen in life again.

The castle's most famous ghost, though, is the Grey Lady, believed to roam the castle to this day. The leading theory for the Grey Lady's identity is that she's Janet Douglas, Lady of Glamis, who was a victim of retribution from King James V. The king was angry at the Douglas family for imprisoning him as a child and decided to exact vengeance on the Lady of Glamis by convicting her of witchcraft. In 1528, Janet Douglas was accused of poisoning her husband (which she was cleared of) and later of plotting to poison the king in 1537. That charge she wasn't able to escape. "Although it was clear that the accusations were false, she was imprisoned in a dungeon at Edinburgh Castle," the Bowes Museum wrote. "While it was easy for James to imprison Janet, convicting her of witchcraft was difficult. To make her 'confess,' James had Janet's family members and servants tortured until Janet gave in and she was then burned at the stake on July 17, 1537."

SCOTTISH SHORTBREAD

Maybe the simplest and most delicious cookie ever made, Scottish shortbread dates back to the twelfth century; the first printed recipe appeared in the 1736 cookbook *Mrs. McLintock's Receipts for Cookery and Pastry-Work*. Mary, Queen of Scots, who lived for a time in Edinburgh Castle, especially loved the cookie. What's also great about this cookie's simplicity is how much fun it is to modify and experiment with new flavors. I love to add fresh rosemary to mine, but lavender, thyme, or citrus zest also work perfectly. One tip: Buy the best quality European butter you can find. It's worth the splurge.

Prep Time: 10 minutes	Cook Time: 35 minutes	Yield: 18 cookies

INGREDIENTS

1/2 cup superfine caster sugar or granulated sugar

2 cups all-purpose flour

1 cup (2 sticks) good-quality European butter, room temperature (see Note below)

INSTRUCTIONS

1. Preheat the oven to 350°F.
2. Line an 8-inch square baking pan with parchment paper.
3. If using granulated sugar, refine it in the food processor for 1 minute before proceeding.
4. In a large mixing bowl, combine the sugar and flour until just incorporated.
5. Add the butter and mix by hand until a dough starts to form, only until everything is fully incorporated. Don't overwork.
6. Press the dough evenly into the baking pan. Prick the surface liberally with a fork, making air vents about halfway through the dough.
7. Bake for 30–35 minutes, until the corners turn golden brown. (These cookies stay relatively pale even when they're done.)
8. Remove the shortbread from the oven and allow to cool for 10 minutes. Slice into bars of your desired size while still warm.

Note: Using salted butter in the recipe is preferable. But if using unsalted butter, add a 1/4 teaspoon salt to the mix.

CHAPTER 3

A TASTE FOR MURDER

FOLEY'S

Few things spawn instant fear more quickly than realizing that we're standing on the very spot where a murder happened. Add in the possibility that we're in a space where *multiple* murders happened, and you can really feel the hair on the back of your neck raise. There's a reason why so many states require sellers of a home or business to disclose if a murder occurred in that space. The idea of death can be a hard thing to live with every day.

It's an interesting juxtaposition as a paranormal researcher; you seek out sites of tragedy but also attempt to have empathy and humanize the victims of such horrors. It took a bit of evolution on my part to start seeing these poor souls as more than just their end. They lived entire lives, presumably filled with moments of joy, love, and triumph.

Rather than remember the victims of homicide by the last few seconds of their lives, I try to celebrate them by thinking about the best ways they lived. And what better way to celebrate that than through food? In the coming pages, you'll read not only about the people who lived in and shaped these places, but also about the dishes people return to again and again to experience a piece of those spots. It's an oddly delicious undertaking.

HINTERKAIFECK FARM

MUNICH, GERMANY

In the days leading up to an unspeakable twentieth-century crime, Andreas Gruber knew something was wrong. Strange things were happening at his family farm, things that seemed off but that he couldn't quite put his finger on.

"Gruber had found footprints leading out of the forest behind his house, yet none leading back [to the woods]," Eric Grundhauser wrote for *Atlas Obscura*. "In addition, he believed that he had been hearing footfalls in the attic and had also found a newspaper that seemed to come from nowhere. His house keys even went missing.

"Despite all of these horror movie clichés," Grundhauser added, "Gruber reported nothing to the police."

In a matter of days, he and his entire family were murdered in one of the most grisly true-crime stories I've ever read. Even more disturbing: The murderer was never caught. And more than a century later, we'll likely never know their name.

The Grubers lived in a tiny village in Bavaria, about forty miles north of Munich, Germany. Andreas Gruber lived with his wife, Cäzilia Gruber, on their family farm with their widowed daughter, Viktoria Gabriel, and her two young children, Cäzilia, age seven, and Josef, age two. Also on the property was a maid, Maria Baumgartner. On the day of the murders, "It had been Baumgartner's first day on the job," Sonya Vatomsky wrote for *Mental Floss*. "The previous maid had abandoned her position due to a fervent belief that the house and farm were haunted."

The details are grisly, and if you'd rather skip the next paragraph, I don't blame you.

All six victims were discovered with horrific head trauma, caused by a mattock, a kind of pickax with a horizontal axe blade on one side and a vertical one on the other. "Gruber himself was said to have had his face 'shredded' and collapsed leaving jagged bone protruding from the wound," Grundhauser wrote.

The four oldest members of the Gruber family were all discovered in the barn, but Josef and Maria were found in the house. The murderer had likely spent several days at the farm between the killings, which happened on March 31, 1922, and the discovery of the crime scene on April 4.

Police launched a massive investigation, arresting dozens of people, though no solid suspects were ever found. They looked at the neighbor who found the family's remains, Lorenz Schlittenbauer, and the possibility that he and Viktoria had a relationship. They even questioned whether her husband, Karl Gabriel, really died (he did, on December 29, 1914, in France). Even more puzzling is the fact that there were substantial sums of money in the home, which were left untouched. "At a loss for leads, the police even decapitated the victims' corpses after their autopsies and sent the heads to Munich where they were given to a clairvoyant who was unable to glean any new facts," Grundhauser added. As for why the former maid believed the house was haunted? She heard phantom footsteps in the attic and felt as though she was being watched all the time.

The home was torn down, and all that remains today is a small memorial to the family at the site. Despite the horror of the crime, which was a massive scandal in Germany at the time, the news didn't make it to America when it happened. In my research, I didn't find a single contemporary newspaper article in English reporting on the murders. Today, it's very different. The Hinterkaifeck murders have inspired books, podcasts, and even a stage production, *Hinter*, which debuted in 2018 in Chicago. In his review, the *Chicago Tribune*'s Chris Jones described the events as "the German equivalent of the crime of the century."

More than one hundred years later, it's unlikely we'll ever know what really happened to that family.

Gruber family memorial

SCHWEINEBRATEN

One of Munich's signature recipes, this roasted pork dish is usually enjoyed during Oktoberfest. One whiff of the delicious aromatics floating around your kitchen while it's slow roasting, and you'll understand why.

Prep Time: 20 minutes | Cook Time: 3 hours | Yield: 6 to 8 servings

INGREDIENTS

1 (2–3-pound) pork shoulder roast with fat and skin still attached (see Note below)

1 teaspoon caraway seeds

2 cloves garlic

2 teaspoons salt, divided

1 teaspoon black pepper, divided

2 tablespoons neutral cooking oil

1 teaspoon whole cloves

3 potatoes, peeled and diced

3 carrots, peeled and diced

1 large onion, diced

12 ounces dark beer, divided

1 tablespoon butter

1 tablespoon all-purpose flour

1 teaspoon cornstarch, optional

INSTRUCTIONS

1. Preheat the oven to 350°F.
2. If your roast has skin attached, score the skin (but not the fat underneath) in a diamond pattern. If your roast is skinless, score the fat in a diamond pattern, taking care not to score the meat itself.
3. Using a mortar and pestle (or a plastic bag and rolling pin) grind the caraway seeds and mash the garlic until fine. Combine the mixture with 1 teaspoon of the salt, 1/2 teaspoon of the pepper, and 1 tablespoon of the oil. Rub the spice mixture on all sides of the roast.
4. Stick the cloves into the scored part of the roast, pressing firmly so they stay in place.
5. Using a Dutch oven or a stovetop-safe roasting pan, heat the pan over medium-high heat and sear the roast for about 1 minute on all sides to seal in the juices.
6. Place the pork in the oven and roast for 30 minutes, then baste with the pan juices. If there isn't much liquid, add 1 cup of water to the pan.
7. Toss the vegetables with the remaining 1 tablespoon oil, 1 teaspoon of the salt, and the remaining 1/2 teaspoon pepper. At the 1-hour mark, baste the roast again, this time with half of the beer. Arrange the vegetables in the pan around the roast.

(recipe continues)

(recipe continued from page 95)

8. After another 30 minutes, baste the roast with the pan juices and stir the vegetables. After another 30 minutes, baste with the remaining beer and stir the vegetables. The roast is done when the internal temperature measures 165°F on a meat thermometer, which will likely take between 2–2½ hours. (If your roast has skin, you may want to finish it for just a minute under the broiler to crisp it further.)
9. Remove the pan from the oven and transfer the pork and vegetables to a platter and cover with foil. It will need to rest at room temperature for at least 15 minutes while you prepare the gravy.
10. Skim off as much fat as you can from the pan juices and strain out the solids.
11. In a medium saucepan over medium heat, melt the butter and whisk in the flour to make a roux. Cook, whisking frequently, for about 3 minutes until golden. Add the pan juices to the roux and whisk to incorporate. Bring to a boil and cook for 10 minutes, whisking constantly, until the gravy is slightly reduced and thickened. If you want a thicker gravy, create a slurry with a small amount of the liquid and 1 teaspoon cornstarch. Add it to the pan and whisk to incorporate. Adjust seasonings to taste.
12. Slice the roast and serve with the gravy.

Note: The success of this dish hinges on getting the right cut of meat. Traditional German preparation means using a pork shoulder with the skin still attached—but if you can't find that, make sure your roast has a substantial fat cap attached to one side.

H. H. HOLMES'S "MURDER CASTLE"

CHICAGO, ILLINOIS, USA

In his thirty-five short years, Herman Webster Mudgett, better known by his alias H. H. Holmes, created enough horror stories to last for centuries. Widely regarded as America's first serial killer, Holmes is a puzzle that is still largely unsolved to this day. Some sources claim he killed as many as two hundred people, though that number is definitely exaggerated considering Holmes himself confessed to murders of people who were still alive at the time of his execution.

But make no mistake: Holmes was a monster of the most terrible sort.

Born in New Hampshire in 1861, Holmes studied medicine in college, where his grotesque crimes started: He worked in the anatomy lab at the University of Michigan and is believed to have robbed graves to procure cadavers for medical study. He moved to Chicago in 1886 and purchased a lot at the intersection of South Wallace Avenue and West 63rd Street, where he built a three-story mixed-use space with retail on the first floor and apartments above.

Holmes was only ever tried and convicted of the murder of one person: his former friend and partner in fraud, Ben Pitezel. Holmes was executed by hanging in 1896 in Philadelphia. Only after his arrest did stories start to emerge about a "murder castle" in Chicago filled with the grotesque mechanisms of torture and mutilation that have followed Holmes into infamy. Newspapers at the time claimed he had outfitted the building with secret passageways, gas chambers, and soundproof rooms to muffle the sounds of his victims' screams.

An 1896 article in the *Chicago Chronicle* described Holmes as a "multimurderer, bigamist, seducer, resurrectionist, forger, thief, and general swindler.

"He allowed no one to block his blood-stained road to wealth, nor was he particular as to the means necessary of the removal of obstacles," the story continued. "Cords or knives, poison or fire, suffocating streams or the deadly lead pipe were all familiar to his ruthless hands. . . . He had a predilection for chloroform, but did not object to nitroglycerin or dynamite when they would best aid his fell purposes, and one of his favorite modes of disposing of women who readily succumbed to his gentle manners and wheedling tongue was to entomb them in the vault of his famous 'castle' in Englewood and asphyxiate them with noxious gases. Nothing was too horrible or too brutal for Holmes to perform."

The outrage at his actions isn't misplaced, but the exploits detailed in the article are definitely exaggerated. After his arrest, Holmes admitted to twenty-seven murders, but that number included some people who were still alive at the time, like Kate Durkee. Eventually, only nine murders could be confirmed, including men, women, and children.

"I was born with the Devil in me," Holmes said. "I could not help the fact that I was a murderer, no more than a poet can help the inspiration to sing."

His exploits, both the mythologized and the real, have been documented in books like Erik Larson's *The Devil in the White City* and inspired *American Horror Story: Hotel*. There was so much interest in Holmes as a true crime celebrity at the time of his death that his "murder castle" was transformed into an attraction called the Holmes Horror Castle, but it burned before opening according to the Crime Museum.

H. H. Holmes

The building was torn down in 1938 and replaced with a US Post Office branch, which is still there today. According to CBS News, part of the building's basement is an original piece of Holmes's building's basement. "Many people say the basement of the Post Office that now occupies the Murder Castle site can be very creepy . . . " Adam Harrington wrote in the story. "They report hearing sounds or seeing shadow figures."

For the PBS special *The Hauntings of Chicago*, Ursula Bielski interviewed employees of that post office. "One employee shared a chilling story of hearing a sound in the basement and poking her head around a corner to see if her colleague was there," she later wrote for American Ghost Walks. "She called out to her but heard no answer, and saw nothing down the hallway but a row of chairs lined up against the wall. A minute later, when she returned to the hallway, the chairs had all been stacked up on top of each other." Employees also report seeing the apparition of a young girl both in the building and outside on the grass.

As part of *The Hauntings of Chicago*, Jeff Mudgett, a descendant of H. H. Holmes, went to the building. "Before I walked down those steps I was a nonbeliever," he said. "Absolutely non. I would have walked into any building in the world. An hour later, when I came out, my whole foundation had changed. I was a believer."

LEMON TOAST

During H. H. Holmes's horrific killing spree, the city was abuzz with the excitement of the 1893 World's Fair. Called the World's Columbian Exposition, the event was of a scale never seen before in America. Forty-six countries participated, and the event drew more than twenty-seven million attendees. Organizers compiled *The "Home Queen" World's Fair Souvenir Cook Book*, which promised "Two thousand valuable recipes on cookery and household economy, menus, table etiquette, toilet, etc. contributed by over two hundred World's Fair lady managers, wives of governors and other ladies of position and influence." Its original recipe for lemon toast calls for very thin slices of bread, but I can't imagine anything more delicious than thick, pillowy slices of bread with this divine lemon sauce.

Prep Time: 10 minutes | Cook Time: 20 minutes | Yield: 4 servings

FOR THE TOAST

6 large eggs

2½ cups milk

2 tablespoons butter

12 slices thick bread (more if using thinner bread, see Note below)

FOR THE SAUCE

6 egg whites, reserved from the toast recipe

1 cup powdered sugar, plus more for dusting

Zest and juice of 2 lemons, some zest reserved for garnish

1 cup hot water

TO PREPARE THE TOAST

1. Preheat the oven to 250°F.
2. Separate the egg yolks from the whites, placing the yolks in a mixing bowl and the whites in a medium saucepan. Set aside the egg whites.
3. Whisk the milk into the egg yolks.
4. Heat a griddle or a large skillet over medium heat. Melt the butter so that it lightly covers the bottom of the pan.
5. Working in batches, dip a slice of bread into the egg mixture, submerging it to fully coat. Transfer the bread slice to the skillet and cook until golden brown, about 3 minutes per side. Transfer the cooked toast to an oven-proof dish, and keep warm in the oven while you repeat with the rest of the bread.

TO PREPARE THE SAUCE

1. Whisk the sugar into the egg whites. Add the lemon zest and juice, reserving a small amount of zest for garnish. (If you like a more lemony sauce, add a bit more zest or juice.)
2. Warm the mixture over medium-low heat, whisking in the hot water gradually so you don't scramble the egg whites. Cook gently until the mixture is lightly bubbling and has thickened a bit, about 5 minutes.
3. To serve, drizzle the sauce over the toast, then garnish with a dusting of powdered sugar and the reserved lemon zest. Serve immediately.

Note: Use slightly stale bread for better absorption and a better final texture.

OMNI MOUNT WASHINGTON RESORT

BRETTON WOODS, NEW HAMPSHIRE, USA

For readers of *Food to Die For*, what is now known as the Omni Mount Washington Resort might sound familiar. In that book, I talked about the remarkable history of the hotel itself: The Mount Washington Hotel was built by industrialist Joseph Stickney as a wedding gift for his wife, Carolyn, in 1902. The hotel instantly became such a hit with New England and New York society that guests paid almost $750 a night in today's money to stay there, about four times the going rate for other New Hampshire hotels. Thomas Edison himself was there to flip the switch and turn on the electricity on its opening day. In my years of investigating and of visiting the hotel, I've seen and heard many spirits and seen furniture move on its own in the haunted Princess Room, number 314.

But the hotel has so many stories to tell that I decided to include it in this cookbook as well. It's also why I find myself going back to visit again and again. Even if I'm not in the Princess Room trying to make contact with Carolyn Stickney herself, I can't get enough of the enchanting atmosphere. I love sitting by the fire in the grand lobby. I love walking the wraparound porch and taking in the mountain view. I love stopping by the portraits of Carolyn and Joseph to pay my respects on the way to dinner in the opulent dining room.

My favorite thing about the Mount Washington is that there's always more to discover about the grand old place. It wasn't until 2017—more than ten years after I made my first visit—that I learned my absolute favorite story about the hotel's history, involving a grisly murder, a case of mistaken identity, and a century of intrigue.

Portraits of Joseph and Carolyn Stickney, hanging in the lobby of the Mount Washington

In 1897, *another* man named Joseph Stickney, an elderly employee of the Great Falls Bank in Somersworth, New Hampshire, was brutally murdered by James Kelley in a bank robbery. "The robber broke the glass in the door leading to the bank and struck his victim with a blackjack, crushing the skull," according to an 1897 article in the Bradford, Vermont, *United Opinion*. "Then ransacking the vault, which was unlocked, the thief secured something over $4000 and escaped. Before leaving the bank, however, the villain cut the old cashier's throat from ear to ear."

I found out about that murder when I was investigating a haunting in Somersworth for an episode of *Kindred Spirits*. (It's the episode where my cohost, Adam, and I find out that the activity of a restless spirit in a family home was coming from a man whose name was misspelled on his tombstone.)

Banker Joseph Stickney, 1897 rendering

Something about the story stuck out to me, besides just the horrific details of the murder. It seemed so familiar. Then I realized: I had seen this banker Joseph Stickney before. His portrait is hanging in the lobby of the Mount Washington.

The Joseph Stickney who built the Mount Washington Hotel died in 1903, five years after the banker Joseph Stickney was murdered nearly one hundred miles to the south. By total accident, the artist of the hotel's portrait unintentionally used the photograph of the banker, not one of the hotel's owner. I don't know for sure when that portrait was commissioned, but I believe it was sometime in the 1980s or 1990s.

In all my years investigating the Mount Washington, I've never made contact with original hotel owner Joseph Stickney. It makes sense—he only lived a year past the opening of the hotel. But I've reached Princess Carolyn (who married a French prince and became a real princess in her later years) many times. She has never mentioned the portraits downstairs in the lobby or indicated that she's unhappy about another Joseph Stickney being memorialized there. I'll have to ask her again next time I go.

For my part, I think it's a happy accident. The banker Joseph Stickney deserved a better end than the one he got. His portrait being at the hotel keeps his memory alive; if not for that mistake, he would likely be lost to time. I don't think the other Joseph Stickney minds either. After all, he's got a whole hotel keeping his name alive.

JELLY OMELET

In *Food to Die For*, the Omni Mount Washington Resort contributed a modern recipe from their legendary brunch. This time around, I'm reaching further back into the past to taste a piece of the hotel's history I've never gotten to experience firsthand. I found a mid-century breakfast menu, and one thing stuck out to me: a jelly omelet. I had to re-create it—and the results were surprisingly delicious.

Prep Time: 10 minutes	Cook Time: 10 minutes	Yield: 2 servings

INGREDIENTS

4 large eggs

1/4 teaspoon salt

1 tablespoon granulated sugar

1/4 cup hot water

1 tablespoon butter, melted, plus 1 teaspoon, divided

3 tablespoons seedless raspberry jam (see Note below)

1 teaspoon powdered sugar

INSTRUCTIONS

1. Preheat the oven to 375°F.
2. Separate the eggs, placing the whites in one medium mixing bowl and the yolks in another.
3. Using a hand mixer, beat the egg whites until they form stiff peaks. Set aside.
4. In the other bowl, whisk the yolks, then add the salt, sugar, water, and 1 tablespoon of the melted butter. When fully combined, carefully fold in a third of the beaten egg whites, then fold in the remainder.
5. In a large skillet over medium-low heat, melt the remaining 1 teaspoon butter. Pour in the egg mixture and cook for 2 minutes, gently tilting the pan so the eggs cook evenly.
6. Place the skillet in the oven and bake about 8 minutes, until the eggs are cooked but not browned.
7. Transfer to a plate and spread the jam on half of the omelet. Fold the other half over and sprinkle with the powdered sugar. Cut into two portions—or keep it all for yourself.

Note: I used raspberry jam in this recipe, but orange marmalade, strawberry jelly, or any flavor you prefer would work.

ROSE HALL

MONTEGO BAY, JAMAICA

Annee Palmer was "a soul that delighted in suffering," Herbert G. de Lisser wrote in *The White Witch of Rosehall.* She lived in the "finest private residence in Jamaica" and was especially known for her cruelty to the enslaved people she owned at her plantation.

Palmer had three dead husbands by the time she was only twenty-five years of age, but she insisted that none of them had met with foul play. In fact, she claimed one of them had tried to murder her before he took his own life.

But Palmer had a secret. She knew the dark arts, learning witchcraft and voodoo from her childhood nanny in Haiti. She would use her knowledge to kill her husbands and to torture and kill enslaved men on her plantation. Eventually, her evil deeds caught up with her, and she was murdered by one of the people she terribly mistreated, her spirit condemned to haunt the property forever.

The legends surrounding Palmer were so pervasive and so convincing that even Johnny Cash wrote a song about her, asking, "Where's your husband, Annie? Where's your number two and three?" For many years, he owned a nearby home, Cinnamon Hill Great House.

The thing is, none of the stories are true.

Rose Hall, however, is a real place, and if you tour the house today, you'll hear the same stories about Annee Palmer, known as the "white witch" of Rose Hall. But it's all based on de Lisser's 1929 book—a novel, not a historical account. That doesn't stop people from trying to reach Annee's spirit though.

Built around 1750, Rose Hall was a sugarcane and cattle plantation, originally owned by George Ash, that housed about 250 enslaved men, women, and children. The house is one of Jamaica's only surviving plantation homes. Today, there's a hotel and White Witch Golf Course on the property, as well as the restored house museum.

Staff will tell visitors the "duppy" story, Jamaican slang for ghost story, about Palmer appearing on the estate, riding her horse in the dark. During the day, you can hear the story. At night, you can see it happen—a reenactment of Palmer's machete murder is part of the experience, as is a dram of a Witches Brew cocktail at the house's Dungeon Bar afterward.

As much as the legends about the white witch aren't true, there's still a lot of residual energy packed onto that land. People who visit claim to see a woman dressed in green velvet around the grounds, sometimes riding a horse. She's spotted dressed in white inside the house. Others claim to hear disembodied screams and footsteps throughout the house, especially in the cellar. "It's a spooky place . . . there's an eerie feeling that comes about you," Keith Stein, director of golf operations at Rose Hall Developments, told CNN. "You do have this sense that overcomes you that something terrible has happened here in the past. You can't miss it."

Annee Palmer's tomb

"WITCHES BREW" RUM PUNCH

A tour of Rose Hall ends with a trip to the dungeon. Unlike in the plantation's dark days, the dungeon now holds a gift shop and bar believed to be spirited in more ways than one. The experience culminates in a taste of Witches Brew, Rose Hall's signature cocktail. While the bar keeps the recipe for Witches Brew a secret, the drink is so good that I couldn't leave it out of this book. I've done my best to re-create the tropical island rum punch here. Maybe I'll have to make a trip back to compare versions.

Prep Time: 5 minutes

Yield: 2 servings

INGREDIENTS

4 ounces orange juice

4 ounces pineapple juice

1 ounce fresh lime juice

1 ounce grenadine or strawberry syrup

3 ounces white Jamaican rum, such as Wray & Nephew White Overproof Rum

3 ounces dark Jamaican rum, such as Myers's Dark Rum

Orange slices and pineapple slices and leaves for garnish, optional

Paper umbrellas for garnish, optional

INSTRUCTIONS

1. In a shaker filled with ice, combine the orange juice, pineapple juice, lime juice, grenadine, white rum, and dark rum. Shake well to chill.
2. Fill two collins glasses with ice, then divide the cocktail between the two glasses. Garnish with fruit slices and paper umbrellas for a vacation feel wherever you are.

RED INN

ARDÈCHE, FRANCE

If I've learned one thing as a paranormal investigator, it's this: Never trust a remote inn run by a husband and wife. I'm kidding, of course, but in my research I've come across some disturbing histories of murderous couples hiding their crimes at tucked-away inns. One of the coolest—er, I mean, *worst* stories I know of is about John and Lavinia Fisher, who drugged travelers in their South Carolina inn with poison tea, robbing them before they died. (If you want to know more, I wrote about them in my first cookbook, *Food to Die For*.)

When I first learned about Pierre and Marie Martin, nineteenth-century owners of L'Auberge de Peyrebeille, in Ardèche, France, that same Spidey-sense in my brain began to tingle. The couple is believed to be the culprits behind the Red Inn Affair—the hotel was more commonly called the Red Inn—which started with the murder of a guest.

On October 12, 1831, Jean-Antoine Enjolras stopped at the Red Inn for the night, but he was never seen alive again. The traveler's body was discovered on October 26 on the banks of the river near the inn, his skull crushed. Suspicion immediately fell on Pierre and Marie Martin and their employee Jean Rochette. Soon, stories started emerging: The innkeepers murdered guests, some claiming as many as fifty victims, to steal their money. The stories got even more grotesque: The Martins, it was said, cooked the bodies of their victims and fed them to other inn guests before killing them as well. Approximately one hundred people testified during the trial. Some people reported sickly smoke coming from the inn's bread oven, conjecturing that bodies had been burned there. Others said they saw human hands in the kitchen's stew pots.

After the crimes were uncovered, L'Auberge de Peyrebeille gained local notoriety. People started calling it "the bloody inn," the "cut-throat," or "the ossuary." In 1833, the French newspaper *Le Constitutionnel* wrote, "These individuals, who ran an inn in Peyrebeille, in the commune of Larrorée, made a living murdering foreigners, especially peddlers, who had the misfortune to stay there."

Pierre and Marie Martin, along with Jean Rochette, were convicted and put to death, executed by guillotine in front of the Red Inn. According to legend, there were thirty thousand people there to witness the deaths. In modern times, the story has come under more scrutiny, largely because of how much hearsay was allowed as testimony under contemporary law during the trials.

The inn is still in operation today and is famous not just for its notorious nineteenth-century crimes, but also for the creative works based on the Martins. In 1831, Honoré de Balzac wrote *L'Auberge des Adrets* based on their story, and there's a 1951 French film inspired by the Martins as well, plus a 2008 remake. A small museum inside the hotel describes the history of the murders. Stopping at the inn, shares French travel website Association Abbe Photo, is a time to reflect on "all those travellers who had the bad fortune to stop there and never leave."

"The place retains its aura," French website Le Progrès published. "The interior darkness, the haunting smell of polish, and the period furnishings, along with the deep, theatrical voice of the virtual guide, transport us to another time."

Inside the Red Inn

ARDÈCHE CHESTNUT SOUP

The chestnuts in Ardèche—called *châtaigne d'Ardèche*—are so prized that they have a Protected Designation of Origin in France, the same way champagne can only come from the country's Champagne region. So make sure to use the best prepared chestnuts you can find. Since there are so few ingredients in this elegant soup, the quality of the chestnuts will make all the difference.

Prep Time: 10 minutes	Cook Time: 25 minutes	Yield: 4 servings

INGREDIENTS

1 tablespoon unsalted butter

2 shallots, diced

1 bay leaf

1 sprig fresh rosemary

1/2 teaspoon salt, or more, to taste

1/4 teaspoon pepper, or more, to taste

1 pound roasted, shelled chestnuts

2 1/2 cups chicken or vegetable broth

1/4 cup heavy cream

Crème fraîche for garnish

Fresh chives, minced, for garnish

INSTRUCTIONS

1. In a medium stockpot over medium heat, melt the butter and sauté the shallots until soft, about 4 minutes. Add the bay leaf, rosemary, salt, and pepper and cook another 30 seconds.
2. Add the chestnuts and broth. Cover and simmer over medium-low heat for 20 minutes. Remove from the heat and discard the rosemary and bay leaf.
3. Using an immersion blender, blend the soup until smooth and velvety. (If preparing ahead or planning to freeze, stop here and finish the recipe immediately before serving.)
4. Stir in the cream and adjust the spices to taste. Serve garnished with crème fraîche and chives.

BOBBY MACKEY'S MUSIC WORLD

WILDER, KENTUCKY, USA

Before it closed for a rebuild, a sign on the wall at Bobby Mackey's Music World read: "WARNING TO OUR PATRONS: This establishment is reported to be Haunted. Management is NOT responsible and cannot be held liable for any actions of any Ghosts/Spirits on these premises."

With a warning like that, there's pretty much no way the place *isn't* full of ghosts, right?

The legends about Bobby Mackey's, a bar and concert venue just over the Kentucky line from Cincinnati, started seven decades before the club even opened. In 1896, a twenty-three-year-old woman, Pearl Bryan, was discovered murdered in an especially grisly way just two miles away from the building. Her body was found, but her head was missing and was never recovered. Among the speculation around what could have happened to Bryan's head, a theory became popular: that it had been thrown down the well in the basement of the building that later became Bobby Mackey's. It was the first macabre association with the place, but it's far from the last.

A former distillery, the building that housed Bobby Mackey's first became a bar in the 1930s and opened as a nightclub called Primrose Country Club in 1940. In 1942, Buck Brady bought Primrose and turned it into a bar with illegal gambling. His operation was so successful that he ran afoul of crime syndicate the Cleveland Four. When an enforcer for the Four turned up dead nearby in 1946, suspicion turned to Brady; they ran him out of town and took control of Primrose. It rebranded as the Latin Quarter and became the target of frequent police raids in the 1950s and '60s. Over the years, there were deaths in the building, enough so to gain it the nickname "the bloody bucket."

Bobby Mackey and his late wife, Janet, purchased the building in 1978. Mackey, a country musician, turned the place into Bobby Mackey's Music World, a performance venue and bar. Inside, there are reported to be more than forty ghosts. The first to tell Mackey of the paranormal activity was Carl Lawson, the caretaker who lived above the bar. "Carl began telling him stories: stories of being watched, of noises and phantom footsteps parading across the dark dance floor after everyone had left, of presences prowling through the basement," Asher Elbein wrote in *The Bitter Southerner.* "Bobby, though not himself inclined toward supernatural terror, listened with growing alarm. 'I said, "Carl, I don't want to hear that. I don't want nobody to know nothin' about that. Here I am, putting everything I got in here. I didn't want to be scaring people off before we got started!"'"

But word got out. Mackey's friend Doug Hensley wrote a book about the activity there, the 1991 *Terror at Music World.* The book became a sensation, prompting the Mackeys and Lawson to appear on *Jerry Springer* and *Geraldo.*

The strange occurrences continued. When Mackey bought the property next door in 1992 to build a less haunted honky-tonk, a two-hundred-foot fissure appeared in the earth, making it impossible to build there. In 2024, the current location was closed down; Bobby Mackey's relocated while Bobby and wife, Denise Mackey, are building a new location, which at the time of this writing they project to open in 2026. Part of me wonders if the spirits will visit the new building. Only time will tell.

The basement was the most active part of a very active building. Downstairs were dressing rooms for performers, a cell for gambling debtors, a staircase to nowhere, bullet holes in the walls, and of course, that well. Because it's so shallow, there's no way Pearl Bryan's head would have gone unnoticed. But that doesn't stop the headless spirit of a young woman from allegedly appearing in the space. Some people even believe the well is a portal to hell. Carl Lawson claimed to have seen two men hanging from gallows down there and to have seen a half-man, half-goat appear from the well.

In 1993, J. R. Costigan sued the business, claiming that he had been assaulted—but not by anyone living. He said he was assaulted by a ghost. If I'm being honest, though, he sounds like he was asking for it. "Costigan said he was walking around the men's room, daring the ghost to show himself, when the dark-haired apparition suddenly appeared, punched and kicked him, then disappeared," Pat Reeder wrote in *The Skeptic.* Costigan said that the ghost who assaulted him had a noose around his neck, raising the possibility that his attacker was one of the men hanged for Pearl Bryan's murder. The man demanded a thousand dollars in damages and a sign posted in the bar—hence that unsubtle warning about ghosts.

Pearl Bryan

THE MARILYN

Bobby Mackey's Music World was a true honky-tonk, where the beer was always cold and the music was always playing. Before the bar was closed to rebuild in a new location, they gave me a recipe for one of their signature cocktails, the Marilyn, which is Denise Mackey's personal favorite. When you sip it, crank the stereo loud.

Prep Time: 5 minutes

Yield: 1 serving

INGREDIENTS

1 1/2 ounces cherry vodka

1 1/2 ounces strawberry schnapps

1 1/2 ounces cranberry juice

Lemon-lime soda such as Sprite, as a topper

Two maraschino cherries for garnish

INSTRUCTIONS

1. Fill a pint glass with ice. Add the vodka, schnapps, and juice. Stir to combine.
2. Top with soda and garnish with two cherries on a cocktail skewer. Enjoy.

DOUBLE EAGLE RESTAURANT

MESILLA, NEW MEXICO, USA

Imagine a bond so strong that it can last centuries beyond death. I think it's possible—and I think it just might be happening, even today as you're reading this, in New Mexico. Inside the walls of the opulent Double Eagle Restaurant, a former home filled with antiques, historic portraits, and glittering chandeliers, a ghostly love story is still unfolding.

The story is as sad as it is romantic.

In 1849, the well-to-do Maes family built the family home that is now the Double Eagle Restaurant in Mesilla, New Mexico. The eldest son, Armando Maes, fell in love with Inez, a beautiful girl with lustrous dark hair who worked for the family. Knowing his mother would not approve of a match with someone below his station—and with a servant, no less—Armando tried to keep their relationship a secret, but Señora Maes discovered the affair and reacted in the worst possible way. Upon discovering the two of them together in Armando's bedroom, she took her sewing scissors and stabbed Inez. In an attempt to protect his love, Armando covered Inez with his own body, and his mother accidentally stabbed him, too. Inez died on the spot, but it took Armando three days to succumb to his wounds.

"It is not known what happened after that," the restaurant's website reads, "but Mesilleros say the Señora did not speak from that day forward. Her last spoken word had been her dying son's name."

The incident occurred in what's now the Carlota Salon, once Armando's bedroom, where the lovers are believed to still spend time today, leaving their ghostly impressions behind on the furniture.

In an attempt to protect his love, Armando covered Inez with his own body, and his mother accidentally stabbed him, too.

There's nearly 175 years of history in the building, which remained a private residence for more than a century after Armando and Inez's deaths.

Besides the ghosts, the Double Eagle is full of other time-earned curiosities. The restaurant is full of antique chandeliers and art and has a dining room with an eighteen-karat-gold ceiling. Outside on the patio, there's a newel post where Billy the Kid carved his name (the Kid was tried and convicted in Mesilla in 1881).

"In 1988, a couple celebrating their engagement were the last patrons in the restaurant one night," Mike Cook wrote in the *Las Cruces Bulletin*. "They left an unfinished bottle of wine in the Carlota Salon. The manager, Bill, was the last employee in the building. He left the wine on the table and 'told the ghost to have a good time,' [owner Buddy] Ritter said. Bill set the burglar alarm and motion detector, locked up for the night and left. The first person in the building the next morning, Bill unlocked the door, turned off the alarms, and upon visiting the Carlota Salon, discovered the wine bottle empty and lying on its side—there was no stain on the tablecloth—and two broken glasses."

Ritter also pointed to two Victorian armchairs in the Carlota Salon. People don't often sit in them, and yet the fabric shows continuous wear consistent with the shapes of teenagers. "There's got to be some reason they're wearing out," he told the *Las Cruces Bulletin*. "The room is really alive."

Sign for Double Eagle Restaurant

CARNE CON CHILE VERDE

The Maes family built the home that now houses the Double Eagle in 1850, and it remained a private residence until 1972. This century-old New Mexico recipe is one that likely would have been prepared in the family home in the past. It's adapted from *Historic Cookery* by Fabiola C. Gilbert, a 1958 circular from the New Mexico College of Agriculture and Mechanic Arts Agricultural Extension Service. Serve it with rice or tortillas.

Prep Time: 10 minutes	Cook Time: 1 hour 20 minutes	Yield: 4 servings

INGREDIENTS

1½ pounds stew beef, cubed

2 cups beef broth

2 tablespoons neutral cooking oil

1 cup canned chopped green chiles

1 teaspoon salt

2 cups diced fresh tomatoes, with the liquid

INSTRUCTIONS

1. In a Dutch oven or high-sided skillet, combine the beef and broth. Simmer over medium-high heat for about 30–40 minutes, until tender. Strain the beef and set aside.
2. In the same pot, heat the oil over medium-high heat and then brown the cooked beef, about 2 minutes per side.
3. Reduce the heat to medium-low, and add the chiles, salt, and tomatoes. Gently simmer for 30 minutes and serve.

HARE AND HOUNDS PUB

ISLE OF WIGHT, ENGLAND, UK

If there's one thing that never fails to fascinate me in my weird and spooky job, it's how we collectively deal with the more difficult parts of life. Of course, I'm talking about death.

More specifically, I'm talking about the apparently universal impulse to turn terrible stories about murder into macabre little songs and poems, like this one:

Michal Morey is dead
For chopping off his grandson's head.
He is hung on Arreton Down
For rooks and ravens to peck down.

And here I was thinking Lizzie "Lizbeth" Borden was the only one with a poem written about allegedly murdering her family. Like Borden, Morey wasn't definitely the culprit. And like Borden, we'll never really know the full story of what happened.

In 1737, Michal Morey (sometimes spelled Micah or Michael) was arrested for the murder of his grandson James Dove. The boy had been orphaned and lived with Morey and his wife, Beth, on the Isle of Wight, a British island just off the coast of Portsmouth, across the English Channel from Omaha Beach. He was fourteen years old, and according to accounts, had lately come into a small inheritance. In June of that year, Dove and Morey were seen going into the woods together, but the boy never reemerged.

"Not being able to offer any explanation for his grandson's disappearance, a warrant was issued for Michal Morey, who absconded for about one week, but was taken into custody at the end of July 1736 and held in Winchester awaiting trial," according to Wight Online. The boy's remains were found months later, having been placed into two leather bags and hidden in the woods. His body was so badly decomposed that he was only identifiable by his clothing.

Morey never confessed, and there was never any solid evidence linking him to his grandson's murder, but he nonetheless was convicted in 1737 and executed. "According to the law his fate was then to hang in chains from a gibbet erected in his home parish of Arreton for a prescribed length of time—this gruesome practice being intended as a deterrent against crime," the site added. A gibbet is a kind of gallows where executed criminals would be chained up for public display. The spot where Morey's remains were on display, now known as Michal Morey Hump, was close to the Hare and Hounds Pub, which dates back to about that same time. In fact, it's said that the timber from the gibbet was used to make the main roof beam inside the pub's original taproom.

"The gibbet-post, complete with a notch cut in it beside the date of his execution, can be seen in the pub, and the spirit of Michael is said to roam nearby," according to *Wightlife* magazine. *The Isle of Wight County Press* has written that Morey's ghost has been reported roaming Gallows Hill where he died, walking with an axe in hand. Inside the pub, that rhyme about Morey is on display, along with a real human skull. For years and years, that skull was believed to be Morey's—though it has been more recently revealed to be of prehistoric origin.

PLUM DOUGHNUTS

Isle of Wight's plum doughnuts are a legend unto themselves. The treat, which showcases the island's famous wild plums, was popular for centuries before all but disappearing in the early twentieth century. James Rayner includes a version of an 1845 recipe in his *Historic Isle of Wight Food* cookbook, and my version owes a debt to Rayner's recipe and the historic original.

Prep Time: 30 minutes, plus at least 1 hour 45 minutes rising time | Cook Time: 30 minutes | Yield: 10 doughnuts

INGREDIENTS

2 ripe red plums, pitted and diced into bite-size pieces (see Notes below)

2 teaspoons powdered gelatin

2¼ teaspoons (1 packet) instant yeast

2 tablespoons warm water

2½ cups bread flour, sifted, plus more for dusting

¼ cup firmly packed light brown sugar

1½ teaspoons allspice

½ teaspoon ground cinnamon

¼ teaspoon ground cloves

¼ teaspoon ground mace

½ teaspoon salt

¼ cup (½ stick) unsalted butter, cubed and softened, plus more for greasing

1 cup whole milk

Neutral cooking oil, for frying

Powdered sugar, for dusting, optional

INSTRUCTIONS

1. In a medium saucepan over medium heat, cook the plums until soft and broken down, about 10 minutes. Remove from the heat and stir in the gelatin. Set aside until ready to use.
2. In a small bowl, combine the yeast and warm water. Let sit for 5 minutes to activate.
3. In a large mixing bowl, combine the flour, sugar, allspice, cinnamon, cloves, mace, and salt. Stir in the butter and the yeast mixture. Slowly add the milk, stirring until a soft, not-too-sticky dough forms (you may not need all the milk).
4. Turn out the dough onto a floured surface and knead until smooth.
5. Grease the bowl with the butter, then put the dough back in and cover loosely. Allow to rise until doubled in size, about an hour. (If you're prepping the dough the night before, refrigerate overnight and allow to come to room temperature before proceeding, at least 30 minutes on the counter.)
6. Turn out the dough and then punch it down to release the air. Divide into 10 balls of equal size. Flatten a ball into a disc, then spoon about a tablespoon of plum filling into the center. Close the dough around the filling and pinch the seam closed. Place on a parchment-lined baking sheet. Repeat with the remaining 9 balls.
7. Cover the doughnuts loosely and allow to rise until doubled, about 45 minutes.
8. In a stockpot or Dutch oven over high heat, heat the oil to 365°F–375°F. Fry the doughnuts in batches until golden brown, turning to cook evenly, about 5–6 minutes.
9. Remove to a baking rack to cool and drain. Dust with powdered sugar before serving, if using.

Notes: The original 1845 recipe called for a whole wild plum in the center of each doughnut, but the island's plums are only about 1 inch in diameter, much smaller than what you'll find in the grocery store today. For this recipe, I've made a fruit filling. Unlike their American cousins, these doughnuts lean more savory. If you prefer a sweeter treat, dust the tops with powdered sugar before serving.

MARY GALLAGHER CORNER

MONTREAL, QUEBEC, CANADA

Look for 242 Williams Street today in Quebec's largest city, and you won't find anything except a few markings in the pavement in front of a vacant lot. But the address and the intersection close to where the building once stood reflect one of the darkest events in Montreal's history.

Mary Gallagher was a resident of Montreal's most impoverished and disease-ridden neighborhood, Griffintown, built by Irish immigrants who fled the Irish Potato Famine and began arriving in Canada in 1847. Gallagher and her close friend, Susan Kennedy, were prostitutes who were often spotted around the neighborhood together. They would also share accommodations, with Gallagher sometimes entertaining her clients at the home Kennedy shared with her husband, Jacob Mears.

The night of June 27, 1879, began as many others did. Gallagher brought a client, Michael Flanagan, back to Kennedy and Mears's house, where the four drank round after round of whiskey. However, what happened as the night wore on remains unclear. In retellings, neither Flanagan nor Kennedy could give a clear account of what occurred. Mears said he left the home, disgusted that the women were drinking and entertaining a man. Flanagan said he stumbled from the home drunkenly the next morning, too foggy to remember anything that happened. But hours after, a blood-covered Kennedy was discovered in the house with Gallagher's mutilated body, her head removed and a bloody axe nearby.

A detective on the scene, who was a war veteran, said that he had seen people gruesomely murdered before, "but none as frightfully as this," according to Alan Hustak's 2005 *The Ghost of Griffintown: The True Story of the Murder of Mary Gallagher.*

Flanagan and Kennedy were tried, but only he was acquitted. According to *The Ghost of Griffintown*, after they had examined Gallagher's body, investigators concluded, "There is no doubt the victim was slain by a woman. A man would have been more precise. No man would have vented his rage in such a haphazard manner." Despite the scene where Kennedy was found alongside Gallagher's body, there was only circumstantial—and not direct—evidence that Kennedy was the murderer.

The death of an impoverished, immigrant prostitute wouldn't normally capture the public's attention, but Gallagher's killing was an anomaly. Hers was the first murder in Montreal in two years. Plus, the murder was allegedly committed by another woman—even more unusual, especially at the time. Hundreds of people visited the crime scene while it was still under an active investigation, and thousands more followed the trial. Though her guilt is in question today, Kennedy was convicted of the murder. She was imprisoned in a two-by-five-foot jail cell in Kingston Penitentiary, where she spent eleven years in solitary confinement until she died of tuberculosis.

After Mary Gallagher's death, it didn't take long for people in Griffintown to claim they saw the ghost of a headless woman in a black gown, who would appear every seven years on the anniversary of her murder. In the mostly Irish community, Gallagher became a legend, a cautionary tale told to misbehaving children. Parents would threaten their kids with a visitation from "Headless Mary" if they didn't do as they were told. Some would even leave her little gifts in the hopes that she'd leave them alone.

Whether she truly does appear every seven years is a divisive subject. In *The Ghost of Griffintown*, one soul claimed to have seen her three times: in 1937, 1956, and 1998. In his retelling, the witness said he "looked up one night and saw a house appear . . . and in the yellow light through the upstairs window, like a lamp, I saw a figure standing there, and it asked me, 'Will you help me look for my head?' I said, 'Yes.' And then she asked me to close my eyes, and I could feel something, like a rising up around me. And when I opened my eyes, the house had vanished and she was gone."

But the last reported sighting—at least, the last one reported in a newspaper—was in 1928. In the years after that sighting, the Irish community dispersed, and Griffintown became a more industrial area. In 1990, local priest Father Thomas McEntee tried to gather former Griffintown residents together to try to spot Gallagher. "McEntee transformed the legend by encouraging Griffintowners to actively seek and welcome the ghost," Arwen Jean Fleming wrote in *David Marvin's Griffintown,* "claiming that if there were no more Irish left in Griffintown to greet her, Gallagher's spirit would no longer find her way back to the site, instead forced to wander without a head or a home, forever."

But the Irish in Griffintown, it seems, are always thinking of Mary Gallagher: At McKibbins Irish Pub on Bishop Street, her story is printed on the front of every menu, keeping her legend alive.

COLCANNON

A traditional Irish dish, colcannon was first referenced in print by a Welsh writer in 1735. But the dish likely dates back to the earliest introduction of potatoes in Ireland and would have been a staple in immigrant kitchens in Griffintown. The version I've adapted comes from the 1830 cookbook *The Cook's Oracle; and Housekeeper's Manual* by William Kitchiner, M.D.

Prep Time: 10 minutes	Cook Time: 30 minutes	Yield: 4-6 servings

INGREDIENTS

2 pounds potatoes, peeled and roughly cubed

1 tablespoon salt, plus more, to taste

8 tablespoons butter, divided, plus more for greasing

3 cups shredded green cabbage or other hardy greens

3 scallions, finely sliced, white and green parts separated

1 cup milk or cream

1/2 teaspoon black pepper, more or less, to taste

INSTRUCTIONS

1. In a large saucepan, place the potatoes and salt, and cover fully with water by an inch or so. Bring to a boil over medium-high heat. Cook until the potatoes are fork-tender, about 15–20 minutes. Drain in a colander and set aside, allowing the potatoes to rest for at least 5 minutes.
2. As the potatoes cool, return the pan to the stove. Melt 2 tablespoons of the butter over medium heat. Add the cabbage and the white parts of the scallions. Sauté lightly until softened, about 4–5 minutes.
3. Add the milk to the pan. Heat until warm, about 1 minute more.
4. Remove the pan from the heat and add the potatoes to the cabbage mixture. Mash until the mixture is smooth, adding 4 more tablespoons of the butter incrementally as you go. If the potatoes aren't smooth enough, add a dash more milk (keep in mind, the potatoes will absorb more liquid after they sit for a few minutes).
5. When the texture is smooth, mix in the green scallion slices, reserving some for garnish. Season the mixture to taste with salt and pepper.
6. Transfer the mixture to a serving dish. Make a hollow in the center of the mixture, add the remaining 2 tablespoons butter as a topping that will melt as you serve, and garnish with the remaining scallions.

Notes: In America, colcannon is popular around St. Patrick's Day in March, but in Ireland, it's traditionally enjoyed on Halloween. The dish isn't just delicious, it's portentous: If a person found one of the hidden trinkets inside colcannon on Halloween night, it was believed to foretell that person's coming year. A ring meant an impending marriage; a coin meant wealth was coming soon.

CHAPTER 4

SPECTRAL SAVORINGS

The idea of "dining with ghosts" takes on a special connotation when the presence of spirits in a culinary establishment is as welcome as the food itself. The locations in this chapter have resident ghosts that aren't necessarily going to terrify you while you dine, but the stories of these spirits are tragic and mysterious, the perfect bits of history to share over a candlelit dinner. So often, when a new restaurant or bar sets up in an old building, that structure comes with its share of stories. Some are horrifying. Others detail crimes that have haunted the place, where the residents have passed down jaw-dropping gossip for generations. When I sit down at these kinds of places, I wonder: Do these spirits watch as we dine, listening in as people tell their history? When the lights go out and the last dish is stacked away, did the energy of the evening leave those spirits feeling more . . . alive? And when we prepare these dishes in our homes, do we invite a bit of their energy into our own kitchens? I hope so. And I hope you'll find out for yourself.

FAIRMONT EMPRESS HOTEL

VICTORIA, BRITISH COLUMBIA, CANADA

Reigning over Victoria's Inner Harbor, the Fairmont Empress looks like it could be a castle in Europe. From its perch on the southeastern edge of Vancouver Island, the hotel has breathtaking views of the water and the Washington State coast beyond. Inside, its stately turn-of-the-century atmosphere echoes its history of hosting royalty and the rich and famous for more than one hundred years. And underneath that, there's the whisper of those who have come before and those who have never left.

Opened in 1908, the Empress was named after Queen Victoria, who was also for a time the Empress of India. That royal inspiration attracted real royalty through the decades. Queen Elizabeth II visited many times, as did Princess Margaret, the Queen Mother, and William and Catherine, the Prince and Princess of Wales. It has hosted Hollywood royalty, too: John Wayne, Katharine Hepburn, and Barbra Streisand have all stayed at the Empress, and it's where Shirley Temple took refuge amid threats of kidnapping in California.

One of the hotel's most famous stories, though, involves a scandal and a murder. After architect Francis Rattenbury designed the Empress and the nearby British Columbia Parliament Buildings, the fame and praise went to his head. In the 1920s, he became involved with a young woman, Alma Pakenham, while still married to his wife, Florrie Rattenbury. Florrie died of cancer not long after the divorce.

"People blamed Rattenbury [for Florrie's death]," historian John Adams told *The Washington Post* in 2018.

"The couple fled to England, where Alma eventually began an affair with her handsome seventeen-year-old chauffeur, George Stoner, who eventually bludgeoned Rattenbury to death," Liz Langley wrote in that *Post* article. On his own testimony, "Stoner was convicted and given a death sentence that was later commuted to life; Alma was acquitted but took her own life before hearing George had been spared."

Francis Rattenbury, 1924

Today, people say that Rattenbury—Langley describes his apparition as "a man in period dress on the staircase to the lower lobby"—has returned to the site of his greatest triumph, hoping to overhear praise of his design.

Another ghost often reported is that of chambermaid Lizzie McGrath, who fell to her death in 1909. She had been in the habit of stepping out onto the fire escape to say her prayers every night but, on the night of her death, didn't realize the contractor had removed it earlier in the day.

Talking to the Victoria *Times Colonist*, Adams shared the story of an elderly woman who passed away in a sixth-floor room. "Adams says that after reports of strange events—an unexplained chill, the feeling of a hand on a shoulder, a mirror reflecting a woman who wasn't there—the hotel left her room locked for several years," Jack Knox wrote. "Then, after the room made way for an elevator shaft, nearby guests began telling stories of someone knocking on the door in the wee hours. Some saw an old woman seeking help finding her room; she would vanish when they were unable to help her."

But the hauntings aren't just confined to the Empress in Victoria. As Adams added, "there are ghosts everywhere in the city."

EMPRESS 1908 ELDERFLOWER ROSE GIN TRIFLE

This delicate (and boozy!) trifle comes courtesy of the Fairmont Empress, from the hotel's Executive Pastry Chef Gerald Tan. Chef Tan is renowned for his contributions to the hotel's famed Afternoon Tea service, which serves more than four hundred guests a day in the summer season. This dessert is labor-intensive but results in a lightly sweet confection with notes of white chocolate, ripe fruit, and delicate botanicals that's worth the effort.

Prep Time: 1 hour, plus chilling time | Cook Time: 1 hour | Yield: 8 servings

FOR THE VANILLA WHITE CHOCOLATE GANACHE MONTÉE

1/2 teaspoon powdered gelatin

1 tablespoon cold water

1 cup best-quality white chocolate

2 cups heavy cream

2 tablespoons granulated sugar

2 teaspoons vanilla bean paste (or extract)

FOR THE STRAWBERRY COMPOTE

1 cup granulated sugar

1 tablespoon fruit pectin

2 cups fresh strawberries, trimmed and quartered, plus more halved for garnish

1/4 cup Empress 1908 Elderflower Rose Gin

PREPARE THE VANILLA WHITE CHOCOLATE GANACHE MONTÉE

1. Bloom the gelatin by combining it with the water in a small mixing bowl. In a large mixing bowl, place the white chocolate. Set both bowls aside.
2. In a medium saucepan over medium heat, warm the cream, sugar, and vanilla paste until just under simmering, being careful not to boil it.
3. Turn off the heat then pour the mixture on the white chocolate. Add the bloomed gelatin and whisk until smooth.
4. Transfer the mixture to a container, then cover and refrigerate for at least 6 hours or overnight.
5. The next day, whip the mixture until soft peaks form. Reserve until ready to use.

PREPARE THE STRAWBERRY COMPOTE

1. Mix together the sugar and pectin (this step will prevent clumping later).
2. In a heavy-bottomed pot, place the strawberries and the sugar-pectin mixture. Add the gin.
3. Cook on low heat until the strawberries are soft, about 6–8 minutes. Cool.

(recipe continues)

(recipe continued from page 135)

FOR THE VANILLA GENOISE SPONGE CAKE

6 large eggs

$^{2}/_{3}$ cup granulated sugar

$^{3}/_{4}$ cup cake flour

$^{1}/_{4}$ cup cornstarch

FOR THE ELDERFLOWER ROSE GIN SYRUP

$^{1}/_{8}$ cup granulated sugar

$^{1}/_{8}$ cup water

$^{1}/_{4}$ cup Empress 1908 Elderflower Rose Gin

Strawberry powder for garnish (see Notes below)

PREPARE THE VANILLA GENOISE SPONGE CAKE

1. Preheat the oven to 325°F.
2. Using a stand mixer, whip the eggs and sugar until the mixture is very light and fluffy. Remove from the mixer.
3. Sift the cake flour and cornstarch.
4. Gently fold the flour mixture into the whipped eggs, one third at a time, until well incorporated but not deflating the eggs.
5. Line a 16 x 12-inch baking sheet (also called a half-sheet) with parchment paper. Spread the mixture onto the prepared baking sheet.
6. Bake until the cake springs back when lightly touched, about 15–18 minutes. Cool to room temperature.

PREPARE THE ELDERFLOWER ROSE GIN SYRUP

1. In a small saucepan over medium heat, warm the sugar and water until all the sugar is dissolved, about 5 minutes.
2. Cool then add the gin.

ASSEMBLE THE TRIFLE

1. Brush the cake generously with the elderflower rose gin syrup.
2. In a trifle dish or a deep bowl, spread the compote on the bottom.
3. Cut the cake into cubes then layer them on top of the compote.
4. Spread the whipped vanilla white chocolate ganache montée on top.
5. Garnish with some fresh strawberries on top and dust with strawberry powder.

Notes: You should be able to find strawberry powder online, but if not, make your own by grinding freeze-dried strawberries in the food processor.

If you want to save yourself a step, buy a sponge cake rather than making your own.

EMPRESS

POOR RED'S BAR-B-Q

EL DORADO, CALIFORNIA

The story couldn't have been written any better if it were fiction: A man won a run-down bar in a game of dice and transformed it into an institution that's still going strong eighty years later. But turns out this story is absolutely true.

In a 1945 game of dice, Red Sadler won a local dive called Kelley's Bar that had been around since 1927. He and his wife, Opal, turned it into Poor Red's, a roadside barbecue joint between San Francisco and Lake Tahoe that became so popular, Frank Sinatra and the rest of the Rat Pack were known to stop in from time to time. The current owners bought the restaurant in 2016 and elevated Poor Red's from a barbecue roadhouse to the epicurean destination it is today, which has won dozens of awards for its refined comfort food. Still, there are portraits of "Poor Red" and "Rich Opal" in the bar, which also has incredible room-length murals of the history of El Dorado.

I would love Poor Red's even if it weren't haunted; it's close to my hometown, and I've been going there for the excellent food my friend Chef Dean Hiatt has been churning out of the kitchen for years. Lucky for me, though, the place is definitely haunted. When I investigated the restaurant for my six-part documentary about the ghosts of El Dorado, *Historically Haunted*, I spoke to Red himself, who likes to stick around the restaurant and keep an eye on things.

I chose El Dorado for my first *Historically Haunted* deep dive because, for a tiny town of fourteen hundred people, it has an enormous amount of spooky history, much of it stemming from the area's Gold

Rush past. El Dorado, California—named after the mythical city of gold—was one of the earliest gold mining towns in the country. (The town of Coloma, where the first gold that sparked the rush was found, is only twenty miles away. You can read about Coloma, and the nearby Cary House Hotel that financed an expansion with the gold dust in its floorboards, in *Food to Die For*.) The building that houses Poor Red's dates back to the 1850s and was right there on Main Street to witness all the highs and lows. Before it became a bar, the building was a Pony Express stop and is believed to have been a brothel as well.

In 1852, the *Sacramento Union Leader* reported on a sermon given by a local reverend speaking against "gambling, horse-racing, licentiousness, fighting, and pretty much all the rest of the evils with which society in California is contaminated." And a lot of it—I mean, a *lot*—was happening in El Dorado County, where the rough mining life led to conflicts and even violent acts, like murders and lynchings. In October 1855, a local serial killer named Mickey Free was hanged after he was caught robbing more successful miners and murdering prostitutes. Free was known to stalk the roads between Gold Rush towns like Coloma and Placerville (read about both places in *Food to Die For*), a sort of Wild West highwayman who would murder and rob those who had found gold.

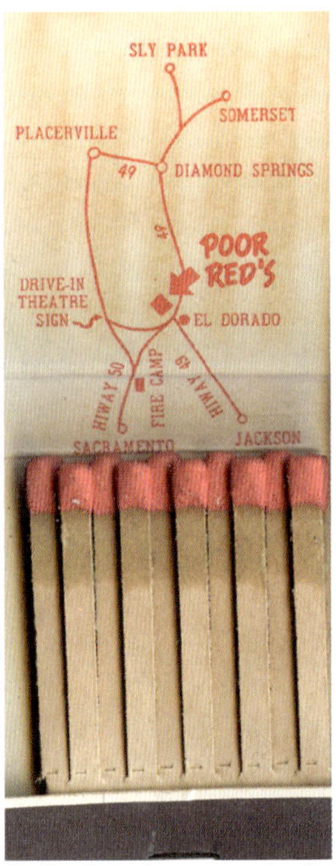

1970s matchbook from Poor Red's

He was hanged alongside Jeremiah Crane, a totally different kind of criminal. Crane had moved to California and earned his room and board tutoring the children of the Newnham family. He fell in love with eighteen-year-old Susan Newnham, despite her father forbidding the match. Crane, in possibly the most misguided show of affection in the history of time, decided the two should be united in heaven if they were forbidden to be together on earth. "Pulling away from an embrace with his beloved, he shot Susan in the head," Jerrie Beard wrote for *Style Magazine*. "The shot was not fatal, however, and she fled back toward her house. He then shot two more times bringing her to the ground, but not killing her. He carried her into the house and placed her on a sofa where she lingered for five days before expiring."

For the staff at Poor Red's, paranormal experiences are a near daily occurrence. People regularly catch objects moving on their security cameras in the middle of the night, hear disembodied voices, and see the jukebox turn itself on. Often, they'll hear footsteps upstairs in the space believed to be a former bordello—even though the upstairs was sealed off years ago.

GOLDEN CADILLAC

Poor Red's Bar-B-Q has been famous for its Golden Cadillac cocktail for decades—so famous, in fact, that Galliano used the recipe in advertising campaigns for the liqueur in the 1960s. The restaurant serves so many of them that it's the number one buyer of the liqueur in the world. According to Poor Red's, the bar goes through a bottle about every hour and a half. The legend goes like this: A newlywed couple stopped into the restaurant and asked bartender Frank Cline to make a cocktail to match their new gold car. He did and poured the libation into two glasses: a champagne coupe for her and a highball for him. Today, every Golden Cadillac is served side by side in those glasses. This recipe comes courtesy of Poor Red's executive chef, Dean Hiatt.

Prep Time: 5 minutes

Yield: 1 serving (in two glasses)

INGREDIENTS

2 ounces Galliano liqueur

1 1/2 ounces white crème de cacao

1 1/2 cups ice

1/2 ounce half and half

INSTRUCTIONS

1. In a blender, combine the Galliano, white crème de cacao, and ice. Blend on high.
2. While the blender is running, stream in the half and half to create frothiness. Add only enough half and half to preserve the gold color and keep the consistency like a thin milkshake.
3. Pour into a coupe glass first, then pour into a highball glass as the sidecar. Serve side by side.

Note: When the coupe glass is empty, do the "Cadillac tap" by slowly and gently tapping a corner of the highball glass on the bar top to break up the frozen top of the sidecar, then refill the coupe.

FIVE FISHERMEN RESTAURANT

HALIFAX, NOVA SCOTIA, CANADA

At 11:40 p.m. on April 14, 1912, the RMS *Titanic* hit an iceberg and sank only three hours later. This maritime disaster still shocks the world more than a century later and is the subject of movies, books, museum exhibits, and even a Broadway musical.

But in the moment, the biggest priority was helping those who had been on the ship. Survivors went to New York, but victims went to Halifax, Nova Scotia, the closest city to the wreck, which happened five hundred miles offshore.

Hundreds of people eat dinner at the epicenter of the recovery mission for those who died with the sinking of the *Titanic*. But macabre history isn't the only reason to visit the Five Fishermen Restaurant. People also go for Five Fishermen's really great seafood . . . and for the ghosts.

Originally built as a school in 1818, the building that houses Five Fishermen is a protected heritage site because it was the country's first national school, a progenitor of public schools in the country. Once the population outgrew the space, the building became Halifax's Victoria School of Art and Design, started by Anna Leonowens, the former governess whose memoirs inspired the semi-biographical novel by Margaret Landon, *Anna and the King of Siam*, about Anna's life. The book was adapted into the musical, *The King and I*.

The next tenant that moved into the building was John Snow & Co. Funeral Home, which opened in 1883. In the days after the *Titanic* tragedy, Snow was tasked with running the recovery mission for remains. The undertaking (sorry, I had to) was overwhelming. Snow called in reinforcements from all over the area and ordered the holds and tanks of ships to be filled with ice to preserve the bodies until they could be embalmed.

Snow's mission recovered 306 bodies, including the body of John Jacob Astor, one of the richest men in the world. Snow decided that 116 of those people had to be buried at sea because of the condition of their remains. "Every body had on a lifebelt," Snow described, "and bodies floated very high in the water in spite of sodden clothes and things in pockets . . . Some had on their pajamas, two or three skirts, two pairs of pants, two vests, two jackets, and an overcoat. In some pockets we found quantities of meat and biscuits. In most every man's pocket were found quite a bit of tobacco and matches and vials of whiskey. Many people had keys to their stateroom and lockers."

Most of the remains went to a local ice rink better equipped to deal with the sheer volume of coffins and relatives coming to identify remains, but the wealthiest passengers went to Snow's. About 150 deceased passengers' remains were unclaimed. Today, they're buried across three cemeteries in Halifax.

The *Titanic* wasn't the only disaster that John Snow & Co. Funeral Home had to manage. Five years later, two thousand people died in an event that came to be known as the Halifax Explosion, when the French SS *Mont-Blanc* collided with the Norwegian SS *Imo* in Halifax Harbor. The collision ignited the cache of explosives inside *Mont-Blanc*, and the ensuing fire and pressure wave caused massive damage to the harbor and surrounding areas. After the Halifax Explosion, Snow's is said to have conducted funeral services for thirty to forty people a day.

The funeral home is still operating today, more than 135 years after its founding, but no longer in that historic building on Argyle Street. Since 1975, the building has been home to the Five Fishermen Restaurant, which has an understandably haunted reputation.

According to restaurant representatives, staffers regularly see glasses flying off shelves and cutlery falling off tables, feel pockets of cold air, watch taps turning themselves on and off, and hear disembodied voices—not to mention experience full-bodied apparitions seen by both staff and customers.

"We say you can stay late, but never alone," restaurant manager Wallace Fraser told CTV News in 2017.

Since this book is filled with tales of true crime, I couldn't stop myself from digging into any crimes that occurred onboard the *Titanic* before it sank. Turns out there were plenty of criminals aboard, both in the passengers and crew, convicted for crimes like thievery, bigamy, spying, and kidnapping, as well as "preaching illegal religious ceremonies, and protesting as suffragettes," as James T. Bartlett wrote for suspenseful stories and true-crime hub *CrimeReads*. Christopher Shulver, who worked in the boiler room, signed up as "J. Dilley" for the sailing to avoid his criminal background following him. George McGough, another boiler room "fireman," had been convicted of murder in 1900 and committed the act again aboard the *Titanic*, pushing shipmate John Dwyer off a landing to his death only twenty feet down. McGough miraculously survived the wreck—and went to prison for manslaughter.

THE FIVE FISH EXPERIENCE

Nova Scotia is a premium source of fresh seafood, which is why the chefs at the Five Fishermen don't have to alter their ingredients much to create a delicious meal. This recipe is inspired by their iconic dish, the Five Fish Experience: five kinds of fish, served over tomato risotto, and finished with a lobster velouté sauce.

Prep Time: 10 minutes | Cook Time: 1 hour | Yield: 4 servings

FOR THE TOMATO RISOTTO

3–4 cups vegetable broth

2 tablespoons unsalted butter, divided

1 medium white onion, diced

1 teaspoon sea salt

½ teaspoon black pepper

1½ cups arborio rice

½ cup dry white wine

1 cup diced fresh tomatoes

½ cup grated Parmesan cheese

FOR THE LOBSTER VELOUTÉ

2 tablespoons unsalted butter

1 tablespoon plus 1 teaspoon all-purpose flour

1 cup lobster stock (see Notes on page 146)

Pinch of white pepper

TO PREPARE THE TOMATO RISOTTO

1. In a small saucepan over medium heat, warm the vegetable broth until it reaches a low simmer. Keep at a very low simmer until ready to use.
2. In a large skillet over medium heat, melt 1 tablespoon of the butter, then add the onion, salt, and pepper. (Be careful with adding extra salt, the shellfish will add natural salinity later.) Cook for 5–7 minutes, until the onion is translucent but not brown.
3. Add the rice, and cook another 2 minutes, stirring frequently (this step will toast the rice and deepen the flavor of the risotto).
4. Add the wine and tomatoes. Cook about 5 minutes, stirring often, until the liquid has mostly evaporated. Add 2 cups of the vegetable broth, and cook for about 5–7 minutes, stirring often, until most of the liquid is absorbed. Repeat with ½ cup more broth, then the remaining ½ cup broth if the risotto can absorb it. You want firm yet tender grains, so you may not need all the broth in the end.
5. Remove the rice from the heat and stir in the Parmesan and the remaining 1 tablespoon butter. Cover to keep the risotto warm until ready to serve.

TO PREPARE THE LOBSTER VELOUTÉ

1. In a medium saucepan over medium heat, melt the butter. Whisk in the flour to make a roux, stirring constantly for about 2 minutes. Don't allow the mixture to brown.

(recipe continues)

(recipe continued from page 145)

FOR THE SEAFOOD

2 tablespoons unsalted butter

8 jumbo shrimp, shelled and deveined

8 sea scallops, side muscle removed

1 pound Nova Scotia halibut, cut into 4 portions

12 littleneck clams (see Notes below)

2 lobster tails, cut lengthwise in half

1/2 teaspoon salt

1 teaspoon black pepper

2. Whisk in half of the lobster stock, stirring until the mixture is totally smooth, then add the remaining stock and a pinch of white pepper. Bring the mixture to a boil, whisking constantly, then lower the temperature and cook at a low boil for about 2 minutes until thickened. (If the mixture is too thin, whisk in 1 teaspoon butter mashed together with 1 teaspoon flour.) Remove the sauce from the heat and cover until ready to serve.

TO PREPARE THE SEAFOOD

1. In a large skillet, melt the butter. Add the shrimp, scallops, halibut, clams, and lobster. Season lightly with salt and pepper.
2. Cook the shrimp and scallops about 2–3 minutes per side, the clams about 3–4 minutes until they open, and the halibut and lobster about 3–4 minutes per side, until opaque and cooked through. As each ingredient is fully cooked, remove from the pan.

TO ASSEMBLE THE DISH

1. Divide the risotto between 4 plates, top with equal portions of the seafood, and finish with a swirl of velouté.

Notes: When you make this dish, try to get the freshest, best-quality seafood you can, preferably from Nova Scotia.

Littleneck clams often have residual sand. To encourage them to release any residual sand, several hours before cooking (or even the day before), submerge the littleneck clams in salted water and refrigerate.

You should be able to find lobster stock from a specialty grocery store or fishmonger. But if the stock remains elusive, it's relatively simple to make your own. Simply simmer lobster shells in about 2 cups of water for about 30 minutes. Freeze any leftover stock to make this dish again—you'll definitely want to.

If you have any leftover velouté, you can freeze it for up to 3 months.

LEMP MANSION

ST. LOUIS, MISSOURI, USA

One of St. Louis's grandest homes, the Lemp Mansion, was built in 1868 and housed generations of one of the city's wealthiest families for nearly a century. According to many who have walked its halls, the Lemps never truly left.

Johann Adam Lemp emigrated from Germany in 1836, settling in St. Louis in 1838. He ran a grocery store, where he made a name for himself selling his German-style lager beer, much lighter than the widely available English ales. In 1840, Lemp started a beer company; the first location of the Lemp Brewery was located where the south leg of the city's iconic Gateway Arch now stands.

Lemp Brewery became so popular so quickly that in just five years it moved to a larger facility, with limestone caves underneath where beer could be kept cold and an aboveground beer garden called Lemp's Cave. When the elder Lemp died in 1862, his son William took over the company. As Kathy Weiser-Alexander wrote for the website Legends of America, "By the 1870s the Lemp family symbolized both wealth and power, as the Lemp Brewery controlled the St. Louis beer market, a position it maintained until Prohibition."

William and Julia purchased the mansion in 1876. The Italianate home had a few architecturally unique features: an atrium for exotic plants and birds, an observation deck, and—according to the mansion's staff—underground tunnels connecting the home to the brewery caves. These tunnels even featured a theater, a swimming pool, and a bowling alley. Lemp Brewery grew to be one of the first beers to be distributed nationwide. William's daughter Hilda married into another storied beer family, the Pabsts. Son Billy married Lillian Handlan, known as the "Lavender Lady" because of her habit of wearing the color every day, down to her horse's accessories.

William J. Lemp

But by the turn of the century, the family's fortunes took a turn. In 1901, William's son Frederick, the heir apparent of the family business, died of heart failure. William mourned his son until 1904, when he died in a bedroom at Lemp Mansion of a self-inflicted gunshot wound to the head.

William's firstborn son, Billy, took over the brewery, but he failed to grow and expand the business the way his father had. Alongside his and Lillian's lavish spending, Billy also threw decadent parties in the brewery caves, including hiring prostitutes for his friends. The couple eventually divorced in a bitter dispute.

In the years following William Sr.'s death, Lemp Brewery continued to decline until Prohibition, when it closed for good. Billy took his own life in 1922. The following year, daughter Elsa—one of the wealthiest women in St. Louis—died of a self-inflicted gunshot wound to the heart (though some question this account and suspect her husband was looking for a payout, as he allegedly didn't call for a doctor for thirty minutes and servants changed their stories after the fact). Billy's brother Charles died by suicide in 1949, in the same room in Lemp Mansion where Billy had ended his life. He was the only Lemp to leave a note, which read: "In case I am found dead, blame it on no one but me." According to mansion representatives, that's when the ghost stories started: Neighbors would report seeing Charles walking the street after his death.

After the last Lemp to live in the mansion died, in 1950, the building went through new lives of its own—among them a boardinghouse and a temporary residence for children from a nearby pediatric hospital—before Richard Pointer bought the home in 1975 and opened the Lemp Mansion Restaurant and Inn.

While restoring the ceiling's frescoes, a worker named Claude Breckwoldt told the *St. Louis Post-Dispatch* that he was on the job late one night when he "had this sensation that someone was staring at me. . . . There was no doubt. I got chills up and down my back. My hair stood on end. Until then, I never believed in ghosts." Today, paranormal activity is part of the mansion's allure. People report hearing disembodied voices, seeing shadow figures, and hearing the piano play on its own. In the dining room, the site of the office where Billy and Charles died, people have seen an apparition of a man sitting down to dinner, only to vanish when approached. Glasses are said to levitate on their own. Some claim to have seen the apparition of Lillian, the Lavender Lady, in the room.

The last remaining Lemp sibling, Edwin, died in 1970 at the age of ninety. As his last wish, his butler burned the Lemp family documents in a blaze.

MAYFAIR SALAD DRESSING

This salad dressing recipe, provided by the Lemp Mansion, is the restaurant's take on the classic Mayfair salad dressing served by St. Louis's Mayfair Hotel during the 1904 St. Louis World's Fair, adapted by Chef Reed Miller and Richard Pointer. As the restaurant notes, "the inclusion of the celery rib and onion, often omitted from later versions, results in a thicker, creamier dressing that has become a well-loved tradition by generations of diners." Serve it over a simple salad of crisp romaine lettuce.

Prep Time: 10 minutes | Yield: 1½ cups

INGREDIENTS

½ small white onion, roughly chopped

1 small rib celery, roughly chopped

1 egg

2–3 anchovy fillets (use more or less according to your preference)

½ teaspoon white pepper

½ teaspoon salt

1½ teaspoons granulated sugar

1½ teaspoons granulated garlic

1½ teaspoons lemon juice

1½ teaspoons yellow mustard

1–1½ cups salad oil (such as canola or vegetable oil)

INSTRUCTIONS

1. In a blender or food processor, combine the onion, celery, egg, anchovy fillets, white pepper, salt, sugar, garlic, lemon juice, and yellow mustard. Blend on high until well combined.
2. With the blender or food processor running, slowly stream in the oil until you achieve your desired consistency (you may not need all the oil).
3. Serve immediately or refrigerate until ready to use.

Note: Consuming raw or undercooked eggs may increase your risk of foodborne illness, especially if you have certain medical conditions

THE COURT OF TWO SISTERS

NEW ORLEANS, LOUISIANA, USA

It's not hard to find a ghost in New Orleans. In fact, if you just stand still, chances are that in what's commonly referred to as the most haunted city in America, it's pretty likely a spirit will come to you. But even so, in a city as undeniably full of spirits as New Orleans (in the air *and* in your glass), there are certain places that just feel different. Charged with energy. Vibrating on a different level.

The Court of Two Sisters is one of those places—and I'm not just saying that because people claim to see fairies and elementals in the restaurant's jazz-filled courtyard.

Tucked away on Royal Street, a quieter part of the historic French Quarter than nearby Bourbon, the restaurant's iconic antique lantern lights the way inside: "Famous Historical Court of Two Sisters Restaurant," it reads, "Since 1832." The restaurant isn't quite that old, but the legend is. Originally built as a shop with a home above it in 1832, 613 Royal Street became "The Shop of Two Sisters" in 1886, when sisters Bertha Angaud and Emma Camors opened a boutique selling women's fineries. After they closed the shop sometime around 1904, the building changed hands often, along with the business inside.

In 1940, local restauranteur Jimmy Cooper bought the building, opening up the Court of Two Sisters. But Cooper also brought a bad reputation and a dangerous temper with him. He married New Orleans socialite Amelie "Diddie" Woolfolk in 1951, but they separated less than a year later, with Diddie living in a separate apartment above the restaurant. On November 30, 1952, Diddie was discovered in her apartment, murdered. She "had been choked into unconsciousness, revived and beaten again with a blunt object which fractured her skull," according to Orleans parish coroner Dr. Nicholas J. Chetta, the *Cincinnati Post* reported on December 1 of that year.

Mardi Gras, 1963

Suspicion immediately went to Cooper, who was tried for the crime and acquitted in 1954. Immediately after leaving court, he threw a party at the restaurant. After the verdict, the story continued, "Bedlam broke loose in the jammed courtroom," and "shrill cries and yells pierced the air and a group of women admirers surged toward the exuberant dapper restauranteur." According to a January 22, 1954, article in the *Daily Clintonian*, Cooper "flashed a big smile and boomed out, 'Gee, it's great to see that the people believe in me.'" Indeed, he had a fan club.

The murder was never solved, but two years later, Cooper died in his apartment above the restaurant under mysterious circumstances, which could have been anaphylaxis but also could have been poisoning.

In 1963, Joe Fein Jr. bought the restaurant, and the third generation of the Fein family still runs it today. Every day there's a jazz brunch, and every evening there's a Creole dinner. It's as charming and transportive today as it ever was, giving visitors a glimpse into good old-fashioned New Orleans hospitality: rich food, lively music, and plenty of good cheer.

Aside from the Coopers' stories, other mysterious tales surround the restaurant. Legend has it that the real name of the courtyard's wishing well is the "Devil's Wishing Well" because famed voodoo priestess Marie Laveau reportedly practiced her rituals there. Those same legends also claim that notorious pirate Jean Lafitte killed three men in duels on the same night in the restaurant's courtyard. The sisters, too, are rumored to be present in the restaurant to this day, watching over the space they loved. They're sometimes spotted together in the courtyard late at night and are said to leave those who glimpse them with feelings of happiness.

NEW ORLEANS BARBECUE SHRIMP

In a city famous for all kinds of dishes, New Orleans barbecue shrimp is a standout. Originally invented at Pascal's Manale in 1953, this spicy and savory shrimp dish—which isn't actually "barbecued" at all—has become ubiquitous in the city. Here's an adaptation of the Court of Two Sisters's famous recipe.

Prep Time: 5 minutes | Cook Time: 20 minutes | Yield: 4 servings as an appetizer, 2 as an entree

INGREDIENTS

24 large shrimp, heads and shells intact

1 cup (2 sticks) melted unsalted butter, divided

1 cup water

2 tablespoons black pepper

1/2 teaspoon cayenne pepper

2 tablespoons chopped fresh Italian parsley

French bread, for serving

INSTRUCTIONS

1. Preheat the oven to 375°F.
2. Spread the shrimp in an 8 x 10-inch baking dish, placing them in a double layer.
3. Pour 1/2 cup of the melted butter and the water over the shrimp, then sprinkle with the black pepper and cayenne pepper. Pour the remaining 1/2 cup melted butter on top.
4. Bake for 10 minutes. Remove the shrimp from the oven, stir, and bake another 10 minutes, until the shrimp are fully pink. Remove from the oven, sprinkle with parsley, and serve with crusty French bread.

GRILL HOUSE RESTAURANT

ALLEGAN, MICHIGAN, USA

If all you know about lumberjacks came from Paul Bunyan, I've got news for you. Unlike the mythologized folktales of the larger-than-life logger and his trusty blue ox, Babe, the real exploits of loggers are gritty, filled with peril, and mostly frozen.

In the winters of the late 1800s and early 1900s, men would layer on their warmest clothing and venture into the woods to harvest the lumber that was building America's Western expansion. An epicenter of that logging was in Michigan's forests, where white pines could reach 150 feet high and span four feet across. Harvesting the trees was backbreaking work and, much like the gold mining happening in California at the time, equally as dangerous. Along with the tempers that could rise in such rough conditions, the work itself was highly risky. Even today, with much more advanced equipment and ready access to emergency care, logging is still one of the most dangerous jobs in the country.

"Logging was winter work because only by turning trails and roads into ice could the massive logs be hauled to the riverbanks where they would be floated to sawmills once ice had broken up," journalist

Barry Wood wrote of the Michigan lumber camps. "Camps housed up to one hundred men. The workday began before dawn and continued until after dark six days a week. Sundays were for sharpening axes and saws, laundry, card playing, and drinking. It was not unusual for one or two men to be killed on the job each winter."

Originally built in 1836, the building once known as Hubbard House goes by another name today: the Grill House Restaurant. At one of Michigan's most unique restaurants, you choose a protein then head to the grill yourself to cook your meal. Downstairs, there's a rough-hewn Rock Bar in the house's basement. Back in the 1800s, though, the town of Allegan barely existed.

Dr. Samuel Hubbard, who built the two-story yellow house with its green roof and long porch, established the Allegan Company that eventually founded the town of Allegan. Hubbard House not only acted as a company headquarters, but it also doubled as a lumberjack boardinghouse. Legend has it that in 1847, a brawl broke out among the "jacks," as they called themselves, and one was stabbed to death. According to the restaurant legend, the man was buried on the property, his grave unmarked, and his name lost to time.

"Jack, the name given to our friendly resident, has shown himself on numerous occasions," the restaurant website shares of its ghost. "He has all too frequently been known to move chairs and leave candles burning. Dimming the lights, changing radio stations, opening and closing doors, and rattling dishes are other parts of his repertoire. On rare occasions a single shot of whiskey, Jack's drink of choice, will even be found sitting on the Rock Bar, acting as a haunting reminder of our supernatural companion."

According to restaurant legend, the murdered man was buried on the property, his grave unmarked, and his name lost to time.

Though everyone knows Jack, he seems to be a friendly presence. "It's fun to have a resident ghost," co-owner Marcia Wagner told *Michigan Beverage Journal* in 2008. "Although I wouldn't exactly call him a tourist attraction, he does make life here a little more interesting."

MOLASSES COOKIES

Harvesting timber is backbreaking work today, let alone with nineteenth-century tools. Lumberjacks could eat as much as eight thousand calories a day, often from molasses-rich foods like these simple, delicious cookies that were a staple in the camps; in New England, we call them Lumberjack Cookies. This recipe is adapted from Maureen Fischer's *Nineteenth-Century Lumber Camp Cooking*.

Prep Time: 10 minutes, plus 1 hour chilling time | Cook Time: 10 minutes | Yield: 3 dozen cookies

INGREDIENTS

2 cups granulated sugar, divided

1/2 cup (1 stick) unsalted butter, softened (see Note below)

1 egg

1/2 cup molasses

2 cups all-purpose flour

1 teaspoon baking soda

1/2 teaspoon ground cinnamon

1/2 teaspoon ground ginger

1/4 teaspoon ground cloves

1/4 teaspoon salt

INSTRUCTIONS

1. In a medium mixing bowl, mix 1 cup of the sugar and the butter. Add the egg and molasses, stirring by hand until combined.
2. Add the flour, baking soda, cinnamon, ginger, cloves, and salt. Stir to combine, then cover the dough with plastic wrap directly touching the surface, and chill at least 1 hour.
3. After 1 hour, preheat the oven to 350°F.
4. Place the remaining 1 cup sugar in a small mixing bowl.
5. Roll the dough into 1-inch balls, working quickly to avoid warming the dough too much. If necessary, run your hands under cold water intermittently. Drop each dough ball into the sugar bowl, roll to coat, then transfer the dough to a baking sheet lined with parchment paper.
6. Bake for 11–13 minutes, until golden brown (the dough is already dark, so you'll have to keep an eye on the cookies so you don't overbake). Let them rest on the baking sheet for 5 minutes before moving to a cooling rack.

Note: A historically accurate version of this recipe would have used lard—so if you're looking for 100 percent historicity, use that instead of butter.

THE *DELTA KING*

SACRAMENTO, CALIFORNIA, USA

It's hard to believe now, but there was a time when it was too difficult to comfortably make the drive between San Francisco and the state's capital, Sacramento. Though it's only about a ninety-minute trip today, in automotive transport's early days, the journey was a long and arduous one. Roads were largely unpaved, and cars couldn't drive very fast; the river crossing in particular raised issues because of the lack of bridges. The preferred way to get from one city to the other was by riverboat on the Sacramento River. By the mid-1920s, wealthy residents were ready for an upgrade. Enter the *Delta King* and *Delta Queen*, sister boats designed to make the overnight trip a luxury experience.

"You can take pride in knowing that in all the world there are no finer stern-wheeled vessels afloat," *San Francisco Chronicle* travel journalist Sam G. Mortland said when they launched in 1927, according to the *Stockton Evening and Standard*. "I have been up and down the Nile many times, but I want to say that even Egypt has nothing in the line of a floating palace which can surpass the *Delta King* and *Delta Queen*. Travelers from all over the world will ride into interior California on these boats and they will not forget their magnificence. These boats will be great advertising mediums for California."

The boats each had eighteen suites (or thirty-six single rooms with bathrooms), sixty single rooms, and room for sixty automobiles in addition to freight. The boat would disembark from Sacramento at 6:30 p.m. on every night except Sunday and arrive in San Francisco at 5:30 a.m. the next morning. On board there was fine food, dancing to a live jazz band, gambling, and even drinking at a time when Prohibition banned it.

But as much as the boats themselves were luxurious, the area they traversed wasn't. The waterfront in Sacramento where passengers would board was a dangerous place, known for its criminal activity from impoverished residents. In 1908, just up the river from the city's waterfront, Joseph Plaraino murdered Antonio Capollo in a robbery gone wrong, dumping his body in the Sacramento River

River Lines advertisement, 1940

in what a contemporary newspaper account in *The Press-Democrat* describes as "one of the most atrocious murders in the history of the county." Another murder happened in 1924, on the seventy-fifth anniversary of California's discovery of gold: A twenty-two-year-old man, D. L. Ingram, attended the Sacramento festivities but ultimately attacked a stranger, killing him and disposing of his body in the water. He later turned himself in to authorities, saying he didn't even know his victim's name.

In January 1929, a San Francisco man was seriously assaulted while boarding the *Delta King*. "John Franklin, forty-one, of this city in the hospital with a possible fractured skull as the result of an alleged attack upon him by two men aboard the Sacramento River steamer *Delta King*," the *Sacramento Bee* wrote. "Franklin told the police that two men who boarded the steamer with him at Sacramento entered his room and demanded his money. When he refused, they attacked him but overlooked $190 sewed in his clothing."

Once the state built bridges in the San Francisco Bay, car travel was much easier, and the boats eventually went out of business and were conscripted into service in World War II. The *Delta Queen* went East for refurbishment and became a pleasure boat on the Mississippi and Tennessee Rivers, eventually becoming a floating hotel in Chattanooga, Tennessee. (It's currently closed for refurbishment.) The *Delta King* stayed in Sacramento, although it fell into disrepair before being rehabbed in the 1980s and becoming a permanently docked floating hotel on the waterfront.

Old Sacramento has become a tourist destination, but underneath the signs for ice-cream shops and souvenirs, the gruesome history is all still there. A lot of people say the ghosts are, too. Old Town has an outsized reputation for paranormal activity, with some even referring to the waterfront as "the haunted river." The *Delta King* is no exception. According to CBS News, "The theater is believed to be haunted by the original captain with employee reports of him sitting in the balcony during performances, footsteps, and water glasses being spilled inexplicably. There are also reports of a young giggling girl who leaves mysterious footprints on the deck and is often bouncing a ball."

The *Delta King* doesn't shy away from that reputation. It hosts regular dinner theater shows called "Murder on the *Delta King*: A Murder Mystery Dinner Show to Die For!" So even if you don't manage to see a ghost when you visit, you can still get the full "haunted river" experience.

CRAB LOUIE

While it's easy to have a delicious meal aboard the *Delta King* today, its original menus have been lost to time—but not those of its sister boat, the *Delta Queen*. I was able to dig up a decades-old menu from the boat, which served a New Orleans–inspired menu (and even had handwritten notes from a server on the best wines to pair with each dish). This chilled seafood dish is a throwback specialty. In 1982, whoever had this particular menu in hand recommended a Chenin Blanc (likely a demi-sec Vouvray), a Johannesburg Riesling, or a bottle of Blue Nun white blend to go along with it.

Prep Time: 15 minutes | Yield: 4 servings, as an appetizer

FOR THE DRESSING

1/2 cup mayonnaise

1 tablespoon ketchup

1 teaspoon sweet relish

1 teaspoon lemon juice

1/8 teaspoon garlic powder

1/2 teaspoon hot sauce (such as Frank's Red Hot or Crystal)

1/2 teaspoon Worcestershire sauce

Pinch of smoked paprika

Pinch of chili powder

Pinch of salt

Pinch of black pepper

FOR THE SALAD

1 head iceberg lettuce, chopped

Assortment of vegetables, such as blanched asparagus, cucumber, radish, grape tomato, and avocado, sliced and diced

4 hard-boiled eggs, shelled and cut into halves or quarters

3/4 pound lump crabmeat

PREPARE THE DRESSING

1. In a small mixing bowl, mix the mayonnaise, ketchup, sweet relish, lemon juice, garlic powder, hot sauce, Worcestershire, smoked paprika, chili powder, salt, and pepper. Whisk until combined.
2. Let the dressing stand for 15 minutes, then taste and adjust the spices. (If you want it less spicy, add a bit more ketchup and relish to balance out those flavors.)

PREPARE THE SALAD

1. Divide the lettuce between four plates. Add the vegetables of your choosing.
2. Layer on the eggs and crabmeat, dress lightly with dressing, and serve.

Notes: Crab Louie has as many local modifications as it has fans: Mix it up with various toppings like cucumber and avocado, or use shrimp or another chilled seafood as your protein instead.

If you're using harder veggies in the salad, like asparagus, you may want to blanch them. Bring a pot of salted water to a boil, cook for 1 minute, then remove the vegetables and place in an ice water bath.

The dressing can be made in advance. Simply prepare it and refrigerate it, covered, for up to a week.

FRAUNCES TAVERN

NEW YORK, NEW YORK, USA

When you step inside Fraunces Tavern today, if you don't pay too much attention to the patrons with their faces in their smartphones, you might just get a glimpse of what Colonial America looked like. The tavern, the oldest building in Manhattan, takes historic preservation to another level. Downstairs, the sprawling network of dining rooms and bars feels like stepping into the past; upstairs, the Fraunces Tavern Museum preserves some of the seminal moments in early American history in the room where they happened.

Built between 1719 and 1722, the three-story brick building that houses the tavern was originally built as (but likely never used as) a private residence and was leased out for balls in its earliest days, before it evolved into a retail and mercantile space. In 1762, Samuel Fraunces purchased the building, opening the Queen's Head Tavern, back when New York was still a British colony and it was common to name things after royalty—in this instance in honor of Queen Charlotte.

Fraunces Tavern wasn't built in New York's Financial District. The Financial District was built around Fraunces Tavern. Brick by brick, New York's history stacked itself as the restaurant watched, daily serving its whiskeys and its roasts, maintaining a piece of the past into the present. In 1768, the New York Chamber of Commerce was established in the tavern, and seven years later, the New York Provincial Congress (the state governing body during the Revolutionary War) did the same. Fraunces's upstairs Long Room is also where, in 1783, George Washington gave his farewell speech to the American army, saying, "With a heart full of love and gratitude, I now take leave of you: I most devoutly wish that your latter days may be as prosperous and happy, as your former ones have been glorious and honorable."

By the time the Statue of Liberty was installed in the Hudson River in 1886, the Fraunces building was already more than 165 years old. In short, it's one of the rarest and most interesting places I've ever seen. And I'm not just saying that because of the ghosts.

In the late 1700s and most of the 1800s, due to ownership and management changes, Fraunces became less of a restaurant and more of a boardinghouse with a bar below. In 1798, ballerina Anna Gardie and her husband were living at Fraunces when she was murdered by him; he was also found dead in what was ruled a murder-suicide.

"Her husband was incredibly jealous," ghost tour guide Marie Carter told NY1 in 2024. "And there are people who work in Fraunces Tavern who say that sometimes when they're in the basement [where] the murder-suicide took place, they can sort of feel this heavy sadness."

Another more recent tragedy struck in 1975, when four people died and fifty were injured in a bombing at the restaurant, for which Puerto Rican nationalist group Fuerzas Armadas de Liberación Nacional claimed responsibility. The terrorists placed a bomb in a suitcase in the restaurant, claiming it was retaliation for a bombing in Mayaguez, Puerto Rico, that they believed was connected to the CIA.

Staff members at Fraunces have reported seeing full-bodied apparitions, feeling sudden changes in temperature, and hearing phantom footsteps. Once, an overnight worker was rattled to his core over noises that he said sounded like a party happening in another room, complete with voices and the clinking of glassware.

"The hauntings have been throughout the day or at night, when the museum has been open or closed," Scott Dwyer, the executive director of the Sons of the Revolution in the state of New York and Fraunces Tavern, told NY1. "All very much unexplained, and all attributed to something that wasn't quite here with us in a human form."

George Washington giving his farewell speech

SAMUEL FRAUNCES'S CARROT CAKE

According to restaurant lore, Samuel Fraunces set his tavern apart by having separate kitchens for savory and sweet foods. One of the earliest recipes ever to be served at the tavern, this carrot tea cake, a simple, sweet confection without the modern tradition of cream cheese frosting, is an adaptation of a historic re-creation from the 1975 cookbook *The Thirteen Colonies Cookbook* and the 2016 *American Cake*, based on Samuel Fraunces's own recipe.

Prep Time: 30 minutes	Cook Time: 50 minutes	Yield: 12 servings

INGREDIENTS

2 cups shredded carrot

¾ cup (1½ sticks) unsalted butter, at room temperature, plus more for greasing

2 cups granulated sugar

4 large eggs

2 cups all-purpose flour

1 tablespoon ground cinnamon

1 teaspoon ground nutmeg

½ teaspoon salt

Fresh whipped cream, for serving

INSTRUCTIONS

1. Bring a pot of water to a boil and place a bowl of ice water nearby.
2. Using a fine-mesh metal colander that fits inside the pot, lower the shredded carrots into the hot water, then boil for 1 minute. Immediately transfer the carrots to the ice water bath to cool, then strain the carrots well and set aside.
3. Preheat the oven to 350°F. Grease a 10-inch springform pan.
4. In the bowl of a stand mixer, combine the butter and sugar. Cream on medium until fluffy, about 1 minute. Add the eggs and continue to mix another 3–4 minutes. Add the flour, cinnamon, nutmeg, and salt, and mix another 2 minutes. Add the carrots and mix until just combined.
5. Transfer the batter to the prepared pan. Bake until a cake tester comes out clean, 45–50 minutes. Leave the cake in the pan until only warm to the touch, at least 30 minutes, then transfer to a serving plate. Top with whipped cream and serve warm.

THE HORSE YOU CAME IN ON SALOON

BALTIMORE, MARYLAND, USA

The Horse, as it's locally known, originally opened in Baltimore's Fells Point in 1775 and is the oldest bar in Baltimore. It's the kind of place that defines "saddle up to the bar" quite literally. The barstools are shaped like saddles, and there's a lot more equine history attached to the place. But there are also legends about the saloon and an author. A very famous, very spooky author.

In Edgar Allan Poe's short but prolific life, he bounced around to places like Boston, New York, and Richmond, Virginia, eventually landing back in Baltimore for what would ultimately be the last few years of his life. Known for his heavy drinking, Poe frequented the saloon in the late 1840s. Local legend has it that the Horse was the last place Poe was ever seen in public before he died. According to the National Trust for

Edgar Allan Poe, 1849

Historic Preservation, after drinking at the bar on October 3, 1849, "he was found, wandering and delirious, and taken to the Washington Medical College, where he died four days later." While it's unlikely that Poe made his last-ever stop at the Horse, it's definitely possible he was drinking there on the day he fell into his delirium.

The Horse "is the only bar in America that can boast the dual attractions of live music every night of the week and the ghost of Edgar Allan Poe," the National Trust continued.

The back half of a pretty salty phrase, "in On" came to new owner Howard Gerber in 1972 when he won enough at Maryland's famous Pimlico horse track to make the down payment on the bar. On its opening day, Gerber had a friend ride through the bar on horseback. It changed hands again in 2006, but the vibe is very much the same, down to the saddle barstools—one of which has a sign that says "Poe's Last Stop."

It's unclear how Poe died, only that his death is "a moment shrouded in horror and mystery," according to the University of Mary Washington. In 1996, Dr. R. Michael Benitez published a study in the *Maryland Medicine Journal* suggesting that the writer died of rabies.

The bartenders at the Horse call its resident ghost "Edgar." They say that the cash drawer in the register flies open on its own, that chandeliers swing overhead with no external prompting, and that the attic has such an intense energy that no employees want to be up there alone. Sometimes employees even leave a whiskey out for Edgar when they close for the night.

"There's a lot of people who don't want to be in here by themselves if they're closing the bar back or something like that," manager Robert Napier told WBAL in 2019. "There's a lot of lights turning on, turning off, TVs turning on and turning off . . . I walked by the bar and a glass is just sitting on the bar, and it just shatters out of nowhere. And I turned around to the guy who was behind me. His eyes were this big and he goes, 'I was working last night, and the same exact thing happened, in the same exact spot.'"

POE FAMILY EGGNOG

Edgar Allan Poe was known to enjoy his drink. While we don't know exactly what he would have sipped at the Horse on the night he was last seen—probably whiskey—we do know his preferred drink: eggnog. No, really. This version is adapted from a Poe family recipe passed down since 1790, which appeared in *A Second Helping of Murder*, among other places.

Prep Time: 15 minutes	Cook Time: 15 minutes	Yield: 8 servings

INGREDIENTS

7 eggs

1 cup granulated sugar

5 cups whole milk, divided

1/2 cup heavy cream

1 1/2 cups brandy

1/4 cup dark rum

Freshly ground nutmeg for garnish

INSTRUCTIONS

1. Separate the egg yolks from the whites, placing the yolks in a medium mixing bowl and the whites in another medium mixing bowl. Cover and refrigerate the whites.
2. To the egg yolks, add the sugar, then beat with a hand mixer until thick and pale, 2–3 minutes.
3. Fill a large bowl with ice water and set aside.
4. In a small saucepan, warm 3 cups of the milk over low heat, about 5 minutes. Temper the egg yolk mixture by slowly whisking 1 cup of the warm milk into the yolks to raise the temperature, then slowly whisk that tempered mixture back into the pan.
5. Simmer until thickened, about 5 minutes, whisking often and being careful not to let the mixture boil. Remove from the heat and whisk in the cream.
6. Place the saucepan into the prepared ice bath. Stir until chilled, about 4–5 minutes, then add in the brandy, rum, and the remaining 2 cups milk. At this point, you can chill the mixture, covered, in the refrigerator, or serve immediately.
7. When ready to serve, beat the egg whites in a stand mixer or with a handheld mixer until soft peaks form. Divide the eggnog into glasses, then top with whipped egg whites and grated nutmeg.

FINN'S IRISH RESTAURANT & TAVERN

KNOXVILLE, TENNESSEE, USA

When Jon Ferrie was in the market for a building to house his new restaurant, he didn't pay much attention to the rumors about hauntings in the Baker Peters House. "I did [hear them]," he told me, "but I didn't really believe in it."

But he definitely does today. "This isn't a Disney haunted house thing," he added. "This is for real."

Finn's Irish Restaurant opened in 2018, serving Irish comfort food. Even before the restaurant opened for business, Ferrie started to experience phenomena he couldn't explain. They've become regular occurrences in the restaurant, both among the staff and the guests. And with the harrowing events that have occurred under the home's roof, I can't say I'm surprised that there's a little unrest.

Built in 1830, the Baker Peters House was first occupied by Dr. James Baker, a local physician and Confederate supporter in the Civil War. When Union troops raided Knoxville in 1863, Baker was killed when Union soldiers fired through the door and hit him. His son Abner, who was a Confederate soldier, returned home in 1865 and shot a man named William Hall, a former Union soldier Abner believed was involved in his father's death. Abner was jailed but never tried. That night, a mob removed him from the jail and hanged him from a tree. A few decades later, the house was sold to George Peters.

Even before the restaurant opened for business, Ferrie started to experience phenomena he couldn't explain.

According to Ferrie, today the Baker Peters House is home to four adult spirits and eight child spirits.

"Dr. Baker built a secret staircase that went down into the basement," Ferrie told me. At night the doctor would shackle and tie up the enslaved people living at his home. He'd often sexually assault the enslaved women, including a woman named Anna, whose presence is in the house today. The eight young children's spirits, Ferrie believes, are the children who resulted from his crimes. Dr. Baker didn't allow those kids to be cared for by their mothers because the women's duty, in his view, was to "his" children upstairs, the ones that belonged to him and his wife. The women's babies who died of neglect are "buried in the basement under the house," Ferrie said.

Another spirit in the house is Richard, a butler. "He continuously walks around the house asking everybody to be quiet," Ferrie said, "because Dr. Baker didn't like any noise whatsoever." The family's matriarch—Ferrie calls her simply "the grandmother"—sits downstairs in a rocking chair in the dining room. The fourth, Ferrie said, "we're still trying to figure out who that is, but he's not very nice." Other than sometimes telling people to "get out," Ferrie said he generally just gives off a cold vibe.

The rest of the spirits, on the whole, are pretty nice, according to paranormal investigations of the restaurant that Ferrie has been part of. "The kids are happy," he said. "Anna's happy. Richard is nasty because he wants everyone to be quiet. The grandmother doesn't really say much. . . . She's just rocking back and forth."

He's been working with local paranormal investigators to learn more about that last spirit, the one with the cold vibe. "I personally sat on the floor with a ball," he said. "I rolled it towards the staircase, the ball stopped dead, and then it rolled straight back to me." He's also seen a barstool move across the room after hours, seen orbs, and heard disembodied voices.

"One of our guests comes in with her daughter every now and then," Ferrie added. "But every time they drive past the restaurant, the daughter sees a man in a Civil War uniform standing, then walking back and forth." Maybe she's got a future as an investigator? After all, a uniformed man who wasn't really there was my first ghost sighting, too.

SCOTCH EGGS WITH STRAWBERRY-SERRANO SAUCE

This sweet and spicy twist on the traditional Scotch egg comes courtesy of Finn's Irish Restaurant. The beauty of a Scotch egg is that it can be eaten anytime: breakfast, lunch, dinner, or as a snack. People eat them warm or chilled. There's simply no wrong way to enjoy one.

Prep Time: 30 minutes, plus chilling time	Cook Time: 30 minutes	Yield: 12 eggs

FOR THE STRAWBERRY-SERRANO SAUCE

1 cup sliced fresh or frozen strawberries

1/4 cup lemon juice

1 cup granulated sugar

1 serrano pepper, seeded and diced

FOR THE SCOTCH EGGS

1 1/2 pounds ground pork

4 teaspoons ground sage

1 teaspoon salt

1 dozen eggs, soft-boiled

3/4 cup all-purpose flour

3 eggs, beaten

3/4 cup panko breadcrumbs

TO PREPARE THE STRAWBERRY-SERRANO SAUCE

1. In a medium mixing bowl, toss the sliced strawberries in the lemon juice. Refrigerate for 2–3 hours.
2. In a large saucepan over medium-low heat, combine the strawberries and their juices with the sugar and serrano pepper. Simmer for 20 minutes, then remove the pan from the heat. Blend the mixture with an immersion blender (or in a conventional blender) until smooth.
3. Refrigerate the sauce at least 4 hours before use.

TO PREPARE THE SCOTCH EGGS

1. To prepare the Scotch eggs, preheat the oven to 350°F.
2. In a medium mixing bowl, combine the pork, sage, and salt. Mix well.
3. Remove the soft-boiled eggs from their shells, taking care to leave them whole.
4. Divide the sausage mixture into twelve 2-ounce portions.
5. Flatten one portion of the sausage mixture and wrap the sausage completely around one of the soft-boiled eggs. Repeat with the remaining eggs.
6. Place the flour, beaten eggs, and panko in three separate bowls.
7. Dredge each sausage-covered egg in the flour, followed by the egg mixture, followed by the panko. Place the eggs on a baking sheet.
8. Bake the Scotch eggs for 11–12 minutes, until the sausage is fully cooked and the panko is browned.
9. Serve warm or chilled with the sauce for dipping.

RED ONION SALOON

SKAGWAY, ALASKA, USA

Walking into Skagway's Red Onion Saloon, nestled in a sleepy corner of southeast Alaska, you'll immediately realize you're somewhere different. Somewhere out of time. Somewhere . . . with bedpans all over the walls as decorations. And somewhere you can order—and receive, and enjoy—a "reindeer fart."

The Klondike Gold Rush–era outpost (which got its name from nineteenth-century slang for a watering hole, and from its red brick exterior) is a singular spot, defined by its history but also very willing to have fun with that legacy. When it opened in 1897, the Red Onion was two businesses: a saloon and dance hall, with an upstairs brothel. While the latter form of entertainment is long gone, the place is as lively as ever. In recent years, the saloon has hosted events like mud wrestling, beach parties with real sand on the floor, and regular live music performances. Back in the day, saloon representatives will readily admit, the entertainment was, well, different.

If you've visited but you're not a local, you likely discovered the place on a cruise stop, like I did on a Strange Escapes Alaskan cruise in June 2022. Today's version of the Red Onion serves pizza and sandwiches, with distinctly Alaskan touches like smoked salmon chowder. The saloon's servers wear period costumes: corsets and petticoats similar to what the ladies up the "stairway to heaven" might have worn back in the building's bordello days.

Upstairs, there's a bordello museum. For twenty dollars, you can get a "quickie"—that is, a tour of the museum. You'll see Gold Rush–era items owned by women who once worked there, including a silver dress found in the floorboards of the building, and hear the history of the Red Onion's exploits. Back in the day, the women were called "dolls," and the bordello worked on a "doll system." Each woman had a doll representing her above the bar. When a doll was on its back, that woman was busy with a customer in a "crib room." After she sent five dollars down a tube to the bar, the doll was placed upright again, because she was ready for her next customer.

But if you're looking for a slightly spookier experience (and let's face it, you definitely are), you can take a Ghosts and Goodtime Girls Walking Tour. You'll be led around Skagway by one of the "fun-loving madams" of the Red Onion, which ends at the museum with a champagne toast and a souvenir garter.

On the tour, you'll learn about notorious characters like local gangster Soapy Smith and vaudeville performer Klondike Kate—and you'll also learn about the saloon's resident ghost, Lydia. A former madam of the brothel, Lydia is believed to have contracted syphilis and, under the fever of the disease, ended her own life. She's said to keep watch over the saloon, taking care of the place she once lived. And she's generally friendly, especially to women. A phantom whiff of perfume indicates her presence, according to restaurant staff, or a cold spot in an upstairs room.

Soapy Smith at the Red Onion Saloon, 1898

"Lydia is like a spiritual hum that is constantly here," general manager Liz Lavoie told *Skagway News* in 2023. "I've never seen her physical form. It's a mojo, you know? An awareness that you're not alone."

The Red Onion's other ghost is a lot less congenial, though. John is more of a troublemaker. He's been known to push people, open doors while staff are changing their clothes, and make a mighty stink to make his presence known. Among the employees, they say that John was a former bouncer who mistreated the "dolls" badly enough and for long enough that eventually, one of them stabbed him to death.

She may be gone in physical presence, but Lydia seems like she's still running the joint. "You have to acknowledge Lydia when you walk into the brothel," museum curator Cori Giacomazzi told *Skagway News*. "If you don't acknowledge her, she can make the rest of your day a little bit difficult. We have that big safe at the back door downstairs in the bar. An employee came in one morning trying to get the money out of the safe. And the damn thing wouldn't open. And then she realized she forgot to say good morning to Lydia. And the minute she did, the safe opened . . . she never forgot again."

REINDEER FART

The signature drink of the Red Onion Saloon, the Reindeer Fart's ingredients are simple yet potent. I haven't stopped thinking about it since I had one during my Strange Escapes cruise to Alaska, and I've done my best to re-create it here. Whip one up any time you want a little "Christmas in your mouth," as the saloon's menu promises. Make sure to toast to your favorite reindeer before you tip your glass.

Prep Time: 5 minutes | Yield: 1 shot

INGREDIENTS

1/2 ounce coffee liqueur, such as Kahlúa

3/4 ounce Irish cream liqueur, such as Bailey's

1/4 ounce peppermint schnapps

INSTRUCTIONS

1. In a standard shot glass, add the Kahlúa. Using the back of a barspoon, gently float the Bailey's on top. Finish with a floater of peppermint schnapps.
2. Drink immediately.

THE CUBAN CLUB

TAMPA, FLORIDA, USA

Of all the haunted places I've investigated in my years of paranormal research, my favorites have always been happy places. It's fascinating to investigate an old asylum or prison—there's usually a lot of activity at places like that—but the energy is heavy, filled with suffering. There's something truly special about the energy of a place that's full of spirits who have chosen to stay (or at least to visit periodically) because they loved the location in life and want to spend their afterlife there. I feel that way every time I visit the Mount Washington Hotel, and I felt that way when I investigated Tampa's Cuban Club.

Still open today after more than 125 years, the club is said to be full of as many as three hundred ghosts. Why? My best guess is because those people spent many happy hours there and have positive associations with the space. Maybe they wanted to spend more time with people they loved after they passed. Maybe they're still doing the same thing, even though they're all in the afterlife now. (I can attest—the party the club threw us when I visited with *Ghost Hunters* was spirited in more ways than one, if you know what I mean.)

Opened as El Club Nacional Cubano, what's now the Cuban Club was built in 1899 as a social club for Cuban immigrants, many of whom had immigrated to the area as part of the cigar boom around Tampa. In the later nineteenth century, high tariffs made it more financially attractive for Cuban cigar producers to build factories in America rather than import their goods from the island nation. Spanish cigar magnate Vicente Martínez-Ybor founded a cigar-manufacturing town near Tampa in 1885, humbly called Ybor City.

Today, Ybor City is a neighborhood in Tampa, parts of which have been lost to time and parts of which have been saved by historic preservation efforts. At its height, the city had about six thousand residents—and Ybor's vision worked. The city was producing more than a million cigars a day in 1910 and had more than two hundred factories in operation. According to the National Park Service, "At the turn of the 20th century, nowhere in the United States was as famous for its cigars as Tampa's Ybor City, which was once known as the 'Cigar Capital of the World.'"

The Cuban Club was a place for Cuban immigrants to gather, socialize, and celebrate their culture. "Its mission was to 'bind all Cuban residents to Tampa into a fraternal group, to offer assistance and help to the sick,'" according to the Cuban Club's history. "The club provided a gathering place for members and served as a unifying force in the Cuban community." Members received health care, English lessons, and death benefits. At one point, the club had seven doctors on the payroll to help treat its forty-five hundred members.

That was all in addition to its social activities. The Cuban Club featured a ballroom, cantina, theater, library, medical clinic, bowling lanes, and even a plunge pool in the basement. Glenn Miller's band played there, as did Tommy Dorsey's. As with any place where large groups of people and large amounts of alcohol combine, tempers would sometimes rise. In 1934, the club saw what the *Tampa Daily Times* described as a "free-for-all fight" where member Belarmino Vallejo was shot and died from his injuries. There were also tensions over politics, including fights between members who supported Fidel Castro's policies in Cuba and those who were supportive of the anti-Castro refugee movement.

Local ghost tour guide Steve Stamberger has said that he believes there are as many as three hundred spirits in the club, largely because they are happy there. Among the reported activity: disembodied singing, the smell of smoke, and the apparition of a man in an old-fashioned suit and white fedora. Sometimes, people say, the elevators run unprompted or refuse to close their doors. The building's theater is said to be haunted by an actor who died by suicide after forgetting his lines on stage.

In *Haunted Ybor City*, Deborah Frethem recounted a story of a former employee in the club, who had just given a tour to a group of college students. "Thinking she had inadvertently left one of the students behind, she went rushing to the theater, some of her tour group following behind her," Frethem wrote. "When she shone her flashlight on the piano, there was no one there, but the blast of sound continued to fill the room. What was really bizarre was that the keys on the piano were actually moving, as if being depressed by an unseen hand."

YBOR CHICKEN

This Cuban-influenced recipe is adapted from *Tampa Treasures*, a 1922 cookbook from the Junior League of Tampa. Don't be nervous about the combination of raisins and olives—the sweetness and saltiness work surprisingly well together.

Prep Time: 15 minutes	Cook Time: 1 hour 40 minutes	Yield: 6 servings

INGREDIENTS

½ cup all-purpose flour

1 teaspoon salt

1 teaspoon black pepper

1 whole chicken, cut into pieces, or 8 assorted bone-in chicken pieces

4 tablespoons olive oil

1 large white onion, diced

1 green pepper, diced

2 cloves garlic, minced

1 large tomato, chopped

1 bay leaf

1 cup raisins

1 cup green olives, pitted and sliced

1½ cups dry red wine

2 cups chicken broth

12 ounces Spanish chorizo, sliced into coins

INSTRUCTIONS

1. Preheat the oven to 325°F.
2. Combine the flour, salt, and pepper in a gallon-sized resealable plastic bag. Toss the chicken in the flour mixture, shaking well to coat.
3. In a large skillet over medium heat, heat the olive oil. Working in batches, brown the chicken, about 3 minutes per side.
4. Remove the chicken to a large casserole dish. To the same skillet, add the onion and cook 5 minutes. Add the green pepper, garlic, tomato, bay leaf, raisins, green olives, wine, broth, and chorizo. Simmer for about 10 minutes, until the veggies are soft.
5. Pour the mixture over the chicken, coating well. Bake for about 1 hour 15 minutes, until the chicken is falling off the bone. Serve immediately.

CHAPTER 5

BEHIND LOCKED DOORS

When imagining the most terrifying location you could visit, people often think of old, abandoned institutions. There is nothing like the feeling of walking down the crumbling hallways of an old asylum or jail. Even if you aren't experiencing true ghostly activity, it's easy to feel haunted by the memories and energy of whatever it is that happened there. I'm a seasoned investigator, and I still sometimes find myself battling my fight-or-flight instinct, wondering what could be around the next corner.

These are some of my favorite places to investigate, but historically, the food that came from those cafeterias wasn't anything to write home about. But surprise: Many of the recipes in this section are surprisingly delicious (remember, the goal of some of these places was rehabilitation, and serving good food was a big part of providing good care). But other recipes? Well, I won't blame you if you take them in historically rather than actually consuming them (I'm looking at you, scrapple).

CRESSON SANATORIUM

LILLY, PENNSYLVANIA, USA

Before doctors developed a vaccine, the tuberculosis epidemic was widespread globally, and America was no exception. Around the turn of the twentieth century, the essentially untreatable respiratory illness was killing about 450 Americans a day. The best hope for a cure was a stay at a sanatorium, where a patient could rest and try to recuperate. The need was widespread, and large facilities (like Waverly Hills, which I wrote about in *Food to Die For*) were filling up as quickly as people could build them.

In 1911, Andrew Carnegie fell ill with typhoid while visiting his family's idyllic Allegheny mountain cottage in Cresson, Pennsylvania. While he was recovering, his mother died from pneumonia; he no longer needed the five hundred acres of land where he intended to build his mother an estate. In his grief, Carnegie agreed to sell the land to the state of Pennsylvania for a dollar if they would build a tuberculosis sanatorium on it.

Cresson Sanatorium took in its first patients in December 1912. Although their illnesses were severe, life at the "San," as locals called it, was relatively pleasant. Patients had their own radio station and newsletter, and the Patients' Social Committee organized events like talent shows and held a weekly "Social Night" with card games and refreshments.

In 1920, Helen Keller and Annie Sullivan visited Cresson, where Keller gave a speech through an interpreter.

"Dear friends, I am glad to be here this afternoon because you are all so bright and full of courage," she said. "The warmth of the sun and the strength of the hills are in your hearts. I cannot see your smile, but I have my own way of telling when others are happy."

Cresson uniquely featured a children's ward where many of the patients were treated preventatively; kids who had been exposed at home could go stay there, often when a parent was being treated in the adults' area of the sanatorium. The ward held as many as 250 children at the height of the epidemic.

Between 1913 and 1964, the six-hundred-bed facility treated about forty thousand patients—but by the 1960s, medical advancements had improved so much that the need for sanatoriums was drastically reduced. In 1964, the San became the Cresson State School and Hospital, treating mentally handicapped patients. In 1973, tragedy struck: A fire broke out, and three patients died of smoke inhalation. Later, authorities discovered that Cresson had been aware of fire code violations for years but failed to address them.

Between 1913 and 1964, the six-hundred-bed facility treated about forty thousand tuberculosis patients.

The hospital closed in 1982 and, in 1987, became Cresson State Prison. Among its most notorious prisoners was serial killer Joseph Kallinger, who murdered one of his sons to collect a life insurance policy and enlisted another son, at twelve years old, to help with a 1974 string of murders. Kallinger had been previously diagnosed

Inside the chapel at Cresson Sanatorium

as a paranoid schizophrenic and, during his trial, said erratic things like that he was being pursued by the Devil and that he was a thousand years old.

Another mentally ill inmate was John E. du Pont, heir to the du Pont family chemical fortune, who was imprisoned for the murder of Olympic gold medal wrestler Dave Schultz. According to *The Washington Post*, du Pont "had razor wire installed in the walls and attic of his house to keep intruders out, complained about mechanical trees moving on his property, and often referred to himself by such titles as the Dalai Lama and Christ child."

The chapel at Cresson Sanatorium

But rather than provide support for incarcerated people suffering from mental illness and disabilities, the prison simply shut them in solitary confinement for nearly every moment of the day. In 2013, a Department of Justice investigation found "that the manner in which Cresson uses isolation on prisoners with serious mental illness violates the Eighth Amendment of the U.S. Constitution." Inmates were punished by having their mattresses taken away, being denied hot food and showers, and not being provided with toilet paper. The prison closed in 2013, and a juvenile facility on the property closed in 2015.

Today, the only reason people come to Cresson is for daytime tours and for overnight paranormal investigations. People report seeing full-body apparitions of former prisoners and staff and being touched by unseen entities. In the chapel, doors slam shut, and some people even report seeing a dark form with claws on the ceiling. In the power plant, the ghost of a boy appears to people; he died from injuries sustained when he fell down a well in 1956. The tunnels under the facilities are especially active for electronic voice phenomena (EVPs), and the prison blocks are absolutely full of shadow figures. Though many people had positive experiences there and it's sometimes possible to make contact with playful kids in the children's ward, the overall energy of the place seems to be dominated by its darker, later years.

SCRAPPLE

Chuck Felton was a patient at Cresson from 1955 to 1956, and he wrote down some recollections of his time there—including one memorably terrible meal. "The main course that evening was scrapple, a Pennsylvania creation, which I hated," he wrote. "I knew it was made out of pork lips, snouts, and cheeks all ground up into some grayish paste, molded into a rectangular block, and sliced into thick slabs. If you omitted the 's' from the name, the remainder pretty much described my evaluation of scrapple."

There are endless variations on this staple farm food because it has traditionally been made with whatever scraps (hence the name) were on hand. With the luxury of sourcing from the grocery store, I went with pork butt and beef liver. It might not be quite as authentic as some purists require, but I think this version is a lot more achievable for home chefs.

Prep Time: 15 minutes | Cook Time: 3 hours, plus setting time | Yield: 10 to 12 slices, depending on thickness

INGREDIENTS

1/2 pound pork shoulder

1 medium onion, cut in half

3 cloves garlic, peeled

6 cups water

1 pound beef liver or offal of your choice

1 1/2 cups yellow cornmeal

1/2 cup buckwheat flour

1 teaspoon paprika

1/4 teaspoon cayenne pepper

1/4 teaspoon nutmeg

2 teaspoons salt

1 teaspoon black pepper

Neutral cooking oil, for frying

INSTRUCTIONS

1. In a stockpot add the pork shoulder, cut into 2 or 3 chunks for ease of cooking. Add the onion and garlic and cover with the water. Bring to a boil over medium-high heat and cook until the pork is very tender, about 30 minutes. You may need to add more water; you're aiming to have about 3–4 cups of pork broth at the end.
2. When the pork is cooked, remove it to a platter, reserving the liquid. Skim the solids out of the stock, including the onions and garlic, and discard.
3. Shred the pork and set aside.
4. Pulverize the liver in a food processor until totally smooth. In a skillet over medium heat, cook the liver for about 3–4 minutes, until grayish and cooked. Allow to cool while the cornmeal is cooking.
5. Bring the broth back to a simmer, and add the cornmeal, buckwheat flour, paprika, cayenne, nutmeg, salt, and pepper. Cook, stirring often, until the cornmeal is smooth and all the liquid is absorbed, about 25 minutes.
6. Add the shredded pork and liver and mix well.
7. Line a loaf pan with parchment paper and transfer the mixture to the loaf pan. Let cool on the counter for 1 hour, then wrap with plastic wrap and refrigerate at least 3 hours, until set.
8. When you're ready to eat, slice off thick slices of the scrapple. Heat a large skillet over medium-high heat, then add a small amount of cooking oil (more or less, depending on how many slices you're cooking). Pan fry for 2–3 minutes per side, until browned.

PENNHURST ASYLUM

SPRING CITY, PENNSYLVANIA, USA

In its seventy-nine years of operation, southeast Pennsylvania's Pennhurst Asylum was characterized by the harshest of patient mistreatment. Its more than ten thousand residents were subjected to what the *Philadelphia Inquirer* described as "medical experimentation, cruel punishments, and constant threats to physical and psychological well-being." Residents were trapped, forced into labor against their will, unable to leave, and unable to control the most basic elements of their own lives.

As another newspaper put it in 1972, Pennhurst Asylum was "the shame of Pennsylvania." But it didn't start out that way.

When it opened in 1908 as the Eastern Pennsylvania Institution for the Feeble-Minded and Epileptic, later called the Pennhurst State School and Hospital, the institution was seen as a progressive place where patients were treated well, and with modern medical techniques. Pennhurst was designed to hold five hundred people, with room for expansion, but the need for support for the mentally ill and disabled who could not live on their own far outgrew the space. The asylum was overcrowded almost from the day it opened.

Pennsylvania's Commission for the Care of the Feeble-Minded forced those with cognitive impairments into Pennhurst to prevent them from procreating and passing down their genes, calling them a "menace to the peace." In a report to the state, Pennhurst's chief physician quoted Henry H. Goddard, a leading eugenicist, by saying: "Every feeble-minded person is a potential criminal. The general public, although more convinced today than ever before that it is a good thing to segregate the idiot or the distinct imbecile, they have not as yet been convinced as to the proper treatment of the defective delinquent, which is the brighter and more dangerous individual."

Aerial view of Pennhurst, 1922

By the early 1960s, the population had ballooned to forty-one hundred patients, and the level of care provided to patients had not, to put it mildly, scaled up with demand. The 1968 documentary, *Suffer the Little Children*, revealed the horrible living conditions and patient mistreatment at Pennhurst. Among the many revelations in the documentary was reporter Bill Baldini's discovery that large American zoos were spending more per day to feed their animals than the state spent on the people in the asylum.

The footage is the stuff of nightmares: adults strapped to crib beds and others in a state of trauma response because of the horrific environment. Doctors giving injections to patients in order to cause the most physical discomfort possible or dosing them with psychotropic drugs as a means of subduing them. Eighty children, aged six months to five years old, discovered in metal cages that hadn't been cleaned of human refuse in days.

Baldini later said that he had trouble keeping his camera crew on the documentary shoot because they were "literally getting sick from what they saw."

About half of the more than ten thousand patients housed in Pennhurst died there, largely due to mistreatment and neglect. What eventually shut down the house of horrors was a complaint filed with the state by patient Terri Lee Halderman. The complaint alleged that the residents "live in inhumane and dangerous conditions, are subjected to unnecessary physical restraints, are given unnecessary and dangerous medication, are consigned to lives of idleness because of lack of habilitative programs, and are subjected to numerous physical injuries resulting from a lack of adequate supervision."

The state ordered Pennhurst closed in 1978, but in 1983, it still housed 640 patients who had been there an average of thirty-five years. At that time, the Department of Justice indicted nine present and former aides for assaulting and abusing patients, including beating patients—some of whom were confined to wheelchairs—and forcing patients to assault each other.

Today, many buildings on the campus have been torn down, as they were deemed unsafe. But for those who want to bear witness to the horrors that happened in this space, the remaining buildings are open for daytime history tours and overnight paranormal investigations.

In the administration building, investigators have said they've picked up disembodied voices and the sound of toilets flushing, though there's no running water in the building. In other buildings, people claim to hear children's voices and EVPs of distressed adults, saying things like "Go away," "I'll kill you," "We're upset," "Why'd you come here?" and "Why won't you leave?" As hard as that is to stomach, I'm grateful the history of the place is still alive in some form for us to learn from.

SHRIMP WIGGLE

I'll admit—reading about the atrocities at Pennhurst didn't make me hungry. But I did manage to find the actual 1951 cookbook that the institution used to prepare its meals, *Large Quantity Recipes* by Margaret E. Terrell, M.A. Everything in that book was written to serve fifty people, but this recipe only called for 2½ pounds of shrimp in the entire dish. Even very small shrimp would only have about fifty pieces per pound, so at the most patients would get two or three small pieces for a whole meal. In my adaptation, I made sure you'll be better fed than that.

Prep Time: 5 minutes | Cook Time: 20 minutes | Yield: 4 servings

INGREDIENTS

2 tablespoons unsalted butter

⅓ cup all-purpose flour

2 cups milk

½ teaspoon salt

¼ teaspoon pepper

1 teaspoon onion juice (or onion powder)

½ teaspoon Worcestershire sauce

1 pound medium or large shrimp, shelled and deveined

¾ cup fresh or frozen peas

Bread or crackers, for serving

INSTRUCTIONS

1. In a Dutch oven or large saucepan, melt the butter over medium heat. Add the flour, and whisk until smooth, cooking for about 1 minute. Slowly stream in the milk, whisking constantly, then add the salt and pepper.
2. Add the onion juice, Worcestershire, shrimp, and peas. Simmer for 15 minutes, until the shrimp is pink and opaque.
3. Serve with bread or on crackers.

NORTH HEAD QUARANTINE STATION

MANLY, AUSTRALIA

In the early days of the Colony of New South Wales, as Australia was once called, ships full of colonists were arriving from all over the globe. With the colonists, in many instances, came ship-borne diseases like cholera, typhoid, tuberculosis, or Spanish influenza. Back then, these conditions were akin to a death sentence not only for the infected person but also for any party who came in contact with them.

In an effort to keep those diseases out of the colony, the local government devised a plan: Everyone arriving to New South Wales, whether a member of a wealthy colonist family or a criminal, would be quarantined until they could be cleared of disease. In 1832, the North Head Quarantine Station was established for that purpose.

But that quarantine was, in a word, terrible. The methods of disease prevention used in the 1800s were sometimes barbaric and would be considered human rights violations today. Worst among them: a carbolic acid shower, where groups of people were stripped of their clothing and placed into a shower block where they would be sprayed with a carbolic acid solution for four minutes. Every person coming into the station was required to have one, as a preventative measure. It certainly would have badly burned in the moment, but for the three days afterward, the side effects got even worse—a person's skin would turn bright red and peel off as though from a severe sunburn.

No wonder North Head is full of ghosts. So many people suffered, and sometimes died, inside those walls. Today, the area is considered one of the most haunted in the world.

"These infectious diseases had no cure," long-time Quarantine Station ghost tour guide Mel Minns told me. "There were no treatments for it. So just even knowing that as a patient, you would've been worried for your life. And also seeing the cemeteries on site, seeing the rows and rows of gleaming white headstones as you go up to your accommodation, I'm sure passengers probably started to worry if that was going to be them."

In the first nine years of the station, more than twenty thousand passengers were detained there, and nearly six hundred died. Conditions for the detainees were equivalent to the class of ticket they held on their arriving ship. First- and second-class passengers enjoyed relatively comfortable accommodations and good quality meals. Third-class passengers slept in dormitories and ate in lots of two hundred at mealtimes. People of color—called "Asiatics" at the station, no matter their ethnicity—had it significantly worse. They slept in tents, ate scant rations of food, and had to cook their own meals in an outdoor kitchen. Access to medical treatment was almost nonexistent, even for those dying of disease. Quarantine would last for weeks or months, depending on a person's illness (or assumed illness); if a person so much as sneezed during their time there, the clock would reset.

The facility officially closed in 1984, but the last time people were quarantined there was 1972, when a plane arrived with people possibly carrying cholera. Those brutal carbolic acid showers were used all the way into the 1960s.

A lot of the paranormal activity is unfriendly, likely because so many people died in terrible circumstances, often kept separate from their families as they watched loved ones die from afar. But not everyone is unfriendly. "The morgue that we have at the quarantine station that we still use on the Ghost Tours has quite a funny resident ghost there," Minns told me. "He's a bit touchy-feely. He's not malevolent though. I quite like him. He's got a bit of a sense of humor."

The gravedigger's cottage is also an area full of activity, where Minns had her first experience while a guest on a ghost tour more than a decade ago. "I had a handbag, and it was draped over my shoulder, and I distinctly remember three really solid tugs on the strap of my handbag," she said. "I turned around expecting that it was my boyfriend, and he was standing on the other side of me. And then I spun around thinking, 'Oh, somebody behind me, some stranger on the group must have done it to try and scare me,' but where I was standing, my back was to the bushes. So there was no one behind me."

Investigators think there are several entities are in that cottage, but especially a "not very nice" man. Younger girls in particular have experiences there. "They seem to be the ones that will pick up on the energy or have some sort of encounter that isn't very pleasant," she explained. "They will often experience stomach cramps or pain, or they will see shadow figures, or they'll have an overwhelming sense of fear, like someone's watching them."

CORNED BEEF

While conditions for most people at North Head were very difficult, the first-class patients had a much more pleasant experience. According to a February 3, 1935, menu from the Canadian Australian Line, reprinted in *Carved into History: Images of Quarantine at North Head*, first-class guests were served soup Française, boiled halibut with anchovy sauce, roast lamb with mint sauce, and corned beef, which I've re-created here.

Prep Time: 30 minutes, plus brining time | Cook Time: 3 hours | Yield: 6 to 8 servings

INGREDIENTS

2 tablespoons whole black peppercorns

2 tablespoons mustard seeds

2 tablespoons coriander seeds

2 tablespoons red pepper flakes

2 tablespoons allspice berries

1 tablespoon whole cloves

5 cardamom pods

6 bay leaves

2 teaspoons ground ginger

1 stick cinnamon

1 gallon water

2 cups kosher salt

1/2 cup granulated sugar

1 tablespoon pink curing salt (see Note below)

1 (5-pound) beef brisket, well-trimmed

INSTRUCTIONS

1. In a dry skillet over medium heat, toast the peppercorns, mustard seeds, and coriander seeds for 2–3 minutes, until aromatic. Lightly grind the spices, either with a mortar and pestle or with a rolling pin and a plastic bag.
2. Add the spices to a glass jar, and then add the red pepper flakes, allspice, cloves, cardamom, bay leaves, ginger, and cinnamon. This is your pickling spice.
3. In a large pot, add the water, kosher salt, sugar, pink salt, and 3 tablespoons of the pickling spice. Bring to a simmer, ensuring that all the salt and sugar are dissolved, then remove from the heat and let cool completely. Refrigerate until cold.
4. Add the brisket and weigh it down with a small plate or overturned bowl so that it's totally submerged in the brine. Cover the pot and refrigerate for 5–6 days, turning the brisket occasionally.
5. When you're ready to cook the brisket, discard the brine and lightly rinse the meat. Add the brisket back to the pot, and cover with water. Add 2 tablespoons of the pickling spice, then bring the pot to a boil, reduce to a simmer, and cook for about 3 hours, until the brisket is very tender.
6. Remove to a cutting board and let rest for 10 minutes. Slice and enjoy.

Note: Pink salt (also called Pink Curing Salt #1) is sodium nitrite, which is an important ingredient for killing any potential bacteria and imbuing the meat with its signature pink color. It's colored pink because, if consumed alone, it can be harmful to your health. Don't substitute pink Himalayan salt; it doesn't have the same antibacterial properties.

RANDOLPH COUNTY ASYLUM/INFIRMARY

WINCHESTER, INDIANA, USA

Originally called the Randolph County Poorhouse, the asylum started as a way to help neighbors in need. As stated on the Official Randolph County Asylum/Infirmary website, it was a place "to care for those unable to work, including the mentally and physically disabled, single mothers, elderly, and orphans." In 1851, if you didn't have family to support you through difficult times, you were on your own.

The Randolph County Poorhouse was largely a farm, where residents would work the three hundred acres, helping to grow the food that fed everyone who lived there. For a long time, conditions were good. A 1911 article in the *Muncie Evening Press* called the facility "one of the best in the state." At any given time, about ninety people would live at the facility, about fifteen hundred total in its lifespan. Over the years, the facility on the site was known as the Randolph County Poor Asylum, Randolph County Poor House, Randolph County Poor Home, Randolph County Poor Farm, Randolph County Infirmary, and Randolph County Home.

Some of the residents had positive experiences at the home. A lumberjack named Jimmy Cantrell was admitted in 1919, after being diagnosed with incurable spinal cancer. He was bedridden and despondent, so the superintendent's daughter Mabel Hull decided to teach him crafts like crochet. Cantrell especially took to lace making and became so well-known for his work that he had a long slate of orders and had his work shown in a national magazine.

"Sometimes I think this isn't a very good kind of work for a man to spend his time on, even if he's in a condition like I am . . . and every once in a while I think about learning to do something more along a man's life," he told *The Muncie Sunday Star* in 1923. "But then I remember that I'm making something useful, for without beautiful things, life wouldn't be much worth living."

Women's hall on the second floor

But for many at the facility, life wasn't as pleasant. Hundreds of deaths occurred at the facility. Some were from age and illness. But many other deaths weren't from natural causes. Some were self-inflicted. Some had freak accidents like falling down the stairs, as happened in 1906, or being hit by a car, which occurred in 1924 and 1941. In 1943, John Oliver Champ died after falling from a second-story window; while it was officially reported as an accident, rumors persisted that he was pushed by two other residents.

In 1994, the facility was purchased from the county by private owners and renamed the Countryside Care Center. When it changed hands, two longtime residents still lived there. John Doty had lived at the facility since 1939. In 1997, *The Indianapolis News* wrote that Doty "had a severe speech impediment, which . . . was enough excuse for his half brothers to declare him stupid and useless and place him here."

Doris Addington, institutionalized since being orphaned at age eleven, had lived in the center since 1945. "In the old days it was like a dungeon here," she said in that article. "Terrible things were done." Misbehaving patients were locked in a second-story jail cell, or in a basement room with barred windows, where Ida Gunkle died by suicide in 1938. At least fifty unmarked graves are believed to be on the property.

The facility closed for good in 2008 and reopened for paranormal investigations in 2016. "We bought it for the history," co-owner Dann Allen told *Journey Indiana.* "The residents came with it."

Today, the poorhouse is a living tribute to those who once lived there, and who may still reside there, even in death. One of the sick bays is now full of dolls as a tribute to Doris Addington, who died there and who loved dolls in life. Some of the dolls belonged to her, and others have been left there in tribute.

Visitors to the poorhouse report hearing and seeing doors close with no explanation, sometimes with doorknobs turning on their own. Sometimes they hear footsteps in the hallways, walking up behind them when no one living is there. The sound of children's laughter is common, as are screams and wails, depending on the part of the building. Those dolls will sometimes move on their own, too. It makes sense—among the spirits believed to be present, one of the most commonly contacted is Doris Addington herself.

BAKED RIBS

While there isn't a lot of information in the historical record about what residents were served at Randolph County Poorhouse except for the vegetables they grew, there is one clue as to a meal they ate. A 1940 article in *The Union City Times-Gazette* revealed during an inspection that, "The food served on the date of the inspection appeared to be substantial, wholesome, well cooked, and well served," it read. "The menu included onions, wilted lettuce, hominy, kraut, baked ribs, dumplings, bread, butter, coffee, and milk. Male and female inmates are served three meals a day in separate dining rooms. A supply of conserved and stored foods make possible a varied menu." Here's a baked ribs recipe that's probably got a little more kick than what the institution would have fed patients—you officially have my permission to serve it in mixed company.

Prep Time: 10 minutes | Cook Time: 2 hours 40 minutes, plus resting time | Yield: 3 to 4 servings

INGREDIENTS

1/4 cup granulated sugar

1/4 cup firmly packed brown sugar

2 tablespoons salt

2 tablespoons black pepper

1 teaspoon dry mustard

1 teaspoon chili powder

1 teaspoon garlic powder

1 rack pork baby back ribs

1 bottle smoky barbecue sauce

INSTRUCTIONS

1. Preheat the oven to 250°F.
2. In a small mixing bowl, combine the granulated sugar, brown sugar, salt, pepper, dry mustard, chili powder, and garlic power.
3. Wash and dry the ribs and remove the membrane from the back with a sharp knife. Coat all sides of the meat with the spice mixture, then wrap tightly in aluminum foil. Place on a baking sheet and bake until cooked through, about 2 hours.
4. Remove from the oven and let rest for 15 minutes.
5. Increase the oven temperature to 350°F.
6. Open the foil, drain the juices, and brush the ribs with barbecue sauce. Return to the oven with the foil open (place the ribs on a baking sheet to save the bottom of your oven). Cook 40 more minutes, brushing frequently with sauce. Slice and serve with plenty of napkins.

BRUSHY MOUNTAIN STATE PENITENTIARY

PETROS, TENNESSEE, USA

Established in 1896, Brushy Mountain State Penitentiary was only the second state prison built in Tennessee. A major economic driver for East Tennessee's Morgan County, just northwest of Knoxville, the prison was one of two main sources of employment in the tiny town of Petros for decades. In fact, with its population of five hundred, Petros essentially grew around the prison.

At that time, the other main job available in the area was coal mining, and the construction of the prison was actually a result of changes to the coal mining industry. For many years, Tennessee employed a common practice called the "convict lease system." Inmates at state prisons were leased out to local coal mines, which served the dual purpose of providing cheap labor to the mining companies and keeping paid workers in line. The logic was that the looming threat of being replaced by an endless supply of inmates would keep the day laborers from speaking out against working conditions or low compensation. (The most gruesome example I've ever seen of convict leasing was at the St. Augustine Jail, which I wrote about in *Food to Die For*, where inmates were called "the product," and they were worked so hard that their lifespan once in the prison averaged just three years.)

In 1891, a group of miners at the Tennessee Coal Mining Company did stand up for better conditions—and the company responded by firing all of them and bringing in convict labor. But in response, the fired workers waged what became the Coal Creek War, wherein the protestors freed the inmate workers from their confines and the coal mines lost significant profits. The state was forced to pay militias to stand against the miners, so they decided it was ultimately less expensive to end the convict labor program altogether. The sudden loss of work meant that the prisoners were forced to spend longer hours in the prison; more space was needed, and Brushy Mountain was the answer.

1892 campaign ad criticizing convict leasing

But the state still fully intended to put the inmates to work. Convicts were sent to work in the neighboring Brushy Mountain Mine, the difference being that the state owned both operations. In 1898, 84 percent of the inmate population at the prison was Black, largely owing to "Black Codes," which imposed outsized punishments for minor infractions like loitering and unemployment.

Brushy Mountain "was known as a brutal and isolated prison, located within a particularly remote section of the Cumberland Mountains," Judah Schept wrote in *Coal, Cages, Crisis: The Rise of the Prison Economy in Central Appalachia*. At times, the prison was so overcrowded that men worked twenty-four-hour rotations in the mines so that two could share a bed in twelve-hour shifts. But the state was largely unconcerned with the living and working conditions because the numbers were good: Between 1903 and 1917, Tennessee made $1.7 million in profit from the mine (about $18 million today).

Punishments for those who resisted were severe. Up until 1965, inmates were whipped with a four-foot leather strap, sometimes so badly that "screams were routinely heard by the townsfolk of nearby Petros," Schept wrote. They were also put into "suspension," hung by their thumbs from an overhead hook. In 1966, the mining ended, and in 1969, Brushy Mountain became Tennessee's first maximum security prison.

Fights among prisoners were common, often resulting in stabbings. A lot of the tension was racially motivated; Brushy Mountain remained segregated until the late 1960s, and in 1982, a group of white inmates staged a coup—with weapons allegedly supplied by guards—and attacked only Black inmates, killing two and wounding two more. When a medic confronted the prisoners, they allegedly responded by saying, "We're not done yet."

The prison closed in 2009 and reopened for tours and events in 2018. Groups can tour the cell blocks by themselves or alongside paranormal investigators. Today, there's a restaurant on site, The Warden's Table, and a distillery. The facility also made its way to Hollywood, appearing in *The Green Mile* and *Ernest Goes to Jail* and being mentioned in *The Firm* and *The Silence of the Lambs.*

When investigators visit, they report a lot of physical contact, including being touched, pushed, and sometimes scratched to the point of drawing blood. Many former inmates are said to make appearances, both as apparitions and in EVPs, including Jack Jett, a prisoner who was stabbed to death as retribution for allegedly snitching on other inmates; Leroy, rumored to be a bully in life, who follows visitors throughout the facility; and James, known to smoke cigarettes if they're left lit in his cell for him.

TURNIP GREENS

In 1969, a group of state senators visited Brushy Mountain and ate a meal there in an employee dining room. "The menu, said to be the same one as the one for inmates, included meat loaf, turnip greens, cold cuts, pinto beans, fruit salad, peach cobbler, and milk, coffee, or tea," *The Tennessean* reported at the time. "A menu for the week posted on a bulletin board showed the luncheon menu repeated at dinner each night." Here's an Appalachian-inspired take on turnip greens.

Prep Time: 30 minutes | Cook Time: 1 hour | Yield: 4 servings as a side dish

INGREDIENTS

1 pound turnip greens, cleaned, stemmed, and chopped

4 tablespoons unsalted butter

4 strips bacon, cut into thin strips, or 1 ham hock

1 medium white onion, chopped

1 clove garlic, minced

1 teaspoon cayenne pepper, more or less, to taste

1 cup diced fresh tomatoes

2½ cups chicken or vegetable broth

Salt and pepper, to taste

INSTRUCTIONS

1. Fill a large pot with the greens and cover with water by 1 inch, then bring to a boil over high heat. (If using a ham hock, add it at this step, then remove it after cooking and shred the meat.) Reduce to a simmer and cook until tender, about 45 minutes. Drain and set aside.
2. In the same pot, melt the butter over medium heat. If using bacon, add it and cook for 5–6 minutes until crispy. To the pot, add the onion, garlic, and cayenne and cook until softened, about 6–8 minutes. Add the tomatoes (and shredded ham, if using) and cook for another 5 minutes, then add the broth. Bring to a boil and cook for 5 minutes, then reduce the heat to a simmer and cook for another 15 minutes, then season to taste with salt and pepper. Add the greens back to the broth and serve hot.

HISTORIC SDG JAIL

CORNWALL, ONTARIO, CANADA

The prison had barely been open two years when the escapes started. SDG Jail (or "Gaol," as it originally spelled its name) opened on Cornwall's waterfront, next to the St. Lawrence River, in 1833. According to legend, the first jail was burned down in 1826 by an inmate incarcerated as a debtor. The new facility only had one cell block, so both men and women, violent and nonviolent, were grouped together.

By 1835, four inmates had already broken out, using embers from the woodstove to burn down the cellblock's wooden door. They disappeared and were never found. The last escape happened in 1995, when Daryl Bolton attempted to escape to see a dying relative. He was found after only thirty minutes. But he's far from the only prisoner who wanted to be free of the walls of the SDG Jail.

Maybe because it was such an old building, and maybe because prison reform wasn't an administrative priority, SDG's conditions in the modern era more closely resembled life as it was in the nineteenth century. Up until 1971, the jail didn't have electricity or plumbing. No lights, no flushing toilets, no running water, no electronic locks. Inmates had been forced to use chamber pots or buckets up until that point. That change was largely prompted by social protests, what jail representatives describe as "outrage at the horrendous living conditions prisoners would have had to endure while incarcerated." In 1980, prisoners staged a short-lived hunger strike to protest breakfast being cut back from two eggs to only one. (It didn't work. The one egg mandate stood.)

Up until 1971, the jail didn't have electricity or plumbing.

The prison expanded over time, but the facility was still inhumanely crowded, especially because of its unusually small cells (so small, in fact, that offenders couldn't easily walk inside them). In addition to the original cell block, an expansion in 1869 added "Hell's Angels," now called that because of its incarceration of members of the motorcycle gang in the 1960s; and the "Windowless Room," where solitary confinement dungeons were found in 1936. The only access for those dungeons was via trapdoors in the floor, where prisoners were lowered in. The final expansion happened in 1985, adding an area called "Hotel California" for its "luxuries" of adequate space to walk and toilets inside cells.

The cellblocks, though, only comprised half of the building. The other half was the governor's offices and residence. On the other side of a complex filled with murderers and violent offenders lived the family of the man responsible for those inmates. While the wives of governors generally worked as matrons or nurses in the prison, the children were kept at a distance—almost. According to the jail's history, "The daughter of the last live-in governor was actually sent away to a boarding school out of fear from threats she was receiving from one of the inmates."

Among SDG's ranks were some of the most notorious and violent offenders in the history of the province. Clark Brown, convicted of murdering his father and younger sister with an axe, was executed in 1879 in front of an audience of seventy-five onlookers. In 1924, Thomas Collison was arrested for murdering Beatrice Thorpe, a woman he had stalked for two years. According to a 1924 story in *The Weekly Advance*, Collison's parents defended his actions, saying "God made Beatrice Thorpe for him, and he had divine right to marry her."

The prison closed in 2002, when only twenty inmates remained. According to jail records, "The severe overcrowding and poor living conditions inside the SDG jail led to the decision to close it as it posed several ethical and physical safety concerns to both the inmates and the workers." In 1997, *The Ottawa Citizen* wrote that "on weekends, impaired drivers bunk up with murderers and armed robbers" because of the intense overcrowding.

Today, SDG is rife with paranormal activity. My guess is that the unrest comes from prisoners who were buried around the prison: To this day, more than one hundred unclaimed bodies of deceased prisoners are still buried on the premises, and many were exhumed and moved in renovations through the years.

People claim to see the spirit of a woman in black who roams the prison and to hear the jangle of phantom keys and chains. Today, tickets to paranormal investigations with local company Phantoms of Yore include the use of investigative equipment, and the tour company reviews and sends footage to you after the fact.

TURNEY KIPPEN'S SKILLY

While I was researching food at SDG, Phantoms of Yore owner Elliot Luijkenaar shared some fascinating information with me—like the fact that inmates used to throw cheese and butter at the ceiling on very hot days, just to see if it would stick. It did—and a lot of it is still there today. A typical prison menu from the nineteenth century in Ontario would have basically included only bread and soup, with a very small amount of beef. But the food that really stuck out to me was mentioned in an 1899 article in *The Freeholder.* A criminal being sent to jail, the story read, "is spending 21 days feasting on Turney Kippen's Skilly." And skilly, a traditionally Irish sailor's food, is essentially just oatmeal made with water in which meat had been boiled. But hey, it's better than hardtack, right? Feel free to skip the meat water and just use water or milk.

Prep Time: 5 minutes | Cook Time: 20 minutes | Yield: 4 servings

INGREDIENTS

4 cups water or milk, or a combination

1 cup steel-cut oats

Brown sugar or dried fruit, for garnish, optional

INSTRUCTIONS

1. The night before serving the skilly, in a medium saucepan over medium-high heat, bring the water or milk to a boil. Add the oats, then bring the mixture back to a boil.
2. Turn off the heat, cover the pot, and leave on the counter overnight. (If using milk, refrigerate the mixture in the pot.)
3. When ready to eat, add a bit more milk or water, and warm gently over medium heat.
4. Garnish with sugar or fruit, if desired, but know that that never would have happened in jail.

TRANS-ALLEGHENY LUNATIC ASYLUM

WESTON, WEST VIRGINIA, USA

When it opened in 1863, the Trans-Allegheny Lunatic Asylum was designed to be an exemplar for mental health care facilities. West Virginia Hospital for the Insane, as it was known then, was designed according to the humane Kirkbride Plan. Dr. Thomas Kirkbride encouraged humane and empathetic care, discouraging the word *lunatic* and preferring to call these facilities *hospitals* and not *asylums*.

Kirkbride called for construction of hospitals that had ample sunlight, sprawling grounds, and comfortable accommodations. But the facility did anything but foster a peaceful healing environment.

At what was later renamed Weston State Hospital by the state, many of the people who were admitted to the facility, especially in its earliest days, didn't have what we would call mental illness today. As Jim Barnes wrote in *The Washington Post* in 2018, "They might have had physical ailments such as asthma, epilepsy, rabies, or tuberculosis. Some had suffered brain damage from being kicked by a horse."

According to West Virginia University's Kim Jacks, doctors at the hospital attributed patients' unconventional behavior to causes like "business trouble," "disappointed love," "desertion by wife," "novel reading," "marriage of son," and "doubt about his mother's ancestors."

The facility's population exploded over just a few years. Originally designed to hold 250 patients, Trans-Allegheny was full by 1871 and had more than seven hundred patients by 1880. By 1935, it held more than fifteen hundred people and in the 1950s held twenty-five hundred. At that time, the ratio of doctors to patients was 1 to 250, and as many as fifty-seven people in a ward had to share one single toilet. Jacks described the hospital in that time as "a dumping ground for unwanted people," especially those with drug and alcohol addictions, who were seen as disgraces to their families. In 1949, Charles Armentrout published an investigation of the patient conditions and disrepair of the facility in *The Charleston Gazette* with the headline: "Cows on Mental Farm are Better Off than Inmates."

Overcrowding conditions in the facility led to more conflicts than the institution's creators could have fathomed. In 1877, the hospital saw its first killing, when a patient beat another patient so badly that a contemporary article in the *Weston Democrat* said that "the head of the poor victim was beaten to a jelly." The article said the perpetrator claimed "he did it by the command of God, who had Himself been trying to kill him, but not succeeding fast enough, had employed him to do it." There were more violent deaths throughout the overcrowded hospital's lifespan. In 1881, an elderly man was beaten to death by his roommate. In 1972, a man hospitalized for alcoholism stabbed another to death. In 1963, there was a murder by a female patient, the only one on record: Wanda Maxine Janes murdered Muriel Creamer, saying the woman "had made improper advances toward her and she feared for her life," according to the *Beckley Post-Herald.*

The most unusual of all of them, though, was in 1987. David Michael Mason and James Woods murdered Dean Metheney, repeatedly hanging him until he lost consciousness, reviving him, and eventually killing him with the metal leg of a bed through his skull. When questioned, according to a tour guide's information provided by Theresa Racer, the men claimed there was a ghost in the room that committed the murder. (Five years later, Mason attacked fellow patient Georgie Edward Bodie, who died of his wounds.)

"Many other patients died by suicide, unable to withstand the barbaric treatments given to them, like insulin-shock therapy, ice-cold hydrotherapy, and 'ice-pick' lobotomies," Tim Barnes wrote in *The Washington Post.* "The Weston facility was one where Walter Freeman, known as the 'father of the lobotomy,' performed the controversial procedures," he added. Those procedures often left patients incapacitated or killed them.

The facility closed in 2004, and thousands of unmarked graves remain on the property. In 2008, the building reopened for historic and paranormal tours under a new name: the Trans-Allegheny Lunatic Asylum. People report seeing shadow figures and full apparitions, as well as unexplained electronic failures. Manager Rebecca Jordan-Gleason reports witnessing forty doors on the fourth floor slam shut at once.

In *The Big Book of West Virginia Ghost Stories*, Rosemary Ellen Guiley wrote that a tour guide "heard a group of ghostly women discussing how to make apple butter." On the first floor, a spirit named Ruth is known to throw things at men, and on the fourth floor, a spirit named Jacob, believed to have been hospitalized for alcoholism, has been heard searching for his beer." Maybe most appropriate for our purposes, there's said to be a ghost named Jack in the kitchen, a former patient who worked there. As Guiley wrote, "Jack is fond of women. In flashlight divination, he will turn a light on when asked if he thinks a woman is pretty."

CRANBERRY CAKE

A big part of the social support at Trans-Allegheny came from local women's clubs, like the Junior Department of the West Virginia Federation of Women's Clubs. "All patients are fed three meals a day for 47 cents and this is quite a feat considering the kitchen and the budget," department chairman of the club, Mrs. Robert Lee, said in the *Raleigh Register* in 1961. That forty-seven cents in 1961 is only about five dollars today. At one point, according to local historians, coffee was pulled from the offerings altogether because of the cost.

This recipe is adapted from *Cookin' in the 80s*, a cookbook published by the West Virginia Federation of Women's Clubs. There's no way to know, but in my heart, I believe someone baked this for a patient in the hospital, and it brought them a little bit of deliciousness.

Prep Time: 10 minutes | Cook Time: 1 hour 10 minutes | Yield: 12 to 16 servings

INGREDIENTS

Butter, for greasing

2 1/2 cups all-purpose flour

1 3/4 cups granulated sugar, divided

1 teaspoon baking powder

1 teaspoon baking soda

1/4 teaspoon salt

Zest and juice of 2 oranges, separated

1 cup chopped pecans

1 cup chopped dates

1 cup chopped fresh cranberries

2 eggs

1 cup buttermilk

3/4 cup vegetable or canola oil

2 tablespoons water

INSTRUCTIONS

1. Preheat the oven to 325°F. Grease a tube pan or Bundt pan.
2. In a large mixing bowl, combine the flour, 1 cup of the sugar, the baking powder, baking soda, salt, and grated orange zest. Add the pecans, dates, and cranberries and stir to combine. Set aside.
3. In a small mixing bowl, whisk together the eggs, buttermilk, and oil. Stir the wet mixture into the dry mixture just until moistened, then transfer the batter to the cake pan.
4. Bake for 1 hour, until a knife comes out clean. Allow to cool in the pan for 1 hour before removing.
5. When the cake is cool enough, turn out onto a platter, then prepare the glaze. In a small saucepan over medium-low heat, combine the orange juice and water. Stir in the remaining 3/4 cup sugar, and cook until the sugar is dissolved, about 3–4 minutes. Let the topping cool slightly, then pour over the cake.

THE LIBERTY HOTEL

BOSTON, MASSACHUSETTS, USA

Since 2007, the Liberty Hotel has been one of the most chic and interesting destinations in Boston. Its 298 rooms are set inside a soaring 1851 structure, where a central rotunda has a ninety-foot-tall atrium and is ringed by catwalks that showcase the preserved historic architecture below. Its restaurants and bars—Clink, Alibi, and Catwalk—offer elevated cuisine and libations. (There's also Scampo, an Italian restaurant and wine bar by noted Boston chef Lydia Shire.)

But the vibe used to be a little different at this hotel—maybe you're noticing a theme?

The Liberty used to be the Charles Street Jail, home to notorious criminals like the Boston Strangler and mobster James Whitey Bulger. When you dine there today, your table will have a clear view of old jail cells or even be inside one. And when you sleep, maybe you'll be sleeping next to a ghost.

In its early days, the jail—sometimes called the Suffolk County Jail—was praised for its design and relative comfort. In 1888, according to Boston's West End Museum, "the National Prison Association named it the best jail in the United States" for its architecture and its efficiency in allowing guards to monitor four stories of cells from its central rotunda.

In its nearly 150 years as a prison, the building held, if we can call it this, a "who's who" of notorious criminals: Frank Abagnale, the former con artist later played by Leonardo DiCaprio in *Catch Me If You Can*, was jailed there. Malcolm X was imprisoned there for a time after being arrested for burglary in Boston's wealthy suburbs. Sacco and Vanzetti, Italian immigrants convicted of murder who were likely innocent and whose executions spawned a worldwide protest, were also held there. Other inmates, or would-be inmates include murderous Harvard professor John White Webster, corrupt Boston mayor James Michael Curley, and mobster Elmer "Trigger" Burke, who was arrested for murder but escaped the jail. In the 1940s, Charles Street Jail held fifty-two German prisoners of war.

But not everyone who crossed the threshold of the jail cells was a dangerous criminal. In 1919, thirteen suffragettes fighting for women's right to vote were imprisoned there after protesting President Woodrow Wilson's visit to the city. One suffragette, Josephine Collins, told the paper that the jail was "warm and comfortable" and there wasn't "anything to complain of."

Indeed, some people did enjoy it there. Businessman George Francis Train "checked in" fifteen times, saying he liked the accommodations, according to the West End Museum. Also according to the museum, "When baseball legend Babe Ruth visited the jail in 1926, he (clairvoyantly) remarked, 'It isn't like a jail, it's like a hotel.'"

Those luxurious reviews didn't last. Conditions deteriorated over the decades, prompting protests from Bostonians outside the jail. According to *The Boston Globe*, an estimated two hundred pigeons lived in the atrium above the dining tables. In 1972, Federal Bureau of Prisons director James Bennett called it a "dehumanizing museum piece." In 1973, inmates filed a lawsuit claiming the jail violated their civil liberties, calling imprisonment there cruel and unusual punishment. Among the complaints: inadequate plumbing, crumbling walls, lack of proper heating, and forced sharing of single-occupancy cells—plus food quality violations that resulted in $250,000 worth of damage, prompted by inmates' soup having bugs in it.

"They were only little black flour bugs," prison superintendent Thomas S. Eisenstadt said at the time. "My wife served me soup with them in it the other day and I didn't riot." (As if you didn't need more proof that he wasn't a great guy: Eisenstadt resigned in 1977 after his lavish personal use of public funds was revealed.)

That year, Judge Arthur Garrity spent a night there to witness the conditions firsthand and concluded that the jail was "a violation of constitutional rights." He closed the prison then, but it took many years to reassign the inmates; it wasn't officially vacated until 1991.

When the prison finally closed, *The Boston Globe*'s David Arnold wrote, "Boston institutions come and go, but few collect as many colorful ghosts, bullet holes, cockroaches, and newspaper clips as the 140-year-old Suffolk County Jail on Charles Street." As for those ghosts, hotel guests have reported seeing apparitions of nineteenth-century men in uniform and hearing the slamming of cell doors. Hotel staff say the kitchen is particularly active, with the clanging of pots and pans and disembodied voices echoing through the space.

Even representatives of the Liberty acknowledge the possible presence of spirits. "The Liberty Hotel's history as the Charles Street Jail sets the stage for its reputation as one of Boston's most haunted hotels," its history reads. "The hotel retains much of its original architecture, including wrought iron bars, the rotunda, and catwalks, making it easy to imagine the spirits of former prisoners still roaming the halls."

BOSTON BAKED BEANS

Way back before inmates were fed bug-ridden soup, the rations for prisoners would have largely been cheap, hearty food like bread and beans. In fact, Boston is so famous for its baked beans, a food that dates back to the seventeenth century, that its nickname is "Beantown." Puritans in the Massachusetts Bay Colony would cook massive pots of the beans on Saturdays so they could observe Sunday as a day of no labor. Today, there's even a candy called Boston Baked Beans, which are peanuts in a sugary red coating. Here's a recipe adapted from The Pot Shop of Boston, which makes the iconic bean pots essential for truly authentic Boston Baked Beans.

Prep Time: 10 minutes, plus overnight soaking | Cook Time: 6½ to 8½ hours | Yield: 8 servings

INGREDIENTS

2 cups dry navy beans

6 cups water

1 teaspoon salt

⅓ cup firmly packed brown sugar

1 teaspoon dry mustard

¼ cup molasses

½ pound salt port or pork belly

1 medium onion, sliced

INSTRUCTIONS

1. Prepare the beans by letting them soak in the water overnight (or by bringing them to a boil, removing from the heat and letting them sit covered for an hour).
2. In a large saucepan over medium heat, bring the bean and water mixture to a simmer, and add the salt. Cover and cook for 1 hour.
3. Drain the beans, and reserve 1¾ cups liquid. To that liquid, add the sugar, mustard, and molasses and mix.
4. Cut the pork into thin slices or cubes.
5. Preheat the oven to 300°F.
6. In a traditional bean pot or Dutch oven, layer a third of the beans, then top with a third of the onions, a third of the salt pork and a third of the liquid. Repeat until you've used all the ingredients.
7. Bake, covered, for 5–7 hours until the beans are soft and have formed a rich gravy. Add more water in the cooking process, if needed.

MALVERN MANOR

MALVERN, IOWA, USA

When I first learned of Malvern Manor, an old, abandoned hotel full of ghosts, I'll admit it: My first thought was of the Haunted Mansion at Disneyland, its "999 happy haunts" filling a once-thriving home. But Malvern Manor, in the tiny town of Malvern, Iowa, isn't that kind of place. Yes, it's filled with spirits who make regular contact with the living. But they're the spirits of real people, many of whom lived troubled existences and whose stories deserve to be told.

Today, Malvern Manor is only open for events and paranormal investigations. When it was first built, sometime around the town's founding in 1869, it was a home for the family of Isaac B. Ringland, a onetime mayor of the town. It became the Cottage Hotel in 1891 and for decades was "the social center of town," as Richard Estep described it in *The Devil's Coming to Get Me.* It changed hands several times, eventually being converted to a nursing home in 1956. Conditions, it seems, were better than expected for the time period. "We don't believe we could have found a more satisfactory place," a resident's relative told *The Malvern Leader* at the time. "The residence is kept immaculately clean. The guests like the good food and excellent care. And there's a homey, friendly atmosphere there that certainly means much to all who stay there."

The nursing home closed because the hallways were too narrow to accommodate hospital beds, and in 1976, Malvern Manor became a home for people with physical and mental disabilities. And over the years, the level of care diminished for the residents staying there. In 2004, the facility failed inspections on thirty different counts, including fire safety issues, missing patient records, poor food sanitation, and incomplete employee training records. It changed hands the following year and shut down again due to more violations.

At the time, according to the *Des Moines Register*, a judge said, "This facility's history is one of constant and numerous deficiencies in repeated surveys and inspections."

In 2004, the facility failed inspections on thirty different counts.

Though medical records are private, it's said that more than one hundred people died in the facility over the years. It sat vacant for more than a decade before paranormal investigator Josh Heard purchased the building.

Now, the twenty-eight-room building belongs mostly to the ghosts. The living are the visitors to the space—and when they visit, they report experiencing intense paranormal phenomena. People hear moans, screams, growls, distant whistling, footsteps, and banging and knocking noises. Others say they hear the sound of something heavy being dragged across the floor. Sometimes it's the sound of children running and playing, and other times it's phantom music with no discernable source. And those are just the noises.

People also see wheelchairs moving on their own, balls rolling across the floor, lights turning on and off on their own, and mysterious shadows.

In room 7, investigators have identified the spirit of a woman "who dislikes the company of males but seems drawn to other women," Richard Estep wrote. He described her as "a screaming woman who had pulled all of her own hair out because she believed that her husband and family had abandoned her." People often report seeing shadow figures peek out of that doorway, and women say they feel their ankles being grabbed.

In room 2, a truly terrifying spirit of a man resides, though investigators have claimed his haunting is residual (meaning that it's more of an energetic imprint than an active spirit). That room was, according to the Paranormal Perimeter, "occupied by a very large, 6' 7" man, in the home's mental health occupant days . . . This man was said to be very crazed, and non-verbal. The large man would scare and chase staff, who were conducting area checks, down the hallways of the Manor." He's believed to have killed two people, and to cast a long shadow, even in life. As Richard Estep wrote, "Staff were said to be so scared of him that they wouldn't even assist him with putting on his shoes in the morning."

On the second floor, a man named Captain Cullers, who was the owner of another hotel in Malvern's early days, is said to haunt room 24. In that room, people report being pushed and shoved and, according to Estep, have "been struck on the arms and legs, hard enough to raise bruises."

A young girl named Inez Gibson, who died in a terrible accident in a nearby home in December 1900, has also been sensed on the second floor. Investigators have heard her identify herself by name, though why she would take refuge at Malvern is unclear—maybe because her own home was torn down, or maybe because she's attracted to all the paranormal activity in the place.

CHICKEN AND DUMPLINGS

When Malvern Manor was known as the Cottage Hotel in 1939, a new restaurant moved onto the property. What was formerly Cuba's Cafe became the Cottage Hotel Cafe, and it advertised its move in the May 4, 1939, edition of *The Malvern Leader*. To welcome new guests, the restaurant held a celebratory "special chicken dinner" at the hotel. What was served at that dinner has been lost to time—but it may have been chicken and dumplings, a staple of the era. My version is inspired by the 1930 *Ames Woman's Club Cook Book* from Ames, Iowa.

Prep Time: 15 minutes | Cook Time: 35 minutes | Yield: 4 servings

INGREDIENTS

6 cups chicken broth

1 whole chicken, cut into pieces, or 8 assorted bone-in chicken pieces

2 bay leaves

1 medium yellow onion, peeled and halved

1 large carrot, peeled and halved

1 1/2 teaspoons salt, divided

1/2 teaspoon black pepper

1 egg

3/4 cup milk

1 1/4 cups all-purpose flour

2 teaspoons baking powder

2 tablespoons cornstarch

INSTRUCTIONS

1. In a large pot or Dutch oven over medium-high heat, combine the chicken broth, chicken, bay leaves, onion, carrot, 1 teaspoon of the salt, and the pepper. Bring to a simmer and cook for 20–25 minutes, depending on the size of your chicken.
2. While the chicken is cooking, prepare the dumpling dough. In a medium mixing bowl, mix together the egg and milk. Add the remaining 1/2 teaspoon salt, the flour, and baking powder. Stir until combined and set aside.
3. Remove the chicken from the pot (shred off the bone, if desired) and discard the bay leaves, onion, and carrot. Spoon a few tablespoons of broth into a small bowl and create a slurry with the cornstarch by mixing the two until combined. Add the mixture to the pot and stir until the slurry is incorporated and the mixture begins to thicken, about 2 minutes.
4. Drop the dumplings on top of the liquid by small spoonfuls of dough. Cover and cook an additional 10 minutes. Return the chicken to the pot to warm it. Season to taste with salt and pepper, if desired, and serve.

POVEGLIA

VENICE, ITALY

The idea was never for Poveglia to become an island of the damned. But has anyone ever really *intentionally* created a place like that? Two boatloads of possibly plague-ridden passengers crossed its shores, and more than two hundred years later, the island is still untouchable, full of legends, horror stories, and more than likely, ghosts.

"Venetians prefer not to discuss the island nor answer questions concerning it," Salvatore Di Vita wrote for *L'Italo Americano* in 2016. "They simply remark that it is harmless to those who keep their distance." Although, he noted, people believe, "while the rest of Venice is governed by Comune di Venezia, the island of Poveglia remains firmly in the jurisdiction of the Devil." Some Italians have a saying: "*Quando muore un cattivo, si sveglia a Poveglia*." Translation? "When an evil man dies, he awakens on Poveglia."

Sometimes called "the island of terror," in 1776 Poveglia became a checkpoint for all passenger and cargo ships coming in and out of Venice, a trading capital for more than a millennium. But in 1793, two ships that were suspected of carrying the Black Plague were detained at Poveglia. By 1805, Poveglia had become an official quarantine station for Venice and remained in use until 1814.

Conditions weren't good for the sick *or* the healthy on the island. "The island had become so overcrowded with plague victims that many of the living, considered to be as good as dead, were simply thrown into the burial pits or onto bonfires to be incinerated along with those already dead," wrote Di Vita.

It lay unused for years after its closure as a quarantine station. In 1922, the government converted the buildings into a psychiatric asylum, which eventually became a nursing home. It finally closed in 1968 and has been abandoned since. At least, it's been abandoned by the living.

"Legend has it that the overgrown island . . . is haunted by the tortured souls of those who were buried there," *The Guardian* wrote in 2014. Other legends speak to its time as an institution. According to *The Sunday Times*, "when it was a mental hospital in the 20th century, the director became possessed by ghosts and performed unnecessary lobotomies on his patients before hurling himself to his death from the belltower."

The myths and ghost stories are likely overblown. Locals say not nearly as many people are buried on the island as the stories claim. But there's at least some truth to some of it. According to *The Telegraph*, "In the undergrowth a Latin inscription on a headstone dated 1793 says, 'Do not dig. Those who suffered contagion in life lie here.'"

It wasn't the only island to be damned by the plague. Nearby, the Venetian island of Lazzaretto Vecchio holds mass graves of those who succumbed to the disease and is regarded as the first plague colony, according to *Smithsonian Magazine.*

In 2014, Poveglia made international headlines when the Italian government auctioned off a ninety-nine-year lease of the island. The highest bidder, Luigi Brugnaro, won the auction for €513,000 (about $723,000 today) but was thwarted by a grassroots campaign.

Poveglia finally closed in 1968 and has been abandoned since.

Poveglia per Tutti (Poveglia for Everyone) was a group founded by Venetians, wherein locals donated €99 each to a fund to counterbid Brugnaro. Because while it had technically been abandoned, Poveglia was still an important place to people who grew up in the city, and they didn't want to see it developed into a luxury hotel or other tourist attraction. "Young people came here to smoke their joints, have sex, have some shade from the adult world," Poveglia per Tutti spokesperson Lorenzo Pesola told *The Telegraph* in 2015. "It's tied to a lot of people's biographies." They topped out at €440,000, but because Brugnaro couldn't raise his bid any higher, it was deemed too low by the local government and denied. He also abandoned the claim so that he could run for mayor and was elected after the sitting mayor was placed under house arrest and resigned after a kickback scandal.

Today, the island sits as it has for decades—abandoned and decaying, but full of a life of its own. Remaining structures include the church, hospital, asylum, bell tower, and staff buildings. The only legal way to access Poveglia is to book a tour through an authorized operator or to apply for special permission.

RISI E BISI

It doesn't get any more simple or delicious than this vibrant Venetian dish—literally translated as "rice and peas"—which is somewhere between a risotto and a soup. In the springtime, use fresh snap peas with their pods. In any season, good-quality frozen peas work just as well. Traditional recipes use pancetta, but for a vegetarian version, omit the meat and bump up the Parmesan (just make sure you're using certified vegetarian Parmesan). Actually, go ahead and bump up the Parmesan anyway. Can you ever really have enough?

Prep Time: 10 minutes | Cook Time: 35 minutes | Yield: 4 servings

INGREDIENTS

4–5 cups chicken or vegetable broth

2 tablespoons extra virgin olive oil

1 medium onion, minced

4 ounces diced pancetta

1 1/2 cups arborio rice

3/4 cup fresh or frozen shelled peas

2 tablespoons minced fresh Italian parsley, divided

1 tablespoon minced fresh mint

3 tablespoons unsalted butter

1/4 cup grated Parmesan, plus more to finish

Salt and pepper, to taste

INSTRUCTIONS

1. In a saucepan over medium heat, warm the broth. Keep the broth on a simmer while you prepare the next ingredients.
2. In a large skillet over medium-low heat, warm the olive oil. Add the onion and cook until it's translucent, taking care not to brown it, about 8 minutes. Add the pancetta, and cook until crispy, another 4 minutes.
3. Add the rice to the skillet, and toast for 1 minute, stirring often. Add two cups of warm broth and simmer for about 15 minutes. As the broth gets absorbed, gradually add more broth in half-cup increments, stirring the mixture occasionally. Eventually, the mixture will slow down its absorption of the broth—that's when you'll know you have enough liquid.
4. Add the peas, 1 tablespoon of the parsley, and the mint. Continue cooking 3–5 minutes more, until the rice is al dente but not too soft.
5. Remove the skillet from the heat and stir in the butter and Parmesan. Season with salt and pepper to taste. Finish with the remaining tablespoon parsley and a sprinkle more of cheese.

CHAPTER 6

UNSAVORY CHARACTERS

When it comes to the darkest of stories, there is almost always a central figure, someone who perhaps seemed completely normal in day-to-day life but hid a ghastly secret or murderous plot. These people are always the most terrifying to think about because they usually skirt through daily life completely undetected. If their horrific crimes are ever uncovered, people around them say things like, "They seemed so normal; it came as such a surprise." Now imagine these unsavory types in ghost form, forever relegated to continue their masquerade of normalcy in the afterlife—or maybe even unchained from the need to continue the charade. Would you rather meet them alive . . . or dead? Personally, I'd rather meet them in spirit form. And truthfully, the macabre part of me would love to share a meal or drink with them and use the opportunity to ask them one simple question: "Why?"

OIRAN BUCHI

YAMANASHI PREFECTURE, JAPAN

Today, there's one remaining commercial gold mine in all of Japan: the Hishikari Mine on the island of Kyushu. But in centuries past, gold mining was a lucrative endeavor around the country, the proceeds of which financed wars and power clashes.

The Sengoku period of the fifteenth and sixteenth centuries was a tumultuous time in Japanese history, marked by infighting between noble families. This led to weakened leadership that gave way to social upheavals, where peasants rebelled against their overlords. One of the wealthiest and most powerful clans was the Takeda, which owned a gold mine near Mount Kurokawa, in the Yamanashi prefecture. The mine was a huge operation, which created rough living conditions in the camps, much like in the mining towns of the Old West. There were miners to dig out the gold, guards to oversee everyone, and courtesans to keep the men occupied in their off hours.

"Not all of the gold that was mined from these hills was used for war," according to the Sengoku Archives. "Some were buried in the hills as offerings to the gods, mainly as offerings for good fortune for the Takeda in battle."

While the clan had prospered under the feudal lord and masterful military leader Takeda Shingen in the earlier part of the sixteenth century, his son Takeda Katsuyori did not fare as well. A massive defeat at the Battle of Nagashino in 1575 left the clan limping along until Katsuyori's death in 1582. In the aftermath, the clan scrambled to cover up its secrets, including the location of the mine, which had been prosperous for more than five hundred years but was beginning to run dry.

"To keep information about the gold from spreading, they targeted the women," according to the Sengoku Archives. "They were afraid that the prostitutes learned information from the men who worked there, which could be valuable in the wrong hands. So they came up with a plan."

Their solution was . . . not good.

Soldiers constructed a platform over the Yanagisawa River, which they told the courtesans would be the location of a dance during a farewell celebration. The women went to the platform to practice the dance, and while they were all gathered there, the men cut the ties securing the platform. All fifty-five women fell to their deaths into the gorge below. Some died on impact, and some were washed downriver and drowned. What happened to the miners and the guards has been lost to time, but it's pretty certain that even if they were executed, it wasn't as brutally as that.

All fifty-five women fell to their deaths into the gorge below.

Today, the Oiran Buchi (the "Courtesan's Bridge" or less elegantly, "Prostitute Gorge") over the Saiko Waterfall is in Chichibu-Tama-Kai National Park. It remains one of the most fabled and allegedly haunted locations in Japan. Visitors to the site sometimes claim they can still hear the screams of the "wailing women" nearly five centuries later.

NYUMEN

This noodle dish comes from the oldest surviving Japanese cookbook, *Ryori Monogatari*, which dates back to 1643. Its title translates to "Narrative of Actual Food Preparation" or "A Tale of Food," and today it's at the Tokyo National Museum. These ingredients should be relatively easy to find at the grocery store or an Asian market, but if not, they're not hard to find online.

Prep Time: 20 minutes, plus soaking time | Cook Time: 30 minutes | Yield: 3 to 4 servings

FOR THE MISO

4 tablespoons white or red miso paste

1 cup water

FOR THE DASHI

2 cups kombu (dried kelp)

8 cups water

2 cups bonito flakes

FOR ASSEMBLY

1 small eggplant, roughly diced

1 tablespoon neutral cooking oil

2 cups leafy greens (like mustard greens, kale, or spinach)

4 green scallions, trimmed and sliced

4 ounces somen (thin wheat) noodles

Black pepper, to taste

$^1/_2$ teaspoon ground sansho pepper (or red pepper flakes)

PREPARE THE MISO

1. In a small saucepan over medium heat, combine the miso and water.
2. Simmer without boiling until the mixture is reduced by about a third. If there are clumps, strain the mixture and let it cool.

PREPARE THE DASHI

1. In a large saucepan, combine the kombu and water. Let soften for 30 minutes, then bring the mixture to a simmer over medium heat. Do not boil.
2. Add the bonito flakes, cook for 1 minute, and then remove the mixture from the heat. Let the broth sit for 10 minutes, then strain and discard the solids. Return the broth to the pot and keep warm. (If using prepared dashi, just make sure you have 8 cups of it warmed.)

ASSEMBLE THE DISH

1. Soak the eggplant briefly in salted water to extract the bitterness, then pat dry.
2. In a medium skillet over medium heat, heat the oil. Sauté the greens, eggplant, and onions until soft, 6–8 minutes. (You can also boil or steam the veggies if you prefer.)
3. While the vegetables are cooking, prepare the noodles. Bring a pot of water to a boil and boil the noodles for 2–3 minutes. Drain, rinse in cold water, and set aside.

(recipe continues)

(recipe continued from page 233)

4. Add the miso to the dashi and bring to just below a simmer. Add the noodles very briefly to rewarm them.
5. Portion the vegetables and noodles into bowls, ladle broth over them, and finish with black pepper and sansho pepper.

Note: If you're short on time, you can buy prepared dashi and skip making your own.

OMNI PARKER HOUSE

BOSTON, MASSACHUSETTS, USA

Even if you've never heard of the Omni Parker House, you've probably tasted some of its food. The Parker House is responsible for those incredibly pillowy, buttery dinner rolls called Parker House Rolls. But the Parker House is responsible for an even more famous baked good: Chef Augustine François Anezin created the Boston Cream Pie for the hotel's 1856 opening. At the time, chocolate was only used in beverages (like Louis XV's drinking chocolate, see page 76) and not in solid foods. Boston Cream Pie changed all of that.

But the Parker House is famous for a lot more than its food. Built by Harvey Parker, at its opening, the hotel was one of the fanciest accommodations in Boston, and it set the standard for luxury hotels in the city. And as such, it has been witness to many important historical moments.

At the Parker House, writers like Ralph Waldo Emerson, Henry David Thoreau, Nathaniel Hawthorne, and Henry Wadsworth Longfellow met for their "Saturday Club" literary salon. The hotel has hosted sports stars like Babe Ruth, celebrities like Judy Garland and Joan Crawford, and politicians like Ulysses S. Grant and John F. Kennedy. Emeril Lagasse cooked in the kitchen, Malcolm X worked as a busboy, and Ho Chi Minh served as a pastry chef.

But there's one guest that, at the time, wasn't obviously of any significance. In 1865, famed Shakespearean actor Edwin Booth was starring nearby in *Hamlet*. During the three-week engagement, his brother John came to town. While he was in Boston, John "was registered at the Parker House and was seen eating in its restaurant," Parker House historian Susan Wilson wrote in *Heaven, By Hotel Standards*. "It's possible that he went to visit brother Edwin, who was playing a successful three-week engagement at the 3,000-seat Boston Theatre. It was reported in the *Boston Evening Transcript* of April 15 that he was practicing his aim: '[A man named] Borland . . . saw Booth at Edwards' shooting gallery [near Parker's], where Booth practiced pistol firing in various difficult ways such as between his legs, over his shoulder and under his arms.'"

Edwin's brother left for Washington the next week. What happened after that changed the course of America. John Wilkes Booth assassinated Abraham Lincoln on April 14, 1865.

Today, some of the hotel's most famous stories stem from spirits who allegedly loved the hotel too much to leave—especially Harvey Parker. In 1992, a bellman named John Brehm, who had been with the hotel more than fifty years, said that he first heard about Parker's ghost appearing to guests in 1941. "They used to say he roamed the halls on the tenth floor annex," Brehm told *The Boston Globe*, as quoted in Wilson's book. Many reported seeing Parker's apparition over the years, but one particular instance happened in 1950. An elderly guest insisted she saw a misty apparition outside room 1078. As it turned toward her, the woman saw it was a heavyset older man with a black mustache who simply looked at her, then faded away. A bit jittery, she reported the incident to security. But when they checked out the tenth floor, security couldn't find anything.

A man died in room 303, and some claim to be able to smell whiskey in that room to this day, or to hear disembodied laughter when staying there.

Seamus Murphy, manager of guest services, told Wilson about an experience during a talk he was giving about the hotel's history. "Well, we were in the Longfellow Room, and I usually spoke from a podium, but there was none there. I went to the storage room on the mezzanine level and heard a gruff voice yell out, 'What do you want?!' I thought it was a houseman at first but there was nobody on the floor. Nobody at all. And the voice sounded just like a bell captain that used to work here. He had been a drinker, and sometimes after work hours, he'd go off to some bar, then wander back into the hotel late at night, and hide out here in some sliding closet. So I thought it was probably him. Yeah, it really sounded exactly like him. Except for the fact that he was dead."

BAKED SCROD

Besides the Boston Cream Pie and Parker House Rolls, the Omni Parker House has another culinary claim to fame: coining the term *scrod*. "The word is generally used for cod or other white-fleshed fish that are the youngest, freshest, smallest, or best of the day's catch," Susan Wilson wrote in *Heaven, By Hotel Standards*. "Unlike cod, haddock, or halibut, scrod is not a type of fish. It's been claimed that when scrod is spelled with a 'c,' it means that the white fish of the day is cod, and when spelled with an 'h' (schrod), the fish is haddock; in reality, restaurants rarely alter their menus to adapt to the day's catch."

Prep Time: 10 minutes, plus marinating time | Cook Time: 10 minutes | Yield: 4 servings

INGREDIENTS

1 cup milk

1/2 cup olive oil

1 teaspoon lemon juice

2 teaspoons Worcestershire sauce

2 cloves garlic, minced

2 teaspoons paprika

1 teaspoon salt

1 1/2 teaspoons black pepper, divided

2 pounds best-quality cod filets

1 cup finely crushed Ritz crackers

2 sticks unsalted butter, melted

1/2 cup white wine

Lemon wedges for garnish

INSTRUCTIONS

1. In a large container with a lid, combine the milk, olive oil, lemon juice, Worcestershire, garlic, paprika, salt, and 1/2 teaspoon of the pepper. Stir well to combine. Add the fish, making sure it's submerged in the milk. Cover and refrigerate at least 4 hours, or overnight.
2. When ready to cook, remove the fish from the refrigerator and drain. Preheat the oven to 400°F.
3. In a mixing bowl, combine the crackers and the remaining 1 teaspoon pepper. Coat the fish on both sides with crumbs, then lay the fish in a baking dish in one layer. Drizzle the melted butter over top of the crackers. Be a little restrained with how much butter you add; you may not need all of it, depending on how many pieces of fish you have. Pour in the wine, making sure to pour around the edges and not directly on top of the fish.
4. Bake until flaky, approximately 12 minutes, then broil for 3–5 minutes to brown the cracker crumbs. Serve hot, with lemon wedges on the side.

Note: The beauty of this dish is its simplicity. Source the freshest fish you can find, and you'll be shocked at how a few ingredients can make such a memorable meal.

CORTIJO DE FRAILE

NÍJAR, SPAIN

It sounds like a Greek tragedy: a woman, headed to the altar in an arranged marriage with a man she doesn't love, escapes before the wedding with her true love. But soon after, he's killed, and she lives out her years alone, with nothing but his memory for comfort.

In 1928, Francisca Cañadas Morales was living with her father at his farm, Cortijo del Fraile, outside a small town called Níjar in Spain's southerly Andalusian region. She was engaged to be married to her sister's brother-in-law, Casimiro Pérez Morales. But she didn't love him. She loved her cousin, Francisco Montes Cañadas. On the day of the wedding, July 24, 1928, the lovers escaped, fleeing on a mule into the countryside, headed for Níjar.

They never made it to safety. Morales's sister Carmen and brother-in-law José Pérez Pinto tracked them down, attacking them on the road. They fatally shot Cañadas and strangled Morales, leaving her for dead on the road. But she survived, living the rest of her days as an outcast in her village, shunned by her family, blamed by everyone she ever knew for causing the tragedy. According to Spanish news site *Ideal*, "The murderer was sentenced to eight years in prison and ordered to pay a fine of one hundred thousand pesetas and another ten thousand to cover costs." Morales would never return to the life she knew before the attack.

The scandal became known as Crimen del Níjar, the Crime of Níjar, and went on to become fodder for famed literary works. Among them was a play called *Blood Wedding*, written by Andalusian literary great Federico García Lorca, which premiered in 1933 in Madrid.

Today, Cortijo del Fraile still stands, now within the Cabo de Gata-Níjar Natural Park, and was designated as a historic site in 2010. The crumbling farmhouse looks like an eerie ghost town, fenced off from the public in a remote location. It's crumbling facade has been featured in Westerns like *For a Few Dollars More* and *The Good, the Bad and the Ugly.*

Morales lived in infamy as "La Coja," or "the lame one," to the age of eighty-four, dying in 1987. She never shared her side of the story or spoke out to clear her name.

Over the decades, journalists attempted to track her down and are still doing so to this day. In 2017, *New York Times* writer Doreen Carvajal went to Níjar looking for Morales's grave to pay her last respects.

"Every time I visit Andalusia, I try to find some trace of the grave of the runaway bride," she wrote. "She never married and was essentially buried in life by the scorn of her village. And every year nothing changes in the essential rural tragedy imagined by García Lorca. A lone cemetery worker offered me a vague hint that Francisca Cañadas's tomb is placed near a soaring cypress tree, a symbol of mourning and hope. But a stone plaque was nowhere to be found. According to the family's wishes, the worker said, it is marked with a false name."

Morales never shared her side of the story or spoke out to clear her name.

Upon reaching the remote ruin, many people report feeling a pervasive sense of eeriness and a heavy energy. I've never visited Cortijo del Fraile on my visits to Spain, and I'm not sure if I'd even find any ghosts if I did get there. Part of me hopes I wouldn't. Morales suffered a terrible loss and lived an incredibly sad life afterward. I hope that, wherever she is now, she's found some peace.

OLLA DE TRIGO

A rich chickpea soup that comes from Almeria, on Spain's Mediterranean coast, *olla de trigo* translates to "pot of wheat." It dates back to the 1600s. A traditional recipe calls for *morcilla*, or Spanish blood sausage, but chorizo is just as delicious and much easier to find. Make sure to use Spanish chorizo, which is dried and cured, for the right texture and flavor.

Prep Time: 10 minutes	Cook Time: 2½ hours, plus resting time	Yield: 8 servings

INGREDIENTS

2 cups fine bulgur (cracked wheat)

1 cup dried chickpeas

14 ounces thick-cut bacon or pork belly, cut into chunks

1 bulb fresh fennel, white parts only, thinly sliced

10 cups water

16 ounces Spanish chorizo, sliced

2 medium potatoes, peeled and cubed

1 teaspoon salt

4 to 6 strands saffron

INSTRUCTIONS

1. In a large pot or Dutch oven, combine the bulgur, chickpeas, pork, and fennel. Cover with the water. Bring to a boil, then reduce the heat to a simmer and cook for another 2 hours. The mixture will thicken significantly. Add more water throughout the process to thin, as needed.
2. After 2 hours, add the chorizo, potatoes, salt, and saffron to the pot. Cook another 30 minutes, then remove from the heat. Let rest for 30 minutes before serving.

LEEDS GENERAL HOSPITAL

LEEDS, ENGLAND, UK

Mary Bateman's strange deeds and purported mystical powers held such sway over the public's imagination that, even in death, she was a major curiosity. People bought pieces of her body as souvenirs and visited her remains on public display. And her powers were so widely believed in that she managed to be convicted of witchcraft nearly eighty years after the practice was outlawed in Britain.

But was "the Yorkshire witch" even a witch at all?

Born as Mary Harker in 1768, Bateman started her life of crime early. She was only twelve or thirteen when she began stealing from the family who employed her as a domestic servant. By the time she was fifteen, she was telling fortunes to supplement her seamstress income. By the time she married John Bateman in 1792, she was buying items from shops in Leeds and charging them to other customers' accounts and collecting donations "for the poor" but pawning them for profit.

By 1799, Bateman had established a reputation as a "wise woman," considered one of the "cunning folk" of the country, who purported to use supernatural means to help people in need . . . for a price. They provided services including "helping people find lost property, curing ailments in humans and animals, and influencing the weather," the York Museum Trust wrote. "English cunning folk were not witches, and they weren't pagan; they used Christian prayer alongside charms and spells." Her cons got bigger and more ambitious. Bateman invented two wise women, Mrs. Moore and Miss Blyth, who corresponded with Leeds residents via mail. The only person allowed to contact them was, you guessed it, Mary Bateman, who collected (and pocketed) the postage for every letter she didn't actually send.

Bateman's biggest con, and the one that ended her life, was her treatment of Rebecca and William Perigo. "In May 1807 she told the Perigos they were about to fall sick from an illness that God had in store for them," according to the York Museum Trust. "To preserve them from this illness they had to follow Miss Blyth's instructions. If they didn't follow the instructions perfectly, death was certain. Mary began to send them a series of white powders, with instructions to mix them into a pudding and eat it all. She guaranteed this would save them. They couldn't let anyone else eat any of the pudding, not even animals. They had to destroy any that was left over, and they weren't allowed to consult with a doctor, as Mary told them the doctor could not help them."

Illustration of Mary Bateman mixing poison, 1809

After six rounds of powders, Rebecca died, but William, who didn't eat the last one, survived. He discovered that Bateman had been conning them when he opened up his mattress expecting to discover the charms and gold coins Bateman said she had sewn into it to promote good health, only to find pennies and scrap paper. Bateman was tried for murder and witchcraft—though the "witchcraft" part was an exaggeration from the gossipy local broadsheet—and hanged in 1809. While Rebecca Perigo's murder was the only one Bateman was tried for, it's believed that she poisoned many others as well.

After her death, Bateman's celebrity only grew. Five thousand people attended Bateman's hanging, and many followed her coffin on its journey to Leeds General Infirmary (now Leeds General Hospital).

Once there, Bateman's body was on display, and over twenty-seven hundred people paid to view it. Medical students later paid to watch the dissection of her corpse, and the following day, men and women attended special dissections divided by intensity. Eventually, her skeleton was on display for many years in the medical school. But the fascination didn't stop there. Her skin was dried and sold as magic charms and used as binding for books. A book about her, *The Extraordinary Life and Character of Mary Bateman*, sold enough copies that it was in its twelfth printing in just two years.

Aside from being the site of Mary Bateman's gruesome death spectacle, Leeds General Hospital is rumored to have more chilling tales associated with it. It's where hospital employee Andrew Milburn allegedly took a phone photo of the "Snapchat ghost" in 2015, and other workers have reported having ghostly encounters there. "I used to work at the Leeds General Infirmary in the 1980s and the worst part for me was under the Brotherton Wing near the operating theatres," Paul Duckworth told the *Yorkshire Evening Post* in 2023.

"One day I heard and partially saw someone pass the room where I was working," he added. "I thought it was a work mate and [was] waiting for him to pass again but he never did—there was no way out without coming back past me—very spooky."

Mary Bateman hasn't been reported as a paranormal presence in the hospital. But if she was inclined to appear, she'd probably charge you a shilling first.

FAT RASCAL

Yorkshire has many signature foods that have made their way around the world—Yorkshire pudding, anyone?—but none is more deliciously cheeky than fat rascal. Similar to scones, these dense breads are studded with fruit and nuts. Yorkshire bakery Betty's popularized these treats as "fat rascals" in the early 1980s, based on the traditional "turf bun" that dates back to the fifteenth century. Here's my adaptation of Betty's fat rascal, by way of website Traditional Yorkshire Recipes.

Prep Time: 10 minutes	Cook Time: 20 minutes	Yield: 6 pieces

INGREDIENTS

2 cups self-rising flour

1/4 teaspoon allspice

1/8 teaspoon ground nutmeg

1/4 teaspoon ground cinnamon

1/4 teaspoon ground cloves

1/8 teaspoon ground cardamom

1/3 cup granulated sugar

1/2 cup (1 stick) unsalted butter, cubed, plus more for greasing and serving

3/4 cup dried fruit, such as cranberries, raisins, currants, or diced apricots

1 egg, beaten

3/4 cup milk, plus more for brushing

1 teaspoon lemon juice

1/4 cup sliced almonds

1/4 cup candied cherries, chopped

INSTRUCTIONS

1. Preheat the oven to 375°F. Grease a baking sheet or line it with parchment paper.
2. In a medium mixing bowl, combine the flour, allspice, nutmeg, cinnamon, cloves, cardamom, and sugar.
3. Cut in the butter until the mixture resembles damp sand.
4. Add the fruit (depending on what you're using, you might want to cut it into smaller pieces), egg, milk, and lemon juice. Mix only until just combined.
5. Divide the dough into six portions, and roughly shape into rounds. Dot the top of each with the almonds and cherries, then press lightly with the bottom of a glass to flatten out into a thick disc.
6. Brush the top of each disc with milk. Bake for 20 minutes until golden brown and serve warm with butter.

HOTEL ST. FRANCIS

SAN FRANCISCO, CALIFORNIA, USA

In 1921, Roscoe "Fatty" Arbuckle was at the height of his fame. The comedic silent film actor was widely beloved, inking a deal with Paramount for $1 million a year in 1920 (about $16 million today). He was a mentor to Charlie Chaplin and Bob Hope and even helped Buster Keaton transition from vaudeville performer to movie star. "He had magical comic timing," Arbuckle biographer Stuart Oderman told the BBC. "He was one of the all-time greats."

But at the end of that year, Arbuckle's career came to a crashing halt when he became embroiled in the first major celebrity scandal to hit the fledgling Hollywood film industry.

Over Labor Day weekend in 1921, Fatty Arbuckle found himself in a party in room 1219 at the Hotel St. Francis. He and Virginia Rappe, a struggling actress, ended up alone in a bedroom together. Minutes later, her screams echoed through the room. Party guests found Rappe fully clothed on the bed, but in agony. Arbuckle swore he had only gone into the room to use the bathroom and carried Rappe to the bed because she was in pain, where she had fallen to the floor. Rappe, however, had a different story. "He did this to me," she said.

The actress had long suffered from chronic cystitis, a bladder inflammation, and fell into a state of delirium, likely from the pain. Three days later, when she still had not recovered, friend Bambina Maude Delmont took Rappe to the hospital. Delmont told the doctors that Arbuckle had sexually assaulted Rappe, later saying in the press, according to the San Francisco Bar Association: "I could hear Virginia kicking and screaming violently and I had to kick and batter the door [to 1219] before Mr. Arbuckle would let me in. I looked at the bed. There was Virginia, helpless and ravaged. When Virginia kept screaming in agony at what Mr. Arbuckle had done, he turned to me and said, 'Shut her up or I'll throw her out a window.' He then went back to his drunken party and danced while poor Virginia lay dying."

Virginia Rappe with a dog, c. 1920

Doctors found no evidence of sexual assault. Rappe died a day later, from peritonitis from a ruptured bladder. Arbuckle was charged with first-degree murder, but the charge was changed to manslaughter. Even before the case went to trial, presiding Judge Sylvain Lazarus doubted Arbuckle's culpability. "I do not find any evidence that Mr. Arbuckle either committed or attempted to commit rape," he said. "The district attorney has presented barely enough facts to justify my holding the defendant on the charge which is here filed against him." But he added that, essentially, he was willing to make an example out of the actor for the greater good of a strengthened morality. "We are not trying Roscoe Arbuckle alone; we are not trying the screen celebrity who has given joy and pleasure to the entire world; we are actually, gentlemen, trying ourselves," he said. "We are trying our present-day morals, our present-day social conditions, our present-day looseness of thought and lack of social balance."

The scandal tore through Hollywood and through the newspapers nationally. "This was the first scandal in Hollywood with box office implications," film historian Cari Beauchamp told the BBC. "Everyone had believed the stars were covered in fairy dust. Now that illusion was shattered, and studio bosses were terrified it would destroy Hollywood itself."

There were many issues with the case against Arbuckle, chiefly among them that Delmont had admitted to attempting to extort money from the actor. Two trials ended in a hung jury, and a third trial exonerated Arbuckle, but his career never recovered. He limped along for another decade, trying to regain his standing in the industry, but died in 1933 at age forty-six of a heart attack.

Today, room 1219 is known to be the most haunted room in the historic hotel, now known as the Westin St. Francis Hotel. People claim to see the spirits of both Virginia Rappe and Fatty Arbuckle in the room. Twenty-nine years later, noted vaudevillian Al Jolson died in the same room, when he suffered a heart attack during a poker game. Guests also claim to see his spirit, eyes downcast, as though unwilling to break his gaze from his final hand of cards.

COFFEE CUSTARD

One of America's first celebrity chefs, Victor Hirtzler, led the culinary program at the St. Francis from its opening in 1904 to 1926. In 1919, he published the *Hotel St. Francis Cook Book*. In it, he provides a year's worth of menus for breakfast, lunch, and dinner. On April 10, he suggests a dessert of coffee custard, which I've adapted here—but I think it would work just as well for something sweet at brunch.

Prep Time: 20 minutes, plus infusing time | Cook Time: 30 minutes | Yield: 6 servings

INGREDIENTS

1 cup ground coffee

2 cups milk

3/4 cup heavy cream

4 egg yolks

1/2 cup granulated sugar

2 tablespoons brandy or cognac

Whipped cream, for serving

Chocolate shavings, for serving

INSTRUCTIONS

1. In a medium saucepan over medium-high heat, bring the coffee grounds and milk to just under a boil. Turn off the heat and let the mixture infuse for 30 minutes.
2. Strain out the coffee grounds and discard. It's okay if some grounds make it through. You'll be straining again. Add the cream to the mixture and bring to a simmer. Set aside.
3. Preheat the oven to 325°F.
4. In a small mixing bowl, whisk the egg yolks, then add the sugar. Temper the egg mixture by whisking in a small amount of the warm mixture to raise the temperature of the eggs, then slowly whisk the tempered egg mixture into the saucepan. Add the brandy.
5. Strain the custard mixture again. You will have a smooth, creamy mixture, ready to pour.
6. Divide the custard between six ramekins, cover each with foil, and place the ramekins in a casserole dish or high-sided baking dish.
7. Create a bain-marie by pouring hot water into the baking dish (but not into the custard ramekins) until the water comes halfway up the sides of the ramekins. Bake for 35–40 minutes, until the custard has set.
8. Let cool to room temperature with the foil in place, then refrigerate at least 2 hours before serving. Serve topped with whipped cream or chocolate shavings, or both.

OYSTER BAY BAR & CASINO

DEADWOOD, SOUTH DAKOTA, USA

You can't book a room at the Fairmont Hotel in Deadwood, South Dakota, anymore. But you *can* get a glimpse of what was once the most notorious brothel in the most notorious Wild West town. The Fairmont, home to Oyster Bay Bar & Casino since at least 1878, still offers oysters and gambling like it did in the old days. Today, it also offers nightly ghost tours of the upstairs rooms, said to be haunted by figures of the Old West past.

Like other mining towns, Deadwood essentially popped up overnight after gold was discovered in South Dakota's Black Hills. In 1875, according to the city's history, miners "set up camp in a gulch full of dead trees and the town of Deadwood [was] born." The city was officially laid out in 1876, and some estimates put its population as high as ten thousand people in that first year alone. Its reputation quickly grew as a center of boozing, gambling, and prostitution. That July, some of the most famous names of the Old West arrived in town, including "Wild Bill" Hickok and Calamity Jane.

But Hickok's stay in Deadwood would be cut short. On August 2, 1876, the notorious gambler, showman, and gunfighter was shot in the back while playing poker at Nutall and Mann's Saloon No. 10.

His friend Colorado Charlie Utter paid for his burial plot, with a sign that read, "Wild Bill, J. B. Hickok killed by the assassin Jack McCall in Deadwood, Black Hills, August 2, 1876. Pard, we will meet again in the happy hunting ground to part no more. Goodbye, Colorado Charlie, C. H. Utter."

Wild Bill Hickok, 1873

That saloon has a different home now, but its location at the time of Hickok's murder was directly next door to the Fairmont Hotel. It's said that the ghost of Jack McCall, Hickok's killer who fled Deadwood only to be captured and hanged by Dakota Territory authorities, haunts the hotel to this day.

Gold mining was drying up by the end of the nineteenth century, but Deadwood lived on. People pivoted to the less lucrative hard rock mining but continued to populate the city because of its legalized gambling and widespread prostitution. The last four of Deadwood's brothels weren't shut down until 1980.

In 1989, Ron Russo purchased the Fairmont Hotel and stayed in the building while renovating it. In a YouTube video, he said that in 1995, "While I was asleep in my two room apartment, I was awoken at, it happened to be 3:33 a.m. in the morning, and I was startled by an apparition that walked into my bedroom. She was about five foot, eight inches, she had beautiful red hair, she was in a green dress, and she stood in front of my bed about five or six feet from me, and she just looked at me . . . for a good five minutes.

"Later on after I did some research and some history of the building, I found out that there was a girl named Margaret Broadwater, and Maggie fit the general description of the same girl that I saw in my room," he added. "It turns out that Margaret Broadwater jumped out of the window in 1907 after she had an argument with her lover." At the time of her death, Broadwater was pregnant and was despondent over being abandoned by her lover. According to Russo, she jumped from the third floor but landed on a muddy spot in the alley and didn't die for three days afterward.

There are other spirits rumored to be in the building, including a remorseful man who ended his own life after accidentally killing another man and a young boy roaming the casino floor.

Russo sold the hotel in 2021 to David Barth, who opened one of his family's A&B Pizza restaurants in the space, but it still serves some of the old favorites. Today, in addition to those oyster shooters, you can get a slice to power you up before your ghost tour.

BAKED OYSTERS

Oysters might not be your first association with South Dakota cuisine. But in Deadwood's earliest days, when the town was flush with cash from gold mining, people wanted to splurge on shellfish during what food historian Clyde MacKenzie has called "the great oyster craze." Oysters would be farmed in Louisiana, then packed in ice and sawdust and shipped up the Mississippi River. Favored preparations varied wildly, but one of the most popular was baked oysters.

Prep Time: 15 minutes	Cook Time: 20 minutes	Yield: 1 dozen oysters

INGREDIENTS

12 large fresh oysters

2 tablespoons unsalted butter

1/2 cup heavy cream

1/4 teaspoon salt

1/4 teaspoon black pepper

1/8 teaspoon ground nutmeg

1/4 cup plain breadcrumbs

2 tablespoons grated Parmesan cheese

INSTRUCTIONS

1. Preheat the oven to 400°F.
2. Shuck the oysters. Discard the flat top shell and pour the liquid into a medium saucepan. Leave the oyster in the shell, but make sure to cut the adductor muscle under the oyster so it's easy to remove later when it's time to eat. Place each oyster on an oyster dish or in rock salt (see Note below).
3. To the saucepan with the oyster liquid, add the butter and cream. Add the salt, pepper, and nutmeg, and bring just to a simmer, whisking often.
4. Divide the mixture between the 12 oysters, carefully pouring some into each. Finish by sprinkling the breadcrumbs and cheese over the top.
5. Bake for 15 minutes and serve immediately.

Note: If you don't have an oyster dish, fill a small baking dish with rock salt and nest the shells in that to keep them steady while they bake.

THE TEN BELLS

LONDON, ENGLAND, UK

In 1888, London was in a panic over a series of murders that were taking place in the city's East End. A serial killer was attacking prostitutes in London's Whitechapel district—cutting their throats and disemboweling the women in gruesome ways. Between August and November of that year, five women were murdered: Mary Ann Nichols, Annie Chapman, Elizabeth Stride, Catherine Eddowes, and Mary Jane Kelly. These victims collectively became known as "the canonical five." Another six were killed between November 1888 and 1891, but it's not definite that those are linked to the same man.

To this day, Jack the Ripper's identity isn't known. But those who want to learn more about the crimes can visit locations closely associated with the killings. First among all of them is the Ten Bells pub. Housed in the Spitalfields neighborhood, the Ten Bells has been a "historic East London boozer," as its website describes it, since the 1790s.

Both Annie Chapman and Mary Jane Kelly were regulars at the pub, and other women were seen there shortly before their murders. Annie Chapman had been married to John Chapman, and they had three children together. One was born crippled, and another died young. The couple coped with those events through drink and eventually separated. After John's death and the loss of her income from him, Annie earned her living—really, earned her drinking money—through handiwork and sometimes prostitution.

Annie Chapman, 1869

Less is known about Mary Kelly, who is believed to have been abandoned by her parents. Kelly, according to East London History, "plied her trade or had her 'pitch' outside the pub for many years." The night before she was murdered, one of the last people to see her alive had spent some time with her in the pub over drinks. It's assumed she was killed in her home probably soon after she left the pub that night.

There are also theories that the killer frequented the pub. "It has often been supposed that Jack the Ripper himself visited the pub," according to London's Jack the Ripper Tours, "either to fortify himself against the cold on his wanderings in the late night and early morning, or to find his unfortunate victims." The pub is only a short walk from the site of Flower & Dean Street—now erased by redevelopment but in 1888 a notorious slum that modern analytic techniques have suggested as the most likely place where the Ripper based himself in Whitechapel.

Today, Jack the Ripper is one of the world's most notorious murderers, and his misdeeds are some of the most persistent and mythologized crimes in history. Tours of the East End regularly take people to places associated with the murders. They also, more often than not, stumble across some unexplained phenomena on their journeys. The Ten Bells has more than its fair share of paranormal activity. Annie Chapman is believed to still haunt the pub, as does a mysterious man.

According to Jack the Ripper Tours, "In the late 1990s, staff living in the pub complained about alarming encounters they'd been having with a ghostly old man dressed in Victorian clothing. After awaking with an uneasy feeling in the middle of the night, they would turn over to find this phantom lying beside them in the bed, but as soon as they cried out, he disappeared."

SUNDAY ROAST WITH GRAVY

The British Sunday roast is a tradition that dates back to as early as the 1700s. People would place a large cut of meat in the oven before leaving for church and then add the vegetables when they got home for the last bit of cooking. Serve this roast with horseradish sauce, fresh peas, and Yorkshire pudding for a truly authentic experience.

Prep Time: 30 minutes | Cook Time: 90 minutes | Yield: 8 servings

FOR THE ROAST

- 1 (3-pound) beef roast
- 1 tablespoon salt, divided
- 1 teaspoon black pepper, divided
- 2 pounds assorted carrots and parsnips
- 3 pounds potatoes (such as Russet or Yukon Gold)
- 1/4 cup olive oil
- 3 cloves garlic, minced
- 1 1/2 tablespoons fresh or dried rosemary, chopped

FOR THE GRAVY

- 2 cups beef broth
- 1 tablespoon Worcestershire sauce
- 1 tablespoon cornstarch
- 1/2 teaspoon salt
- 1/4 teaspoon black pepper

PREPARE THE ROAST

1. Pat the roast dry with paper towels, then season with 2 teaspoons of the salt and 1/2 teaspoon of the pepper. Place the meat in a roasting pan. Let the roast sit at room temperature while you prepare the vegetables.
2. Wash and peel the carrots, parsnips, and potatoes. Chop them into roughly 2-inch pieces. In a large bowl, toss the vegetables in 3 tablespoons of the olive oil, the remaining 1 teaspoon salt, and remaining 1/2 teaspoon pepper.
3. Preheat the oven to 375°F.
4. In a small mixing bowl, combine the garlic, rosemary, and the remaining 1 tablespoon olive oil. Rub all over the roast, then arrange the vegetables around the beef.
5. Place the beef in the oven, and roast for 30 minutes to create a crust.
6. Lower the oven temperature to 275°F. Use a meat thermometer to check the roast's internal temperature after 40 minutes, but it may take an hour or more to get to doneness. This roast is best at medium-rare (125°F), but you can cook it slightly longer if you prefer. Remember, as the roast rests outside the oven, it will cook more.
7. When the roast is done cooking, remove it to a platter and arrange the vegetables around it, tenting with foil to keep it warm. Reserve the pan drippings.

PREPARE THE GRAVY

1. Add the pan drippings to a medium saucepan. Add the beef broth and Worcestershire, and bring to a boil.
2. In a small bowl, create as slurry with the cornstarch and a few tablespoons of the broth mixture, stirring until smooth, then slowly add that into the pan, whisking as you go.
3. Add the salt and pepper. Simmer for about 10 minutes, until thickened.
4. Adjust seasonings to taste, then serve alongside the roast.

HOTEL MONTE VISTA

FLAGSTAFF, ARIZONA, USA

You know the feeling—you walk into a historic hotel, and your Spidey-sense just goes off. You *know* there are more guests in the building than just the living ones. Many hotels would prefer not to talk about their resident spirits, maybe because the owners think it's bad for business, or maybe because they're trying not to scare people. But it's always more fun (to me, and if you're reading this book, probably to you, too) when a hotel embraces its spookiness.

The Hotel Monte Vista, in Flagstaff, Arizona, is definitely in the latter category of historic accommodations. The hotel is full of legends and history. It's also, they claim, full of ghosts.

The Monte Vista has an especially unique origin story. In the 1920s, with increasing tourism to the area, Flagstaff residents felt they needed a high-end accommodation to attract even more guests with deep pockets. Private citizens started a fundraising campaign, added to by novelist Zane Grey, and by June 1926 they had $200,000 to build the Hotel Monte Vista (about $5.8 million today). It officially opened for business on January 1, 1927. While the hotel was originally slated to be named the Community Hotel as a nod to its origins, that plan changed, and the hotel held a contest for a new name: the winner was a twelve-year-old kid who selected Monte Vista, according to the hotel's history.

In its early days, the hotel was home to a post office and to KFXY, a radio station run by Mary Costigan, the second woman to ever be granted a radio broadcasting license. Because the hotel opened during Prohibition, Monte Vista couldn't legally serve alcohol—so it opened up a "newspaper publishing house" that made its own booze and served cocktails on the sly. Local officials caught on in 1931 and shut down what's now the Cocktail Lounge until 1933, when Prohibition was repealed.

Underneath the Monte Vista is a network of tunnels that connected Flagstaff businesses underground. According to the hotel, more than just transportation took place there: "Opium dens, moonshine distilleries, gambling machines, and other relics have been discovered in depths of Flagstaff's underworld." It's also rumored that scenes from *Casablanca* were filmed at the hotel. Bing Crosby, Esther Williams, and Bob Hope have all stayed there.

But more than anything, the Monte Vista is famous for its ghosts. And according to what the hotel told me, there are a *lot* of them. "In 1970, three men robbed a nearby bank and during the robbery, a bank guard shot one of the men," according to Monte Vista representatives. "Despite their injured comrade, they decided to stop by the hotel lounge and have a drink to celebrate. The wounded man bled to death while enjoying his last drink. Since then, both patrons and staff have reported barstools and drinks that seem to move on their own."

Others report waking in the night and sensing the presence of two prostitutes who were allegedly murdered in room 306 in the early 1940s and thrown to the street below. An episode of *Unsolved Mysteries* featured the phantom rocking chair in room 305, which is sometimes seen rocking on its own, and sometimes seen with the ghost of an old woman sitting in it. Sounds of a baby crying have been heard in the basement, and visions of a gaily dancing couple have been seen in the Cocktail Lounge.

Even John Wayne claimed to have seen a ghost at the Monte Vista. One of the hotel's recurring ghostly visitors is a phantom bellboy, who is known to knock on doors, saying "room service," but disappearing before guests can open the door. They've also spotted him outside room 210. According to Monte Vista staff, "John Wayne experienced this ghost while he was a guest of the hotel. Mr. Wayne reported that the ghost seemed friendly, and that he did not feel threatened at all by its presence." But if John Wayne was scared of a ghost, well, that wouldn't be very John Wayne of him.

CHILE COLORADO

Chile Colorado is a robust stew full of spicy peppers that's a signature dish of Mexico's Sonoran region, just south of what are today Arizona and New Mexico. The dish came north with Mexican migrations when the territory was still part of the Central American country and has been served throughout Arizona for as long as anyone can remember. As Sonoran food historian Minerva Orduño Rincón wrote for *The Arizona Republic*, "The cuisine born here is a reflection of desert life and its flavors." Serve this stew with rice or tortillas.

Prep Time: 10 minutes, plus steeping time | Cook Time: 2 hours | Yield: 6 servings

INGREDIENTS

8 cups chicken broth, divided

8 assorted dried chiles, preferably a blend of ancho, guajillo, and pasilla, stemmed and seeded

2 pounds pork shoulder, cubed

1 teaspoon salt, plus more, to taste

1/2 teaspoon black pepper, plus more, to taste

2 tablespoons neutral cooking oil

1 medium white onion, diced

4 cloves garlic, minced

1 bay leaf

2 teaspoons dried oregano

1 teaspoon cumin

1 teaspoon smoked paprika

1 lime, sliced into wedges, optional

Fresh cilantro, chopped, optional

Sliced radishes, optional

INSTRUCTIONS

1. In a medium saucepan, bring 3 cups of the chicken broth to a boil, and add the peppers. Remove from the heat, cover, and let steep for 30 minutes. Blend the mixture in the pan using an immersion blender or transfer to a blender to puree. Set aside.
2. Season the pork all over with the salt and pepper. In a large stew pot or Dutch oven, heat the oil and brown the pork over medium-high heat, 2–3 minutes per side. Add the onion, garlic, bay leaf, oregano, cumin, and paprika. Cook for 1 more minute until the spices are fragrant.
3. Add the remaining 5 cups chicken broth. Simmer for 1 hour, then add the chile puree and cook for about 45 minutes more, until the sauce is a deep red. Season to taste with salt and pepper, then serve with limes, cilantro, and radishes on the side as optional toppings.

MEALS TO KILL FOR

There's nothing I love more than a themed celebration. Actually, I take that back. A creepy and delicious themed celebration is truly a dream come true—especially when I have a cold glass of Chardonnay in my hand.

A CHILLINGLY SPIRITED HOLIDAY

TO START:

Ardèche Chestnut Soup 113

MAINS:

Black Kuba 81
Baked Scrod 238
Schweinebraten 95

DESSERT AND DRINKS:

Buttered Beere 65
Poe Family Eggnog 170
Cranberry Cake 215
Molasses Cookies 159

A GHOSTLY PUB FEAST

TO START:

New Orleans Barbecue Shrimp 154

MAINS:

Irish Lamb Stew 68
Sunday Roast with Gravy 258
Colcannon 129

DESSERT AND DRINKS:

Buttered Beere 65
The Old Talbott Tavern Pie 18
Samuel Fraunces's Carrot Cake 167

APPARITIONS AND APPETIZERS

SAVORIES:

Bagna Cauda 36
Salt Cod–Stuffed Piquillo Peppers 49
Baked Ribs 202
Pork Rillettes 55

SWEETS:

Orange Valley Sponge Cake 44
Scottish Shortbread 88
Cherry Ice 41

DRINKS:

"Witches Brew" Rum Punch 109
The Marilyn 116
Golden Cadillac 141

DINNER WITH THE DEPARTED

TO START:

French Onion Soup 15
Mayfair Salad Dressing 151

MAINS:

Bryndzové Halušky 60
Penne alla Vodka 23
Meat Stew with Polenta and Egg 73

DESSERT AND DRINKS:

Tipsy Charlotte 10
Samuel Fraunces's Carrot Cake 167

THE INSTITUTIONAL TABLE

TO START:

Shrimp Wiggle 195

MAINS:

Corned Beef 199
Boston Baked Beans 218

DESSERT:

Cranberry Cake 215

THE "MOURNING AFTER" BRUNCH

SAVORIES:

Scotch Eggs with Strawberry-Serrano Sauce 175
Scrapple 191
Turney Kippen's Skilly 210
Crab Louie 162

SWEETS:

Jelly Omelet 104
Fat Rascal 246
Coffee Custard 250
Plum Doughnuts 124
Lemon Toast 101
Empress 1908 Elderflower Rose Gin Trifle 135

DRINKS:

Louis XV's Drinking Chocolate 76

A CHILLINGLY SPIRITED HOLIDAY

RECIPES BY COURSE

BIBLIOGRAPHY

CHAPTER 1

Paris Catacombs

"The Catacombs of Paris." *The London Journal* I, no. 6 (April 5, 1845): 82. https://books.google.co.jp/books?id=jHc-AQAAMAAJ&pg=PA82#v=onepage&q&f=false.

Willsher, Kim. "'Bodies Were Dropped Down Quarry Shafts': Secrets of Millions Buried in Paris Catacombs Come to Light." *The Guardian*, March 6, 2025. https://www.theguardian.com/world/2024/oct/19/bodies-quarry-shafts-millions-buried-paris-catacombs.

Shanghai Tunnels

Portland Ghosts. "The Shanghai Tunnels," December 5, 2024. https://portlandghosts.com/the-shanghai-tunnels/.

Saia, Jessica. "The Crazy SF History Behind the Term Shanghai-ed." The Bold Italic. Medium, November 7, 2014. https://thebolditalic.com/the-crazy-sf-history-behind-the-term-shanghai-ed-the-bold-italic-san-francisco-c25d6d95732e.

Web-Foot Cook Book. W. B. Ayer & Co, 1885. https://ia800107.us.archive.org/16/items/webfootcookbook00port/webfootcookbook00port.pdf.

The National Exchange Hotel

Jones, Anthony. Interview by author, telephone, March 2025.

Lyon, Mark. *Haunted Nevada City and Grass Valley*, Windwhistle Press, 2021.

The Old Talbott Tavern

Adams, Kirby. "'I Can't Explain What Is Going on Here.' Inside One of the Most Haunted Spots in Kentucky," *The Courier-Journal*, October 17, 2022, https://www.courier-journal.com/story/life/2022/10/17/old-talbott-tavern-history-inside-one-of-kentuckys-haunted-spots/69505806007/.

Brown, Alan. *Stories from the Haunted South*, University Press of Mississippi, 2004, 98.

Valley Inn Restaurant

New England Historical Society. "The 1673 Murder of Rebecca Cornell and the 'Good Fire,'" August 1, 2023. https://newenglandhistoricalsociety.com/1673-murder-rebecca-cornell-and-good-fire/.

La Cabotina

Agriturismo Le Girandole. "What to See in Triora, the Town of Witches," October 27, 2022. https://www.agriturismolegirandole.com/en/blog/liguria-villages/what-to-see-triora/.

Borghi Di Riviera. "Strigòra a Triora," March 29, 2019. https://www.borghidiriviera.it/en/events/strigora-a-triora/.

The Spaniards Inn

Farrant, David. "The Haunted Spaniards Inn." *The Human Touch Blog* (blog), December 28, 2007. https://davidfarrant.org/the-haunted-spaniards-inn/.

Myers, Daniel. "Stewet Beef." *Medieval Cookery* (blog), November 28, 2011. https://medievalcookery.com/recipes/display.html?stew1001.

Fenestrelle Fort

Lo Bello, Nino. "Italy Fortress Haunted—but the Ghost Is Friendly." *Chicago Tribune*, October 27, 1985. https://www.newspapers.com/image/388480124/?match=1&terms=fenestrelle.

The Morning Chronicle. "The Industrial Condition of Italy." October 19, 1852. https://drive.google.com/file/d/1kh30NLVFnYFI6Fu8xfVe6rx9SNEog_Ke/view.

Newby, Eric. "In the Cottian Alps." *The Observer*, June 11, 1967, sec. Time Off. https://www.newspapers.com/image/258884204/.

Rete Due Sicilie. "To Deny Fenestrelle, Historical Memory Is Attacked," July 9, 2013. https://www.retedue sicilie.it/per-negare-fenestrelle-si-colpisce-la-memoria-storica/.

Winchester Mystery House

San Jose Herald. "Cherry Ice," LXVIII, no. 102, April 28, 1900. https://cdnc.ucr.edu/?a=d&d=SJH19000428.2.132.

Trevelyan, Laura. "The Winchester Rifle–My Family's Part in Shaping the Wild West." *The Guardian*, October 15, 2016. https://www.theguardian.com/lifeandstyle/2016/oct/15/the-winchester-rifle-my-familys-part-in-shaping-the-wild-west.

Winchester Mystery House. "History," March 14, 2025. https://winchestermysteryhouse.com/history/.

Orange Valley

Cox, John. *Ghosts and Other Bermuda Tales*. Self-published, 2025.

Cave of Witches

Pablo S. Quiza. "Zugarramurdi." Accessed August 15, 2025. https://www.pablosquiza.com/zugarramurdi.

CHAPTER 2

Château de Brissac

Château de Brissac. "Histoire Du Château De Brissac," January 9, 2024. https://brissac.net/en/histoire/.

Château de Brissac. "The Castle," January 24, 2025. https://brissac.net/en/the-castle/.

Čachtice Castle

Bartosiewicz, Aleksandra. "Elisabeth Báthory–a True Story." *Przegląd Nauk Historycznych* 17, no. 3 (December 13, 2018): 105–06, 116. https://doi.org/10.18778/1644-857x.17.03.04.

Cawley, Laurence. "Cambridge University Academic's Quest to Clear Elizabeth Bathory's Name," May 28, 2024. https://www.bbc.com/news/uk-england-cambridgeshire-69057709.

Spike, Justin. "400 Years Later, Accounts of Hungarian 'Blood Countess' Remain Shrouded in Mystery and Controversy." AP News, October 30, 2024. https://apnews.com/article/blood-countess-legend-bathory-hungary-slovakia-e732847066ffe69f91812b57df61bf43.

The Red Lion

Miller, Max. "Tudor Buttered Beer." Tasting History, January 14, 2025. https://www.tastinghistory.com/recipes/butteredbeer.

Kyteler's Inn

Williams, Bernadette. "The Sorcery Trial of Alice Kyteler." *History Ireland* 2, no. 4 (1994): 20–24. http://www.jstor.org/stable/27724208.

Bran Castle

Bran Castle Official Website. "Count Dracula." accessed August 16, 2025. https://bran-castle.com/explore/count-dracula/.

Bran Castle Official Website. "Historical Chronology." Accessed September 30, 2025. https://www.bran-castle.com/en/cronologia-istorica/.

Palace of Versailles

Frost, Natasha. "The Scandalous Witch Hunt That Poisoned 17th-Century France." Atlas Obscura, October 5, 2017. https://www.atlasobscura.com/articles/affair-of-the-poisons-france-witch-hunt-occult.

History. "Did Marie-Antoinette Really Say 'Let Them Eat Cake'?," July 14, 2025. https://www.history.com/articles/did-marie-antoinette-really-say-let-them-eat-cake.

Palace of Versailles. "The Ghosts of Trianon," May 2, 2023. https://en.chateauversailles.fr/discover/history/key-dates/ghosts-trianon#back-to-paris.

Palace of Versailles. "Hot Chocolate in Versailles," August 23, 2018. https://en.chateauversailles.fr/discover/history/key-dates/hot-chocolate-versailles.

Houska Castle

CzechTourism. "Explore Houska Castle: Czechia's Mysterious Gateway to Hell." VisitCzechia, October 23, 2025. https://www.visitczechia.com/en-us/things-to-do/places/landmarks/castles-and-ruins/c-houska-castle.

Hrad Houska. "Hrad Houska - Brána Do Pekel," May 15, 2025. https://hradhouska.cz/#historie.

Miller, Nick. "The Real Truth Behind Houska Castle." Discovery UK, December 5, 2022. https://www.discoveryuk.com/mysteries/the-real-truth-behind-houska-castle/.

Morton, Caitlin, and Alex Erdekian. "19 Haunted Castles Around the World That You Can Visit." *Condé Nast Traveler*, August 14, 2025. https://www.cntraveler.com/gallery/haunted-castles-around-the-world.

Schimanski, Annette. "Houska in the Czech Republic." Travel Book, April 4, 2022. https://www.travelbook.de/mystery/burg-houska-tschechien.

Tower of London

Farris, Charles. "Charles II and the Discovery of the 'Princes in the Tower' in 1674." *Historic Royal Palaces* (blog), July 17, 2024. https://www.hrp.org.uk/blog/charles-ii-and-the-discovery-of-the-princes-in-the-tower-in-1674/#gs.mbgi4c.

Gregory, Alden. "The Jewel House Keeper's Ghost: A Spectral Bear at the Tower of London." *Historic Royal Palaces* (blog), October 31, 2024. https://www.hrp.org.uk/blog/the-jewel-house-keepers-ghost/#gs.mbeatn.

Historic Royal Palaces. "The Royal Menagerie at the Tower of London." Accessed October 30, 2025. https://www.hrp.org.uk/tower-of-london/history-and-stories/the-tower-of-london-menagerie/#gs.mbfxqw.

Historic Royal Palaces. "The Story of the Tower of London—Legends and Ghosts." Accessed October 30, 2025. https://www.hrp.org.uk/tower-of-london/history-and-stories/the-story-of-the-tower-of-london/#gs.mbfzuc.

Historic Royal Palaces. "The Tower of London as a Prison—Anne Askew." Accessed October 30, 2025. https://www.hrp.org.uk/tower-of-london/history-and-stories/tower-of-london-prison/#gs.mbg0ld.

Newcott, Bill. "The Living Tower of London." Originally published in *National Geographic*, 1993. https://billnewcott.com/the-tower-of-london.

Edinburgh Castle

Brenkley, Dorothy. "The Gruesome Story of Janet Douglas." *The Bowes Museum Blog*, October 27, 2022. https://thebowesmuseum.org.uk/the-gruesome-story-of-janet-douglas/.

Caldwell, David H. "Edinburgh Castle Under Siege." Historic Environment Scotland Archives and Research. Historic Environment Scotland, November 18, 2019. https://www.historicenvironment.scot/archives-and-research/publications/publication/?publicationid=d6e83199-b05f-4198-a4db-ab090113f99a.

Edinburgh Castle. "History of the Castle." Accessed August 17, 2025. https://www.edinburghcastle.scot/the-castle/history/.

CHAPTER 3

Hinterkaifeck Farm

Grundhauser, Eric. "Hinterkaifeck Memorial." Atlas Obscura, October 27, 2014. https://www.atlasobscura.com/places/hinterkaifeck-memorial.

Vatomsky, Sonya. "The Chilling Story of the Hinterkaifeck Killings, Germany's Most Famous Unsolved Crime." *Mental Floss*, July 24, 2023. https://www.mentalfloss.com/crime/chilling-story-hinterkaifeck-killings-germanys-most-famous-unsolved-crime.

H. H. Holmes Murder Castle

Bielski, Ursula. "Chicago's Murder Castle and the Ghosts of Englewood." *American Ghost Walks* (blog), April 25, 2022. https://www.americanghostwalks.com/articles/king-castle-for-a-haunted-land-chicago-s-murder-ca.

The Chicago Chronicle. "Murder His Mania." May 3, 1896.

Harrington, Adam. "Chicago Hauntings: The Story of H.H. Holmes' Murder Castle, and Sightings in the Basement of the Englewood Post Office Standing in Its Place." CBS News, July 29, 2025. https://www.cbsnews.com/chicago/news/chicago-hauntings-h-h-holmes-murder-castle-post-office/.

Landis, Jacob F. *The World's Fair Recipe Book*, 1893. https://hdl.handle.net/2027/loc.ark:/13960/t12n5mr0f.

Solly, Meilan. "The Enduring Mystery of H.H. Holmes, America'S 'First' Serial Killer." *Smithsonian Magazine*, August 16, 2023. https://www.smithsonianmag.com/smart-news/enduring-mystery-hh-holmes-americas-first-serial-killer-180977646/.

Omni Mount Washington Resort

The United Opinion. "His Throat Cut: Bank Cashier Cruelly Murdered at His Post." April 23, 1897. https://www.newspapers.com/article/the-united-opinion/89269886/.

Rose Hall

Bantock, Jack. "A Murderous Ghost Haunted an Exclusive Jamaican Resort for Centuries. But Could She Survive a Paranormal Investigation?" CNN, August 7, 2024. https://edition.cnn.com/travel/white-witch-rose-hall-jamaica-golf-spc.

De Lisser, Herbert G. *The White Witch of Rosehall. Internet Archive*. Macmillan Caribbean, 1982. https://archive.org/details/whitewitchofrose0000deli/page/78/mode/1up.

Red Inn

Boyer, Claude. "Red Inn." *Abbe Photo* (blog), July 24, 2023. https://abbe.photo/en/lauberge-rouge/.

Chevillard, Thibaut. "Histoires De Procès: La Légende De L'auberge Rouge Et De Ses 53 Meurtres." *20 Minutes*, August 24, 2017. https://www.20minutes.fr/societe/2116075-20170824-histoires-proces-legende-auberge-rouge-53-meurtres.

Joanou, Laurie. "'L'Auberge Rouge' À Peyrebeille." *Le Progrès*, August 10, 2011. https://www.leprogres.fr/actualite/2011/08/10/l-auberge-rouge-a-peyrebeille.

Bobby Mackey's Music World

Elbein, Asher. "Honky-Tonk Haints." *The Bitter Southerner*. Accessed October 16, 2023. https://bittersoutherner.com/honky-tonk-haints.

Reeder, Pat. "The Third Eye." *The Skeptic* 7(12), December 1993. http://www.ntskeptics.org/1993/1993december/december1993.htm.

Double Eagle Restaurant

Cook, Mike. "The Double Eagle Celebrates 50th Anniversary, Almost 175 Years of Mesilla History, Lore." *Las Cruces Bulletin*, August 17, 2023. https://www.lascrucesbulletin.com/stories/the-double-eagle-celebrates-50th-anniversary-almost-175-years-of-mesilla-history-lore,54139.

Double Eagle. "Armando and Inez—Ghosts," accessed August 16, 2025. https://www.doubleeagleonline.com/ghosts-read-more.

Hare and Hounds Pub

Whitmore, Warren. "Isle of Wight Villains: The Grim Tale of Michal Morey–The Murderous Woodcutter." *Island Echo*, September 4, 2022. https://islandecho.co.uk/the-grim-tale-of-michal-morey-the-murderous-woodcutter/.

Wightlink. "The Dark Side of the Wight," October 10, 2025. https://www.wightlink.co.uk/blog/the-dark-side-of-the-wight.

Wightonline. (archived), http://www.wightonline.co.uk/wfiles/wfiles_pages/michalmorey.html#selection-57.0-57.211.

Mary Gallagher Corner

Fleming, Arwen Jean. "David Marvin's Griffintown: An Archival Exploration of a Ghosted Neighbourhood." MA Thesis, Concordia University, 2015. https://spectrum.library.concordia.ca/id/eprint/980525/1/Fleming_MA_F2015.pdf.

Hustak, Alan. *The Ghost of Griffintown*. PDF. Redlader Publishing, 2005. https://www.mes-racines.ca/fichiers/Villes%20et%20villages/Qu%E9bec/06%20-%20Montr%E9al%20AH/Montr%E9al%20par%20ses%20villes,%20quartiers%20et%20arrondissements/Griffintown/The%20Ghost%20of%20Griffintown/The%20Ghost%20of%20Griffintown.pdf.

CHAPTER 4

Fairmont Empress Hotel

Knox, Jack. "Empress Reigns on Haunted-hotel List Thanks to Lizzie the Chambermaid—among Others." *Times Colonist*, January 18, 2023. https://www.timescolonist.com/local-news/jack-knox-empress-reigns-on-haunted-hotel-list-thanks-to-lizzie-the-chambermaid-mdash-among-others-6393028.

The Washington Post. "Like a Good Scare? Here Are Five Haunted Hotels With Stories Fit for True-Crime Files." October 26, 2018. https://www.washingtonpost.com/lifestyle/travel/like-a-good-scare-here-are-five-haunted-hotels-with-stories-fit-for-true-crime-files/2018/10/25/ddd4e70e-d3cb-11e8-b2d2-f397227b43f0_story.html.

Poor Red's Bar-B-Q

Beard, Jerrie. "In History: El Dorado County's Romeo and Juliet." *Style Magazine*, January 27, 2016. https://www.stylemg.com/2016/01/27/100480/in-history-el-dorado-countys-romeo-and-juliet.

Noble, Doug. "Criminal Annals, Part 72–Lynchings at Drytown and Mud Springs." *Doug Steps Out* (blog), May 7, 2020. https://www.dougstepsout.com/2020/05/07/criminal-annals-part-72-lynchings-at-drytown-and-mud-springs/.

Five Fishermen Restaurant

Bartlett, James T. "A Snapshot of the Many and Various Criminals Aboard the Titanic." CrimeReads, April 13, 2023. https://crimereads.com/a-snapshot-of-the-many-and-various-criminals-aboard-the-titanic.

Bundale, Brett. "The Five Fishermen: Halifax Eatery Serves up Fine Seafood and the Odd Apparition." CTVNews, November 29, 2024. https://www.ctvnews.ca/lifestyle/article/the-five-fishermen-halifax-eatery-serves-up-fine-seafood-and-the-odd-apparition/.

Van Beck, Todd. "Call to Duty: The Funeral Director's Response to the Titanic Disaster–1912." *Todd Van Beck* (blog), June 18, 2017. https://www.toddvanbeck.com/call-to-duty-the-funeral-directors-response-to-the-titanic-disaster-1912.

Lemp Mansion

Dickey, Colin. *Ghostland: An American History in Haunted Places*. Viking, 2016.

Cornell, Adrienne. "Lemp Shades." *St. Louis Post-Dispatch*, October 30, 1994. https://www.newspapers.com/image-view/142353100/.

Weiser-Alexander, Kathy. "The Haunted Lemp Mansion in St. Louis." Legends of America. Accessed November 20, 2025. https://www.legendsofamerica.com/mo-lempmansion/.

The Court of Two Sisters

The Cincinnati Post. "TV Beauty Slain, Police Await Laboratory Tests." December 1, 1952. https://www.newspapers.com/image-view/762751709/.

The Daily Clintonian. "James L. Cooper Acquitted by Criminal Jury." January 22, 1954. https://www.newspapers.com/image-view/133586381/

Grill House Restaurant

The Grill House. "The Grill House." Accessed August 16, 2025. https://grillhouse.net/grillhouse/.

Michigan Beverage Journal. "Jack Lives Here," PDF. November 2008. https://grillhouse.net/wp-content/uploads/2011/07/MLBA-ARTICLE-2008.pdf.

Wood, Barry D. "Dangerous Life of Michigan Lumberjacks." *Barry D. Wood* (blog), August 2, 2020. https://econbarry.com/2020/08/02/dangerous-life-of-michigan-lumberjacks/.

***The* Delta King**

Anderson, Scott Thomas. "The Startling Real-life Crimes That Inspired Sacramento's 'Haunted River' Lore." *Sacramento News & Review*, October 28, 2022. https://sacramento.newsreview.com/2022/10/28/the-startling-real-life-crimes-that-inspired-sacramentos-haunted-river-lore/.

CBS News. "Sacramento's Most Haunted Places," October 22, 2012. https://www.cbsnews.com/sacramento/news/sacramentos-most-haunted-places/.

Delta King. "Upcoming Events." Accessed August 16, 2025. https://www.deltaking.com/upcoming-events.

The Stockton Record. "Stockton-Made Million Dollar Palatial Steamers Dedicated." May 20, 1927. https://www.newspapers.com/image-view/843278110/.

Fraunces Tavern

Brosnan, Erica. "Manhattan Tavern Embraces Revolutionary Past and Ghostly Encounters." Spectrum News NY1, October 31, 2024. https://ny1.com/nyc/all-boroughs/human-interest/2024/10/31/manhattan-tavern-embraces-revolutionary-past-and-ghostly-encounters.

Fraunces Tavern Museum. "History." Accessed August 16, 2025. https://www.frauncestavernmuseum.org/history.

The Horse You Came In On Saloon

Flynn, Katherine. "Baltimore's in on Saloon." National Trust for Historic Preservation, September 3, 2015. https://savingplaces.org/stories/historic-bars-baltimores-the-horse-you-came-in-on-saloon.

Franciotti, Jennifer. "244-year-old Haunted Baltimore Bar Has Workers Talking to Ghosts." WBAL, October 31, 2019. https://www.wbaltv.com/article/haunted-horse-you-came-in-on/29655771.

University of Mary Washington Library Guide. "Great Lives 2024: Edgar Allan Poe." March 14, 2024. https://library.umw.edu/c.php?g=1372438&p=10144382.

Finn's Irish Restaurant & Tavern

Ferrie, Jon. Interview by author, May 2025.

The Red Onion Saloon

Munson, Melinda. "Skagway Staff Befriend, Placate Ghosts: Three Local Businesses That Coexist With Their Specters." *The Skagway News*, May 12, 2023. https://skagwaynews.com/2023/05/12/skagway-staff-befriend-placate-ghosts-three-local-businesses-that-coexist-with-their-specters/.

The Cuban Club

The Cuban Club. "History." Accessed November 20, 2025. https://cubanclubybor.com/history/.

Frethem, Deborah. *Haunted Ybor City*. The History Press, 2014.

U.S. National Park Service. "Ybor City Historic District Tampa FL." Accessed November 20, 2025. https://www.nps.gov/places/ybor-city-historic-district-tampa-fl.htm.

CHAPTER 5

Pennhurst Asylum

Downey, Dennis B. "Remembering 'Suffer the Little Children' and Pennhurst's Problematic History." *The Philadelphia Inquirer*, June 22, 2018. https://www.inquirer.com/philly/opinion/commentary/pennhurst-mental-health-pennsylvania-disabilities-20180622.html.

Gutman, Abraham. "Pennhurst: A Timeline of the True Horror Behind the Infamous Haunted House Site." *The Philadelphia Inquirer*, October 25, 2022. https://www.inquirer.com/history/pennhurst-asylum-history-haunted-house-20221025.html.

Law Notes. PDF. Vol. XXII. Edward Thompson Company, 1919. https://books.google.com/books?id=unkqAAAAYAAJ&q.

North Head Quarantine Station

Minns, Mel. Interview by author, April 25, 2025

Randolph County Asylum/Infirmary

Fitzgibbon, Paul V. "Infirmary Invalid Becomes Maker of Exquisite Fancy Work." *The Star Press*. June 17, 1923. https://www.newspapers.com/image-view/251362014/.

Journey Indiana. "If These Walls Could Talk," October 26, 2022. https://www.youtube.com/watch?v=zKjLKJQBjP0.

Muncie Evening Press. "Youngsters Getting Busy at Winchester." November 23, 1911. https://www.newspapers.com/image-view/249323381/.

Official Randolph County Asylum/Infirmary. "Randolph County Historical Timeline," November 13, 2023. https://hauntedrandolphcounty.com/history/.

Shaw, Bill. "Their Refuge, Their Strength." *The Indianapolis News*, March 31, 1997. https://www.newspapers.com/image-view/313471656/.

The Times-Gazette. "Four Recommendations Made By Welfare Department For Randolph County Infirmary." February 6, 1940, Union City edition. https://www.newspapers.com/image-view/654814717/.

Brushy Mountain State Penitentiary

Schept, Judah. *Coal, Cages, Crisis: The Rise of the Prison Economy in Central Appalachia*. NYU Press, 2022.

The Tennessean. "Hazards Found in State Prison." November 4, 1969. https://www.newspapers.com/article/the-tennessean/174428069/.

Thornton, Mary. "Racial Tensions Fuel the Hell in Brushy Mountain Penitentiary." *The Washington Post*, March 4, 1982. https://www.washingtonpost.com/archive/politics/1982/03/05/racial-tensions-fuel-the-hell-in-brushy-mountain-penitentiary/66d787aa-7ac0-4305-8123-84d0a9a76f77/.

Historic SDG Jail

The Freeholder. "News of the Courts." September 8, 1899. https://www.newspapers.com/image-view/1059743954/.

Historic SDG Jail. "Our History." Accessed November 20, 2025. https://www.historicsdgjail.com/our-history.

Trans-Allegheny Lunatic Asylum

Armentrout, Charles R. "Cows On Mental Hospital Farm Are Better Off Than Inmates." *Hinton Daily News*. January 28, 1949. https://www.newspapers.com/image/667555846/.

Barnes, Jim. "In West Virginia, a moving, respectful tour of the Trans-Allegheny Lunatic Asylum." *The Washington Post*. May 25, 2018.

Beckley Post-Herald. "Police Probe Strangling of Weston Patient," May 29, 1963. https://www.newspapers.com/image-view/15830411/.

Guiley, Rosemary Ellen. *The Big Book of West Virginia Ghost Stories*. Stackpole Books, 2014.

Jacks, Kim. "Weston State Hospital." Unpublished master's thesis, West Virginia University. 2008. https://researchrepository.wvu.edu/cgi/viewcontent.cgi?article=1860&context=etd.

Racer, Theresa. "1877 Murder at the Trans-Allegheny Lunatic Asylum." *Theresa's Haunted History of the Tri-State* (blog), October 29, 2017. https://theresashauntedhistoryofthetri-state.blogspot.com/2017/10/1877-murder-at-trans-allegheny-lunatic.html.

Raleigh Register. "Needs at Weston State Hospital Outlined by Junior Clubwomen." November 17, 1961. https://www.newspapers.com/article/the-raleigh-register/171836022/.

Stuhler, Linda S. "Thomas Story Kirkbride 1809–1883—Physician, Psychiatrist and Developer of the Kirkbride Plan." *Social Welfare History Project*. Accessed August 27, 2023. https://socialwelfare.library.vcu.edu/organizations/state-institutions/kirkbride-thomas-story/.

The Washington Post. "In West Virginia, a Moving, Respectful Tour of the Trans-Alleghany Lunatic Asylum." May 25, 2018. https://www.washingtonpost.com/lifestyle/travel/in-west-virginia-a-moving-respectful-tour-of-the-trans-allegheny-lunatic-asylum/2018/05/24/03d476e6-5937-11e8-858f-12becb4d6067_story.html.

The Liberty Hotel

Arnold, David. "Locking Up Charles' Street Jail Colorful Past." *The Boston Globe*, June 18, 1991. https://www.newspapers.com/image-view/439731002.

The Boston Globe. "Militants Think Their Jail Treatment 'Lovely.'" February 27, 1919. https://www.newspapers.com/image-view/430737901.

Iyer, Neil. "The Charles Street Jail." *The West End Museum* (blog), March 20, 2025. https://thewestendmuseum.org/history/era/west-boston/the-charles-street-jail.

The Liberty Hotel. "Liberty Hotel," August 16, 2025. https://libertyhotel.com/.

Cresson Sanitorium

Cresson TB Sanatorium Remembered. "1950's History of Cresson Sanatorium," August 16, 2025. http://www.feltondesignanddata.com/cressontbsanatoriumremembered/id24.html.

Felton, Chuck. "Felton: Day 1." Cresson TB Sanatorium Remembered, August 16, 2025. http://www.feltondesignanddata.com/cressontbsanatoriumremembered/id16.html.

Goldberg, Debbie. "John du Pont Found Guilty, Mentally Ill." *The Washington Post.* February 26, 1997. https://www.washingtonpost.com/wp-srv/local/longterm/aron/dupont022697.htm.

Perez, Thomas E., and David J. Hickton. "Re: Investigation of the State Correctional Institution at Cresson and Notice of Expanded Investigation." U.S. Department of Justice. May 31, 2013. https://www.justice.gov/sites/default/files/crt/legacy/2013/06/03/cresson_findings_5-31-13.pdf.

Solomon, David, and Paul Ruggieri. "Cresson: Remembering Life at the San." WQED. Aired November 21, 2011. https://www.wqed.org/tv/watch/experience/cresson-remembering-life-san.

Malvern Manor

Estep, Richard. *The Devil's Coming To Get Me: The Haunting of Malvern Manor.* CreateSpace, 2018.

Kauffman, Clark. "Safety violations prompt closure of care facility." *The Des Moines Register.* March 30, 2005. https://www.newspapers.com/image/128391298/.

The Malvern Leader. "Editorials." December 6, 1956. https://www.newspapers.com/image-view/182282/.

The Malvern Leader. "We Are Moving!" May 4, 1939. https://www.newspapers.com/article/the-malvern-leader/164528364/.

The Paranormal Perimeter. "Malvern Manor," accessed November 27, 2023. https://www.paraperim-eventide.com/malvern-manor.

Poveglia

Bone, James. "'World's Most Haunted Island' to Be Opened to Public." *The Times*, May 13, 2014. https://www.thetimes.com/travel/destinations/europe-travel/italy/worlds-most-haunted-island-to-be-opened-to-public-mv5lpcnqtw8.

Griggs, Mary Beth. "Lease a Haunted Venetian Island for 99 Years." *Smithsonian Magazine*, April 17, 2014. https://www.smithsonianmag.com/smart-news/lease-haunted-venetian-island-99-years-180951144/.

The Guardian. "How Much? Haunted Island Near Venice Lido Sells for €513,000." March 4, 2018. https://www.theguardian.com/world/2014/may/13/haunted-island-poveglia-venice-sells.

L'Italo-Americano. "Poveglia." Accessed August 16, 2025, https://italoamericano.org/poveglia/.

Richardson, Nigel. "Treasured Island: How Venetians Are Saving Poveglia." *The Telegraph*, December 19, 2015. https://s.telegraph.co.uk/graphics/projects/venice-poveglia/index.html.

CHAPTER 6

Oiran Buchi

The Sengoku Archives. "Sengoku Hauntings: Oiran-buchi." July 3, 2021, accessed August 16, 2025, https://thesengokuarchives.com/2021/07/03/sengoku-hauntings-oiran-buchi/.

Omni Parker House

Wilson, Susan. *Heaven, by Hotel Standards*. Omni Parker House, 2014.

Cortijo de Fraile

Callejón, Diego. "El Auténtico Asesinato Que Inspiró 'Bodas De Sangre' De García Lorca." *Ideal*, January 18, 2021. https://www.ideal.es/almeria/provincia-almeria/autentico-crimen-nijar-inspiro-bodas-sangre-garcia-lorca-20210117121711-nt.html#&ref=https://www.ideal.es/almeria/provincia-almeria/autentico-crimen-nijar-inspiro-bodas-sangre-garcia-lorca-20210117121711-nt.html&ref=https://www.google.com/.

Carvajal, Doreen. "Chasing the Spirit of a Fractured Spain Through García Lorca." *The New York Times*, October 24, 2017. https://www.nytimes.com/2017/10/24/travel/andalusia-federico-garcia-lorca-spain.html.

Leeds General Hospital

Andrew, Laura. "Ghostly Encounters That Happened in Leeds From Eerie Noises to a Ghoul in a Ballgown." *Yorkshire Evening Post*, June 23, 2023. https://www.yorkshireeveningpost.co.uk/news/people/ghostly-encounters-that-happened-in-leeds-from-eerie-noises-to-a-ghoul-in-a-ballgown-4192616.

York Museums Trust. "Prisoner Stories: Mary Bateman." Accessed August 16, 2025. https://www.yorkmuseumstrust.org.uk/blog/prisoner-stories-mary-bateman/.

Hotel St. Francis

The Bar Association of San Francisco. "The Many Trials of Fatty Arbuckle," January 24, 2019. https://www.sfbar.org/blog/sfam-the-many-trials-of-fatty-arbuckle/.

Sheerin, Jude. "'Fatty' Arbuckle and Hollywood's First Scandal." BBC News, September 4, 2011. https://www.bbc.com/news/magazine-14640719.

Oyster Bay Bar & Casino

Deadwood Chamber of Commerce. "History Timeline." Deadwood. Accessed August 16, 2025. https://www.deadwood.com/history/history-timeline.

Isa, Mari. "The Great Oyster Craze: Why 19th Century Americans Loved Oysters." *MSU Campus Archaeology Program* (blog), December 17, 2021. https://campusarch.msu.edu/?p=4962.

Where In the World Is Joe Lee. "Real Ghost Story About the Historic Fairmont Hotel in Deadwood, SD," December 11, 2016. https://www.youtube.com/watch?v=W1pJEQVM2rk.

The Ten Bells

Jones, Richard. "Interesting Facts About the Ten Bells Pub." Jack the Ripper Tour, May 22, 2025. https://thejacktherippertour.com/blog/interesting-facts-about-ten-bells/.

Jones, Richard. "The Ten Bells Pub." Jack the Ripper Tour, August 16, 2025. https://www.jack-the-ripper-tour.com/locations/ten-bells-pub/.

Oakley, Malcolm. "The Ten Bells: A Historic East End Pub With a Modern Twist." *East London History* (blog), March 3, 2024. https://www.eastlondonhistory.co.uk/historic-east-end-pubs-ten-bells/.

The Ten Bells. "The Ten Bells," August 16, 2025. https://tenbells.com/.

Hotel Monte Vista

Hotel Monte Vista. "About—Famous Guests." Accessed August 16, 2025. https://hotelmontevista.com/about/#fam.

Hotel Monte Vista. "The Hotel Monte Vista's Permanent Guests." Unpublished fact sheet, last modified June 17, 2025. Google Docs file.

Rincón, Minerva Orduño. "Chef Minerva Orduño Rincón Is Here to Teach You How to Cook Sonoran-style Mexican Food." *The Arizona Republic*, October 8, 2021. https://www.azcentral.com/story/entertainment/dining/2021/10/07/what-is-sonoran-cuisine-recipe-chile-colorado/5908355001/.

ABOUT THE AUTHOR

Amy Bruni is a professional paranormal investigator, author, podcaster, and TV host. In 2007 she began appearing on *Ghost Hunters*, one of the longest-running and highest-rated paranormal television shows. Now, she's the co-star and executive producer of The Travel Channel's *Kindred Spirits* and host of the true crime podcast *Haunted Road*. Amy is the owner of Strange Escapes, a company offering paranormal excursions to some of America's most notoriously haunted destinations. She is the author of *Life with the Afterlife*, and currently resides in Newport, Rhode Island.

ACKNOWLEDGMENTS

Thank you to everyone who worked on *Food to Die For*—you all understood my deliciously morbid vision, and thanks to that (and the book's subsequent success), we now have *Cuisine to Kill For.*

Thank you to the entire team at Harper Celebrate, particularly Danielle Peterson, Michael Aulisio, and Kara Mannix. You are all an absolute joy to work with, and I feel fortunate to be able to have done so for years now.

My manager, Bill Stankey, for continuing to help me think of new and inventive ways to parlay my love of all things spooky into creative projects. I would not be where I am without you.

Julie Tremaine, my longtime writing partner, friend, and fellow Disney extraordinaire. Sometimes I'm convinced that you know my voice better than I do, and I'm not sure that bodes well for you. Sorry. And sorry you had to cook the scrapple.

Courtney Block, for using her librarian superpowers to pull through some amazing last-minute research for us.

To my longtime partner, Jimmy, and our daughter, Charlotte. You've both been extraordinarily patient and kind, even when I fed you things like Shrimp Wiggle (though Charlotte, I did see you try to feed it our cats, Harry and Fern). Harry and Fern also deserve a shout-out because there is nothing they love more than watching me cook—and boy, did recipe testing for this book give them days of enjoyment, and possibly confusion.

PHOTO CREDITS

Cover photos, all food photography, and photos on pages iii, ix, xii, 50, 90, 130, 184, 228, and 266: Emily Dorio

Page x *Elizabeth Báthory* {{PD-US}} / Wikimedia Commons
Page 3 *Catacombs of Paris* dirk94025 / Adobe Stock
Page 4 *Engraving* Beeldbewerking / iStock
Page 8 *Shanghai Tunnels* Historic Collection / Alamy
Page 12 *National Hotel* Tadd and Debbie Ottman / Wikimedia Commons
Page 13 *National Hotel 1894* {{PD-US}} / Wikimedia Commons
Page 16 *Old Talbott Tavern* {{PD-US}} / New York Public Library
Page 20 *Valley Inn* {{PD-US}} / HathiTrust
Page 24 *Triora* Fondo Paolo Monti / Wikimedia Commons
Page 25 *Street in Triora* dragoncello / AdobeStock
Page 30 *Spaniards Inn* Nigel Harris / iStock
Page 31 *Highwayman* duncan1890 / iStock
Page 34 *Fenestrelle Fort* FotoGablitz / iStock
Page 38 *Winchester House* Ben Franske / Wikimedia Commons
Page 42 *Wreck of the Sea Venture* The Library of Congress / Internet Archive
Page 43 *Stamp* {{PD-US}} / Wikimedia Commons
Page 46 *Zugarramurdi Caves* marktucan / iStock
Page 47 *1991-Zugarramurdi* Ttipi-Ttapa / Wikimedia Commons
Page 53 *Château de Brissac* Jonah Mucchiutti / Adobe Stock
Page 54 *Inside Château Brissac* © Sergi Reboredo. All rights reserved 2025 / Bridgeman Images
Page 58 *Čachtice Castle* Richard / Adobe Stock
Page 62 *Red Lion Inn* Jhsteel / Wikimedia Commons
Page 63 *Henry V* GeorgiosArt / iStock
Page 66 *Kyteler's Inn* peterspiro / iStock
Page 70 *Bran Castle* sichimsergiu / Adobe Stock
Page 71 *Torture Machine* Fotokon / Adobe Stock
Page 74 *Versailles Castle* Sergii Figurnyi / Adobe Stock
Page 75 *Execution of Marie Antoinette* {{PD-US}} / Wikimedia Commons
Page 78 *Castle Houska* dtatiana / Adobe Stock
Page 79 *Inside Houska* Tadehruska / Wikimedia Commons
Page 82 *Tower of London* daliu / Adobe Stock
Page 86 *Edinburgh Castle* nielvdw / Adobe Stock
Page 93 *Hinterkaifeck* {{PD-US}} / Wikimedia Commons
Page 94 *Hinterkaifeck Memorial* Andreas Keller / Wikimedia Commons
Page 98 *H. H. Holmes Castle* {{PD-US}} / Wikimedia Commons
Page 99 *H. H. Holmes* {{PD-US}} / Wikimedia Commons
Page 102 *Mount Washington Hotel* Wangkun Jia / Shutterstock
Page 103 *Lobby Portraits* courtesy of Amy Bruni
Page 103 *Banker Joseph Stickney* {{PD-US}} / Oak Park Vindicator / Newspaper Archive
Page 106 *Rose Hall* Urban Walnut / Wikimedia Commons
Page 107 *Annee Palmer Tomb* Urban Walnut / Wikimedia Commons
Page 110 *Red Inn* {{PD-France}} / Wikimedia Commons
Page 111 *Red Inn Interior* {{PD-France}} / Wikimedia Commons
Page 114 *Bobby Mackey's* Nicolas Henderson / Wikimedia Commons
Page 115 *Pearl Bryan* {{PD-US}} / Wikimedia Commons
Page 118 *Double Eagle Restaurant* K.D. Leperi / Alamy
Page 119 *Old Mesilla* Alyson Hurt / Flickr
Page 122 *Hare and Hounds* © Chris Allen / Geograph
Page 126 *Griffintown 1896* {{PD-US}} / Wikimedia Commons
Page 133 *Fairmont Empress* Dllu / Wikimedia Commons
Page 134 *Francis Rattenbury* {{PD-US}} / Wikimedia Commons
Page 138 *Poor Red's* David Prasad / Flickr
Page 139 *Matchbook* Gravetime / Internet Archive
Page 142 *The Five Fishermen* Lee Brown / Alamy
Page 148 *Lemp Mansion* Paul Sableman / Wikimedia Commons
Page 149 *William J. Lemp* {{PD-US}} / Wikimedia Commons
Page 152 *Court of the Two Sisters* Fotoluminate LLC - stock.adobe.com
Page 153 *Mardi Gras 1963* {{PD-US}} / Wikimedia Commons
Page 156 *Logging* Library of Congress, Prints & Photographs Division, Detroit Publishing Company Collection
Page 160 *Delta King* © Justin Smith / Wikimedia Commons, CC-By-SA-3.0
Page 161 *River Lines Flyer* {{PD-US}} / Wikimedia Commons
Page 164 *Fraunces Tavern* Stuart Monk - stock.adobe.com
Page 165 *Washington Taking Leave* {{PD-US}} / Nathaniel Currier / The Metropolitan Museum of Art
Page 168 *The Horse You Came In On Saloon* jonbilous - stock.adobe.com
Page 169 *Edgar Allan Poe* {{PD-US}} / Wikimedia Commons
Page 172 *Baker-Peters-Rogers House* Tom Bosse / HMbd.org
Page 176 *Red Onion Saloon* Debbie Ann Powell / iStock
Page 177 *Soapy Smith* {{PD-US}} / Wikimedia Commons
Page 180 *Cuban Club* Ebyabe / Wikimedia Commons
Page 187 *Cresson Sanatorium* Sherman Cahal / Adobe Stock
Page 188 *Grace Chapel Interior* Sherman Cahal / Adobe Stock
Page 189 *Grace Chapel* Sherman Cahal / Adobe Stock
Page 192 *Haunted Pennhurst School* AmityPhotos / Alamy
Page 193 *Aerial view of Pennhurst* {{PD-US}} / Wikimedia Commons
Page 196 *Q Station* Regi51 / Wikimedia Commons
Page 200 *Randolph County Asylum Infirmary* OfficialRandolphCountyAsylumInfirmary / Wikimedia Commons
Page 201 *Women's Hall* OfficialRandolphCountyAsylumInfirmary / Wikimedia Commons
Page 204 *Prison* Laura Ragsdale / iStock
Page 205 *Tennessee's Shame* {{PD-US}} / Wikimedia Commons
Page 208 *Cornwall Jail* Carrot top25 at en.wikipedia
Page 212 *Trans-Alleghany Lunatic Asylum* BDphoto / iStock
Page 216 *Liberty Hotel* Steve Rosenbach / iStock
Page 220 *Cottage Hotel* {{PD-US}} / Iowa University Libraries
Page 224 *Poveglia* Aerial Film Studio / Adobe Stock
Page 231 *Oiran Buchi* mapplefan8 / Wikimedia Commons
Page 236 *Parker House* {{PD-US}} / Wikimedia Commons
Page 240 *Cortijo del Fraile* Lalocracio / iStock
Page 244 *Leeds General Infirmary* Tupungato / Shutterstock
Page 245 *Mary Bateman* {{PD-US}} / Wikimedia Commons
Page 248 *Westin St. Francis* Eric Molina / Wikimedia Commons
Page 249 *Virginia Rappe* {{PD-US}} / Wikimedia Commons
Page 252 *Fairmont Hotel* powerofforever / iStock
Page 253 *Wild Bill Hickok* {{PD-US}} / Wikimedia Commons
Page 256 *Ten Bells* Ewan Munro / Wikimedia Commons
Page 257 *Annie Chapman* {{PD-US}} / Wikimedia Commons
Page 260 *Monte Vista Hotel* Pavel Špindler / Wikimedia Commons
Page 276 Author Photo by Wolf Mathewson